Sport and Safety Management

Sport and Safety Management

Edited by Steve Frosdick and Lynne Walley

Staffordshire University

Butterworth-Heinemann
Linacre House, Jordan Hill, Oxford OX2 8DP
A division of Reed Educational and Professional Publishing Ltd

ℝ A member of the Reed Elsevier plc group

OXFORD   BOSTON   JOHANNESBURG
MELBOURNE   NEW DELHI   SINGAPORE

First published 1997

British Library Cataloguing in Publication Data
A catalogue record for this book is available from the British Library

ISBN 0 7506 3281 X

Typeset by David Gregson Associates, Beccles, Suffolk
Printed and bound in Great Britain by Scotprint Ltd, Musselburgh, Scotland.

Contents

Preface

My father first took me to Griffin Park on 18 March 1967. Along with 6339 other people, I saw Brentford beat Rochdale by four goals to nil. I was nine years old and fascinated by the spectacle: the stadium, the sense of belonging to the crowd, the colour, noise and smells, the excitement of the play, the whole atmosphere of the place. So began a lifelong interest in football, crowds and sports grounds.

I continued to visit Brentford regularly throughout my youth and bachelor years in the police service. At the same time, I became involved in policing large crowds on occasions such as football matches, pop concerts and demonstrations. Whilst on duty at a rally in East London on 11 May 1985, I stood outside a television rental showroom and watched in horror as over fifty people burned to death in a grandstand at Valley Parade in Bradford. I was deeply touched by what I saw. In later years, I returned to Brentford as a police inspector and saw at first hand the police response to the 1989 disaster at Hillsborough Stadium, Sheffield and the subsequent reports by Lord Justice Taylor.

In 1992, I was fortunate enough to have the chance to study for a higher degree. I wanted to look in detail at how sporting events are managed, to understand more about why disasters happen and how they might be better prevented. In 1994, having concluded my studies and become a Christian, I felt it was right to leave the police and earn my living as a writer, researcher and consultant in the field of risk management, particularly in the context of sport and safety management. My mission was to make a contribution to knowledge of how to improve safety and reduce the risk of future disasters in public assembly facilities.

In 1995, I began to collaborate with Lynne Walley in the Centre for Public Services Management and Research at Staffordshire University. My interests in safety and accountability dovetailed neatly with her interests in legal liability and we became involved together in organizing a number of seminars dealing with sport and safety management. Several of the contributors to this book were speakers at those seminars, giving valuable insights from a practitioner perspective. We eventually realized that their papers, together with the outcomes of our own research, our collaboration with other academics and our consultancy activities, provided the basis for a publication.

We knew from our contacts in the world of British football that it was an almost daily experience for clubs and the authorities to receive enquiries about safety management. These came from students from diverse disciplines such as sociology, sports sciences and leisure management. At the same time, we were aware that practitioners had been faced with a post-Hillsborough deluge of guidelines on various safety matters, focused on football, yet having equal validity for the wider sports and leisure context within public assembly facilities. We realized too that the popularity of football and the concentration of disasters within the sport meant that the subject of spectator safety in sport would be of interest to the general reader.

This book therefore represents the outcome of five years' research and consultancy work. We hope the book will have a broad appeal, that the effort will have been worthwhile and that we will have been able to support an ongoing process of continuous incremental improvement in sport and safety management.

Steve Frosdick and Lynne Walley
Staffordshire University, November 1996

About the contributors

Alan Beckley, LLB

Alan Beckley has served for twenty-five years in the police service in Surrey, Shropshire and Hereford and Worcester. He currently holds the rank of Chief Inspector, working at Kidderminster divisional headquarters of the West Mercia Constabulary. Postings have varied between large urban areas and small rural towns. Between 1991 and 1995 his role involved planning major policing operations, contingency planning and fulfilling many liaison functions with police and other organizations at national, regional, county and local levels. In 1995, he completed a year-long part-time research project funded by the Home Office on the personal liability of police officers following major and critical incidents. Several articles from the research have been published in national policing magazines. He is working on a Master's degree in Law, and holds several posts in voluntary youth organizations.

Bryan Drew

Bryan Drew joined the Metropolitan Police Service in 1974 and has worked in many areas of London as an operational officer. In 1989 he was selected as one of a small team of officers tasked with establishing the National Football Intelligence Unit (NFIU), where he served until the NFIU became an integral part of the National Criminal Intelligence Service (NCIS) in April 1992. He was worked in the NCIS since 1992, more recently as a Detective Chief Inspector, Head of Specialist Crime. He is a member of the Association of Chief Police Officers (ACPO) Public Order Sub-Committee which deals with policy matters in respect of the policing of football in England and Wales and was a member of the Euro '96 ACPO Steering Group, chairing the Information Technology Sub-Group. He was promoted to Detective Superintendent, Head of the Strategic and Specialist Intelligence Branch of the NCIS in September 1996.

Dominic Elliott, BA (Hons), MBA, MMS Dip

Dominic Elliott has taught and researched in the fields of strategy and crisis management at a number of universities. He is currently a Principal Lecturer in corporate strategy at Leicester Business School, De Montfort University. He is also a visiting lecturer at the Universities of Sheffield and Birmingham. Dominic has taught on a variety of executive MBA programmes and has worked in a consultancy and training capacity with executives from a range of organizations including IBM, the Royal Mail, Philips and the Foreign Office. He has written a number of publications in the fields of strategic and crisis management. His doctoral research examines the development of crisis within the post-war UK Football Industry, with particular emphasis upon the 1970 to 1996 period. Dominic is a Leicester City supporter and thus has had many years experience of the ups and downs of professional football!

Steve Frosdick, MSc, MIIRSM

Steve Frosdick is a company director and a Visiting Fellow at both Staffordshire and Bradford University. He is a Member of the International Institute of Risk and Safety Management and an Associate Member of the Football Safety Officers' Association. From 1992 to 1993, he undertook postgraduate research into stadium safety at the Cranfield University School of Management. He has a number of publications and media appearances in the field of strategic risk management and has completed research and consultancy projects in public safety, policing, corporate strategy and performance review for a number of important organizations, including the British Security Industry Association, Building Research Establishment, National Criminal Intelligence Service, the Police Foundation, and several UK police forces. During 1996, he was commissioned by the English football authorities to edit the training package for stewarding at football grounds. In his spare time, he is a devoted supporter of Brentford Football Club.

Mel Highmore, Dip SM, MIIRSM

Mel Highmore, a Cumbrian (and proud of it), is the Stadium and Safety Manager at Ewood Park, the home of the 1994 to 1995 Premiership Champions, Blackburn

Rovers. Mel has been in the post since 1990 and had an important role in the design and project management of the redevelopment of the stadium. He completed a British Safety Council Diploma in Safety Management in 1993 and is a Member of the International Institute of Risk and Safety Management. Formerly a Chief Inspector in the Lancashire Constabulary, Mel's organizational skills were fully challenged in ensuring the continual use of the stadium during its redevelopment and its maintenance since completion. Changes in legislation for safety management, including the full implementation of Lord Justice Taylor's recommendations for safety in stadia, have all brought additional work and responsibilities for Mel and his colleagues, who are increasingly accountable for public and staff safety and welfare.

Mike Holford, QPM

Mike Holford has been the Safety Consultant for Nottingham Forest FC since 1990. He was a founder and also the first Chairman of the Football Safety Officers' Association. He is widely respected for his pioneering work in football safety and was a member of the working group which produced the English football authorities' guidelines on stewarding and safety management in 1995. During the 1996 European Football Championships, he commanded the three matches held at the City Ground in Nottingham. He was formerly a Chief Superintendent in the Nottinghamshire Constabulary responsible for the policing operations at both Nottingham Forest FC and Notts County FC.

Gerald Mars, MA (Cantab), PhD, FRAI

Gerald Mars, Professor of Risk Managment at the University of Bradford, is an applied anthropologist who read economics and social anthropology at Cambridge and was awarded a doctorate by the London School of Economics. He has held research posts at Oxford and Cambridge Universities and visiting Professorships at the Cranfield University School of Management and the University of Hong Kong. He is currently constructing the Bradford Master's programme in Strategic Risk Management. He has published five books and over forty academic papers, mainly on occupational crime, risk perception and the organization of hotels. He is the joint editor of the International Library of Criminology, Criminal Justice and Penology. In his spare time he carries out selective consultancy and visits to Italy.

John de Quidt

John de Quidt has been the Chief Executive of the Football Licensing Authority since March 1991. During over twenty years in the public service he has held a wide variety of responsibilities. These include over five years working on prison contingency planning, incident management and analysis, and the strategic and tactical management of the prison population. Other areas of work have included the co-ordination of the United Kingdom's European Community policies on all home and social issues, for example health and safety at work, and the regulation and safety of the taxi and private hire industries. He has also played an important role in major inquiries into the protection of individual privacy from the media and into the provision of legal services to the public.

John Sidney

John Sidney is the Deputy Safety Officer at Nottingham Forest Football Club. He is the Secretary of the Football Safety Officers' Association and acted as Secretary to the working group which produced the training package for stewarding at football grounds. He was formerly a Sergeant in the Nottinghamshire Constabulary and for the last eight years of his career served as the Football Liaison Officer at Nottingham, joining Forest on his retirement in February 1995. He is a qualified police instructor with over twenty years' training experience.

Denis Smith, BEd, MSc, MBA, PhD, DASE, FIPD, MIOSH

Denis Smith is Professor of Management at the University of Durham where he is also Head of the Business School's Centre for Risk and Crisis Management. Following a first degree in Geography and Environmental Science, he studied for Master's degrees in Pollution and Environmental Control, Applied Psychology (University of Manchester) and Business Administration (Sheffield Hallam University) and a PhD in Science and Technology Policy (University of Manchester). Before moving to Durham he was Director of Liverpool Business School and has previously held faculty positions at the University of Manchester and Nottingham Trent and De Montfort Universities. He is currently visiting Professor of Strategic

Management at the University of Sheffield and has been visiting Professor in Human Resource Management at the University of Kobe in Japan. Outside of his academic interests he is a non-executive director of Mersey Regional Ambulance Service and a consultant to a number of companies.

Lynne Walley LLB (Hons), MA

Lynne Walley is an academic lawyer with interests in criminal law and juvenile offending and is the Deputy Head of the Centre for Public Services Management and Research at Staffordshire University. She has undertaken research on juvenile cautioning and truancy, and is currently studying for her doctorate on action-based intervention for juvenile offenders. She has completed projects for the Inland Revenue, the Magistrates Association and a number of local authorities. She has presented papers at several international police and criminal justice conferences in the UK and abroad and has been a visiting speaker at the Universities of Keele and of Central England. From 1988 to 1996 she was a visiting law lecturer for Staffordshire Youth and Community Service. Lynne is also the co-author of *Practical Police Management*, which has become a core management text for several police forces and training colleges.

Clive Warne, LLB (Hons)

Clive Warne is a Lecturer in Law and a Safety and Training Consultant to the sport, leisure and security industries. He holds an honours degree in law having graduated from Sheffield University in 1985. As a police Superintendent he commanded the central subdivision of a major northern city and has been involved in police training for many years with expertise in public order training and special events. His passion for commanding large events and his background in training match commanders for Premier League football led to his appointment to the high profile role of safety and security officer at Sheffield Wednesday's Hillsborough stadium. During Euro '96 Clive was a member of the operational planning team for the eight venues and was the operational commander for three of the matches. He has earned widespread recognition and respect for his expertise in crowd management.

Glyn Wootton, MSc, BA (Hons), MTS, MILAM, AFDM, ATT, EASM

Glyn Wootton has worked in the leisure industry since 1985. He has been involved in a wide range of consultancy and research projects in Europe and other continents, and specializes in the development and management of sports facilities, particularly stadia and arena. He is a refereed author and has published numerous articles on leisure management. In 1995 he co-authored the Stadium Management Project's strategy for the training of people involved in the development and management of stadia and arena facilities. He is a member of the British Standards Institution Committee for the development of a European standard for the design and layout of major spectator facilities. He has a Master's degree in Leisure Resource Management and before becoming a consultant worked for four years in the management of local authority managed multi-purpose leisure facilities.

Glyn's chapter in this book was co-authored with Peter Mills, DMS, MInst. SRM Dip., MILAM, who is Principal Consultant of Quality Leisure Management (QLM) Services. Peter specializes in the management of safety and quality in the leisure industry and has guided over two dozen leisure organizations to the ISO 9002 (formerly BS 5750) quality standard. He has worked in the leisure industry since 1976 and is regularly contracted by local authorities, solicitors and insurance companies. He assisted the Sports Council in the development of QUEST, the leisure industry quality standard, for which QLM is also the appointed scheme manager.

Acknowledgements

The management of safety risks in public assembly facilities is a complicated and difficult business. During the course of our travels and research, we have been privileged to meet many of those involved in this field at football grounds and other venues.

We acknowledge the integrity and honestly held convictions of all those who bear the responsibility week by week. Without exception, they have offered us open house to study their safety operation, 'warts and all'. Their names are too numerous to mention but we thank them all for their openness and interested support of our work.

Whilst it is clearly right to include examples of best practice within a work of this kind, one cannot seek to add to knowledge about the theory and practice of sport and safety management without exposing some of the difficulties experienced and analysing the causes of the problems. We hope, therefore, that in presenting our own and our contributors' observations of some of the 'warts', we shall not offend any of those who have granted us such excellent access.

Among the many people without whose help this book would never have been possible, we would like to offer our particular thanks to the following:

- our contributors: Alan Beckley, Bryan Drew, Dominic Elliott, Mel Highmore, Mike Holford, Gerald Mars, John de Quidt, John Sidney, Denis Smith, Clive Warne and Glyn Wootton. We have been fortunate enough to collaborate with all of them in a variety of contexts since 1992 and are enormously grateful for their interested support for our work.
- our publishers: Kathryn Grant, Jonathan Glasspool and Diane Scarlett at Butterworth-Heinemann, who have patiently supported us throughout the production of this book.
- our Staffordshire University colleagues in the Centre for Public Services Management and Research, for valuable administrative help; and Geoff Berry, our Head of Centre, for ongoing leadership and encouragement.

● our spouses: Tania and Andrew, for bearing the respective mantles of 'football widow' and 'research widower' with great forbearance over recent years.

Where appropriate, additional acknowledgements have also been included at the end of the chapters in this book.

Steve Frosdick and Lynne Walley

Foreword

by Jack Crawford

Having been involved in the safety and control of spectators at football grounds, first as a police officer in Liverpool and, for the past nine years, as an adviser to the Football League, I welcome the publication of this book and consider it a privilege to have been invited to pen this foreword.

It is a matter of record that the largest spectator sport in the United Kingdom for over a century has been professional football. It was inevitable, therefore, that the safety management of sports stadia would initially be channelled towards football grounds.

Spectators are the backbone of all sporting events and, as such, the succession of tragic incidents involving death and injury to spectators at major football matches, culminating in the tragic events at the Hillsborough ground in April 1989, rightly brought forward necessary legislation and guidance for ensuring spectator safety.

This resulted in a plethora of advice and publications being produced, presenting those charged with the responsibility of ensuring the safety of spectators at events in their stadia with the unenviable task of deciding which of these were most relevant.

Those involved with the operation of sports stadia needed to recognize the fact that they were required to have a clear understanding of the safety and management of spectators in both normal and emergency situations. This had all become increasingly complicated and what the contributors in this book have done is set out in clear terms some ideas about what needs to be accomplished.

Having said this, much has been achieved since those dark days of the Hillsborough tragedy and the subsequent report by Lord Justice Taylor in January 1990. It is right to say that the standards of safety and comfort for spectators in UK football stadia are now becoming the model for others to follow.

Complacency is the enemy, however, and there was still a need for a comprehensive and practical publication to be produced to pull together all the strands of research, best practice and advice that was now available for the benefit of those directly involved with the safety of our sports stadia. The safety of spectators attending sporting events now extends far beyond the mere practical safeguards on the day. It involves a much greater responsibility for ensuring that those charged with the operational tasks on the day have the means of achieving them. The contents of this book will provide those concerned with some useful ideas on how to discharge their responsibilities.

The list of contributors to the book is impressive with a good blend of the academic and operational experience being evident, and they are all to be congratulated on the excellence of their particular presentations.

An extremely well-presented and written publication offering the necessary advice and guidance to all involved with the safe management of sporting events, written in a style that is easily understood, it should be of great benefit to practitioners, planners and to all those studying or interested in the subject.

PART 1   INTRODUCTION

Overview

Part One introduces and sets the scene for the book.

Chapter summaries

In Chapter 1, Steve Frosdick begins by setting out the background, context and reasons why this book has been written. He goes on to review the debate about football hooliganism, emphasizing that this is not another book about that subject. He concludes by outlining the five parts in which the book is presented: the introduction, accountability for safety, academic research, consultancy and best practice, and a vision for the future.

In Chapter 2, Dominic Elliott, Steve Frosdick and Denis Smith seek to demonstrate the importance of sport and safety management as a subject for social science enquiry. They begin by outlining, with specific reference to British football grounds, the social, historical and economic contexts in which crowd-related disasters are set. They go on to review the radical changes made in response to the Hillsborough disaster, but note that crowd safety problems have nevertheless continued to occur, both in football and elsewhere. They conclude that the failure of 'legislation by crisis' reinforces the need for practitioners to take account of the research findings and good practice outlined in this book.

1 Beyond football hooliganism

Steve Frosdick

This introductory chapter opens by setting out the background, context and reasons why this book has been written. It goes on to review the debate about football hooliganism, emphasizing that this is not another book about that subject. It concludes by outlining the five parts in which the book is presented: the introduction, accountability for safety, academic research, consultancy and best practice, and a vision for the future.

Why this book?

Managing public assembly facilities, particularly sports stadia, so as to provide spectators with an environment in which they can watch events enjoyably and safely, is a highly complex problem. It includes questions of architectural and engineering design, operational management, technological sophistication, health and safety, public order, customer care and an understanding of how people behave in crowds. Whilst no single publication can hope to cover all these aspects, the central theme of the subject is one of risk assessment. Designing, planning and managing a public assembly facility is fundamentally all about identifying the things that could go operationally wrong, working out which things matter the most and putting in place control measures to design or manage them out before they happen. This book therefore addresses the management of safety in sport from a risk assessment perspective.

Because it is football, specifically British football (as Steve Frosdick, Dominic Elliott and Denis Smith argue in the next chapter), which has suffered the disasters and had to learn the resultant lessons, it is inevitable that the book focuses on the experience of football and British football grounds. But the wider setting for the book is in an international world of stadia, arenas and sports grounds in general. These may be collectively referred to as 'public assembly facilities' (PAFs), which, according to Wootton and Stevens [1],

> have a number of characteristic features which require special consideration in their planning, design, management and operation. They . . .

- provide amenities for spectator viewing of sporting and non-sporting events;
- must be accessible, comfortable and safe for a range of users and participants;
- attract large number of spectators attending events of relatively short duration;
- are managed to ensure the safe movement of people in a smooth, unimpeded, fashion in the time before, during and after the event;
- provide pleasurable experiences in an enjoyable and safe way;
- provide a range of ancillary services and amenities to meet the needs and demands of spectators, participants and promoters;
- provide environments to encourage the highest standards for sporting participants within the criteria required by the regulations of that sport;
- may be open to the elements, or may be covered or enclosed in total or in part;
- involve an ensemble of features creating a sense of place and identity;
- contribute to the wider community, through economic, social and cultural benefits;
- adopt a responsible approach towards community aspirations and concerns;
- have the potential to be used for a range of sporting and non-sporting events on single or multiple use basis.

Several chapters in this book provide a historical perspective on sport and safety management. As Inglis [2] points out, however, 'It cannot be emphasised enough, if emphasis were needed, that the death of 96 Liverpool fans at Hillsborough on 15 April 1989 was an absolute turning point'. Thus the book has a particular focus on the nadir of Hillsborough in 1989 as the catalyst for change and subsequent improvement. At the time of writing, the 1996 European Football Championships have just been successfully staged in England in a way that nobody could have envisaged even a few years previously. Thus the book also seeks to provide a position statement on how sport and safety management has got to where it is in 1996.

Finally, whilst much of the book is concerned with the experience of British football, it is argued, as Toft and Reynolds [3] have shown, that since disasters within any single industry (even football) are low frequency events, thus each industry needs to look beyond itself to find the lessons which will enable it to learn the active foresight necessary for improving safety. The experience of British football should therefore be a source of useful learning for all sectors of the international sports and leisure industry.

Going beyond football hooliganism

Having thus established what this book is about, I want to emphasize what it is not about. This is not another book about football hooliganism.

When I started my research into sports safety management in 1992, I quickly discovered that, as Redhead [4], has shown, 'it has become almost impossible to research into the regulation of football without being seen to be an integral part of the discourses about "football hooliganism" '. The safety at sports grounds debate has been dominated by moral panic about football hooliganism, and a brief analysis of the reasons behind this is appropriate in setting the scene for this book.

The focus on football hooliganism has arisen for a combination of factors, including media amplification, and police and academic emphasis. Murphy et al. [5] have undertaken a detailed analysis of press reporting of soccer crowd disorder. They show, from a historical perspective, how the media played a de-amplifying role during the inter-war years and up until the 1950s. Thereafter, through amplification of the extent of the problem, the press, 'played a part of some importance in directing hooligan behaviour into the football context' [6].

For example, the arrest of English supporters outside an Oslo public house before the England versus Norway match on 1 June 1993 drew banner headlines and widespread 'outraged' coverage in the national press [7, 8]. Yet, interviewed on BBC Radio News, Johnny Birmingham, the disc jockey working at the pub, reported that the boisterousness was no different from any ordinary Friday or Saturday night, except that there were over 100 riot police waiting outside!

Historical data from the National Criminal Intelligence Service [9] suggests that, at worst during the early 1990s, only one in every 2500 spectators had been either ejected from the ground or arrested either inside or outside the ground. In terms of arrests, this data indicated a slight reduction on the 1977 Scottish Education Department survey finding of 0.28 arrests per 1000 spectators, reported by Bale [10]. This compared very favourably with the number of arrests in leisure activities on Saturday nights and represented only one-thirteenth of arrests for drinking and driving. Bale concluded that 'given such low figures, the measures used to control spectators seem draconian in the extreme' [11].

The police concern with football hooliganism has remained constant. The police's own research [12] has argued that, since football and disorder have been historically associated with each other throughout the world, a cautious approach and realistic individual assessment of each match are required. Speaking at the 'Grounds for Optimism' conference in Leicester on 24 March 1994, Assistant Chief Constable Malcolm George set out the police view that hooliganism had not gone away, although it had been displaced from inside to outside grounds. Bryan Drew shows later in this book (Chapter 17) the detailed planning, intelligence gathering and operational activities undertaken to ensure that the Euro '96 football championships were kept trouble-free.

It may be argued that the treatment of football hooliganism bears all the hallmarks of the type of moral panic described by Cohen [13]. Like the mods and rockers before them, the football hooligans are folk devils, labelled as deviant by the middle classes, in order to bolster middle-class perceptions of the correctness of their own way of life. The media reinforce this with over-reporting of incidents that do occur and the creation of 'non-stories' where nothing has happened [14]. For example, Buford has shown that during the seven days of the final build-up to the 1990 World Cup in Italy, although nothing untoward was happening, the *Guardian* newspaper carried 471 column inches devoted to football supporters – 'nearly forty feet of reports that said: there is nothing to report' [15].

This moral panic can become a self-fulfilling prophesy. Media reporting suggests the likelihood of hooliganism. Football therefore becomes more attractive to the type of person disposed to violence. The police plan for the trouble anticipated and may be inclined to over-react to minor incidents. Nobody is surprised when serious disorder breaks out, since it was what everybody expected in the first place.

Benjamin and Palmer [16] have shown how, between 1986 and 1993, the Football Trust donated £900 000 to fund research centres at Oxford and Leicester universities. Eight other academic institutions were also named as having funded their own research. The study of football hooliganism had become an academic growth industry. The various discourses have been extensively reviewed elsewhere [17–20]. I do not propose to cover the same ground other than in the brief summary below.

According to Marxists, such as Ian Taylor [21] and John Clarke [22], hooligan behaviour was the only means open for the 'lumpenproletariat' to express its concern at the hijacking of football by big business. This view was criticized as lacking any supporting evidence and indeed as 'a deliberate eschewing of analysis of empirical data of any kind' [23].

For anthropologists such as Marsh et al. [24], rituals and display among young male groups represented an illusion of violence which was misconstrued as hooliganism. This theory was criticized for overlooking the injuries that can and do occur when opposing groups rush at each other [25]. Anthropological studies of single spectator groups, such as that conducted by Armstrong and Harris [26], were criticized [27] for overgeneralizing about hooligan styles from empirical work at just one club.

According to the Leicester sociologists [28–30], the social roots of football hooliganism were to be found in the cultural traditions of the 'rough' working class. The road to eradicating hooliganism was one that addressed the wider issues of social justice. Armstrong and Harris [31] accused the Leicester researchers of failing to scrutinize carefully enough the data upon which their conclusions were based. Illustrating the acrimony of the debate, Dunning et al. [32] responded to Armstrong's temerity by attacking his work and robustly defending their own.

Other studies have taken different approaches, such as the categorization of Italian fans as either fanatics or moderates [33]. A psychological perspective was added by Kerr [34], who sought to provide an understanding of the motivation behind violent soccer hooligan activities.

This focusing of social science enquiry on rival theoretical explanations of football hooliganism, whilst important in helping to generate understanding of the causes of the phenomenon itself, nevertheless does little to assist in the development of public policy. It may also unwittingly have contributed to moral panic and amplification of the real extent of the problem. Duke [35] has stressed the need for an agenda which goes beyond hooliganism, and this book is intended as a contribution to that wider debate.

Introduction to sport and safety management

The book is presented in five parts. This first part continues with Dominic Elliott, Steve Frosdick and Denis Smith's review of the social, historical and economic contexts in which crowd-related disasters are set, and the reasons why radical post-disaster change has failed to prevent a succession of disasters and continued near misses.

Part Two deals with questions of accountability. It examines the concept of risk as a mechanism for attributing blame and, in that context, reviews the emergence of the legal principle of corporate manslaughter liability. It goes on to examine some general issues in liability from the perspective of the police service and concludes by setting out the role of the football industry regulator.

Part Three has a theoretical orientation and reports the results of academic research into sport and safety management. It begins by using crisis management theory to investigate club management attitudes to safety in the British football industry, revealing the difficult context in which safety practitioners have to work. It goes on to use the theory of cultural complexity to explain the tensions which exist between commercialism, safety and order, enjoyment and environmental impact at both the macro level of the British stadia safety industry and the micro level of the individual venue.

Notwithstanding the football club management attitudes and overall cultural complexity revealed in Part Three, the practitioners themselves have made considerable progress. Part Four introduces the results of consultancy and best practice in the areas of stadium design, risk assessment, operational safety management and policing. Several of the chapters have been written by leading practitioners, whose perspective and views are rarely captured in the literature.

Having thus set out the present position, Part Five outlines the editors' vision of where sport and safety management should perhaps be heading in the approach to the millennium. Options are presented for the strategic development of the industry and methodologies offered for undertaking strategic risk assessments and for managing change through the vehicles of programme and project management.

Many of the chapters contain extensive references, which it is hoped will assist the student or general reader who wishes to research the literature more extensively. The book concludes with a useful list of addresses of relevant organizations, associations and professional bodies, who may be able to assist with any further enquiries.

Summary

- Sport and safety management is a complex phenomenon, but its central theme is one of risk assessment.
- British football has had to learn the lessons of repeated disasters. Whilst focusing on the British experience, the book should provide a source of useful learning for the international world of public assembly facilities management.

- The book takes a historical perspective, but has a particular focus on the period between 1989 – the nadir of the Hillsborough disaster – and 1996 – the euphoria of the European Football Championships.
- The safety at sports grounds debate has been dominated by a moral panic about football hooliganism, fuelled by media amplification, police concerns and academic emphasis, but this is not another book about that subject.
- The book is presented in five parts. Part One is the introduction. Part Two deals with questions of accountability. Part Three has a theoretical orientation and reports the results of academic research. Part Four introduces the results of consultancy and best practice, and Part Five outlines the editors' vision of the future.

References

[1] Wootton, G. and Stevens, T. (1995). *Into the Next Millennium: A Human Resource Development Strategy for the Stadia and Arena Industry in the United Kingdom*, p. 6, Stadium and Arena Management Unit, Swansea Institute of Higher Education.

[2] Inglis, S. (1996). *The Football Grounds of Great Britain* (3rd edn), p. 7. Harper Collins.

[3] Toft, B. and Reynolds, S. (1994). *Learning from Disasters: A Management Approach.* Butterworth-Heinemann.

[4] Redhead, S. (1991). Some reflections on discourses on football hooliganism. *The Sociological Review*, **39**(3), 479–488.

[5] Murphy, P., Williams, J. and Dunning, E. (1990). *Football on Trial–Spectator Violence and Development in the Football World*, pp. 96–128. Routledge.

[6] Ibid. p. 126.

[7] Bhatia, S. (1993). England's shame as fans riot in Oslo. *Evening Standard*, 2 June.

[8] Graves, D. and Marks, K. (1993). England fans in pitched battle with police. *Daily Telegraph*, 3 June.

[9] National Criminal Intelligence Service Football Unit (1992). *Summary of Statistics 1991/2 Season Showing Comparison with the 1990/1 Season.*

[10] Bale, J. (1993). *Sport, Space and the City*, pp. 28–29. Routledge.

[11] Ibid. p. 29.

[12] Middleham, N. (1993). *Football: Policing the Supporter*. Home Office Police Research Group.

[13] Cohen, S. (1973). *Folk Devils and Moral Panics*. Paladin.

[14] Ibid. pp. 6–39.

[15] Buford, B. (1992). *Among the Thugs*, p. 276. Mandarin.

[16] Benjamin, D. and Palmer, R. (1993). Football fans put boot into violence 'experts'. *Sunday Times*, 8 August.

[17] Dunning, E. Murphy, P. and Williams, J. (1988). *The Roots of Football Hooliganism – An Historical and Sociological Study*, pp. 18–31. Routledge and Kegan Paul.

[18] Canter, D., Comber, M. and Uzzell D. (1989). *Football in its Place: An Environmental Psychology of Football Grounds*, pp. 107–118. Routledge.

[19] Hobbs, D. and Robins, D. (1991). The boy done good: Football violence, changes and continuities. *The Sociological Review*, **39**(3), 551–579.

[20] Williams, J (1991). Having an away day: English football spectators and the hooligan debate. In *British Football and Social Change – Getting into Europe* (J. Williams and S. Wagg, eds.), pp. 160–186. Leicester University Press.

[21] Taylor, I. (1971). Football mad: A speculative sociology of football hooliganism. In *The Sociology of Sport: A Collection of Readings* (E. Dunning, ed.), Cass.

[22] Clarke, J. (1978). Football and working-class fans: Tradition and change. In *Football Hooliganism: The Wider Context* (R Ingham, ed.), Inter-Action Imprint.

[23] Op. cit. 19. p. 554.

[24] Marsh, P., Rosser, E. and Harre, R. (1978). *The Rules of Disorder*. Routledge & Kegan Paul.

[25] Op. cit. 18. p. 113.

[26] Armstrong, G. and Harris, R. (1991). Football hooligans: Theory and evidence. *The Sociological Review*, **39**(3), 427–458.

[27] Op. cit. 4. p. 481.

[28] Williams, J., Dunning, E. and Murphy, P. (1984). *Hooligans Abroad: The Behaviour and Control of English Fans in Continental Europe*. Routledge.

[29] Op. cit. 17.

[30] Op. cit. 5.

[31] Op. cit. 26.

[32] Dunning, E., Murphy, P. and Waddington, I. (1991). Anthropological versus sociological approaches to the study of soccer hooliganism: Some critical notes. *The Sociological Review*, **39**(3), 459–478.

[33] Zani, B. and Kirchler, E. (1991). When violence overshadows the spirit of sporting competition: Italian football fans and their clubs. *Journal of Community and Applied Social Psychology*, **1**(1), 5–21.

[34] Kerr, J. (1994). *Understanding Soccer Hooliganism*. Open University Press.

[35] Duke, V. (1991). The sociology of football: A research agenda for the 1990s. *The Sociological Review*, **39**(3), 627–645.

2 The failure of 'legislation by crisis'

Dominic Elliott, Steve Frosdick and Denis Smith

This chapter seeks to demonstrate the importance of sport and safety management as a subject for social science enquiry. It begins by outlining, with specific reference to British football grounds, the social, historical and economic contexts in which crowd-related disasters are set. It goes on to review the radical changes made in response to the Hillsborough disaster, but notes that crowd safety problems have nevertheless continued to occur, both in football and elsewhere. The chapter concludes that the failure of 'legislation by crisis' reinforces the need for practitioners to take account of the research findings and good practice outlined in this book.

Introduction

Since the days of the Roman Empire there has been some recognition of the problems associated with managing crowds at large events. The architects and builders of the Rome Colosseum, constructed to accommodate 50 000 spectators, incorporated some eighty entrance/exit points; demonstrating that even the Romans were aware of basic crowd safety ideas. For many centuries the Colosseum remained unique in Europe until the development of professional sport during the nineteenth century and the associated rapid growth in crowd and venue sizes. High profile disasters such as the fire at the Summerland leisure complex, Isle of Man in 1973 and the crowd crushing at Hillsborough, Sheffield in 1989 have illustrated the great potential for accidents where many people are gathered together. As a result of a series of incidents, concern for crowd safety has been growing and with these concerns we have also seen the emergence of a growing literature dealing with the problems of managing crowds in 'complex space' [1].

The first point to emphasize is that, regardless of their behaviour, the potential for disaster exists where large crowds congregate, particularly where such gatherings occur within artificial complexes and structures. The crowd crushing resulting in the 173 deaths that occurred in 1943 at the Bethnal Green Tube station in London had a number of close similarities with the Ibrox Stadium disaster in Glasgow in 1971, where some 66 people lost their lives as they left the ground on the infamous Stairway Thirteen. In both instances the immediate cause of the incidents was directly related to the sheer weight of numbers of people moving through a confined space. The response of legislators, as we shall argue, has frequently dealt only with the immediate causes of such incidents, often ignoring the more significant, underlying causes. These include social, historical and economic factors and it has been argued that the implementation of technical solutions to socio-technical problems has done little to prevent the recurrence of crowd-related disasters [2]. Although recent interest in issues of crowd safety has focused largely upon the football industry, the result of a series of high profile incidents involving multiple fatalities and injuries, it is argued that the lessons from these disasters apply to all venues where large numbers congregate.

The particular problems associated with crowd safety within the football industry can be traced back to the emergence of British football as a mass spectator sport. In the nineteenth century, when many of today's stadia were first built, crowd safety was not considered an important issue. As Inglis [3] comments:

> A century ago clubs did virtually nothing to protect spectators. Thousands were packed onto badly constructed slopes with hardly a wooden barrier in sight. About the best that can be said of the early grounds is that with only ropes around the pitches there was little to stop a build up of pressure sending hundreds pouring onto the pitch.

Given the combination of the size of crowds at some matches and the poor facilities inside stadia, it was only a matter of time before disaster struck. In 1902, at an international match played between Scotland and England, 25 spectators died and a further 500 were injured when a temporary stand collapsed at Ibrox Park, Glasgow.

Evidence of at least forty-four UK-related incidents involving deaths and multiple injuries up until 1989, the watershed of Lord Justice Taylor's reports into the Hillsborough disaster [4, 5], have been gathered together from several sources [6–11] and are shown in Table 2.1. Two (marked [#]) occurred in rugby league grounds,

Table 2.1   Disasters and incidents involving United Kingdom stadia or supporters

Venue	Year	Fatalities/injuries	Disaster/incident type
Valley Parade (Bradford)[#]	1888	1 dead, 3 injured	railings collapse
Blackburn	1896	5 injured	stand collapse
Ibrox (Glasgow)	1902	26 dead, 550 injured	collapsed temporary stand
Brentford	1907	multiple injuries	fence collapse
Leicester	1907	multiple injuries	barrier collapse
Hillsborough (Sheffield)	1914	70–80 injured	wall collapse
Charlton	1923	24 injured	crowd crush
Wembley	1923	1000 + injured	crowd crush
Burnley	1924	1 dead	crowd crush
Manchester (City)	1926	unknown injuries	crowd crush
Huddersfield	1932	100 injured	crowd crush
Huddersfield	1937	4 injured	crowd crush
Watford	1937	unknown injuries	crowd crush
Fulham	1938	unknown injuries	crowd crush
Rochdale Athletic Ground[#]	1939	1 dead, 17 injured	roof collapse
Burnden Park (Bolton)	1946	33 dead, 400 injured	crowd crush
Shawfield (Clyde)	1957	1 dead, 50 injured	barrier collapse
Ibrox (Glasgow)	1961	2 dead, 50 injured	crowd crush on Stairway 13
Oldham	1962	15 injured	barrier collapse
Arsenal	1963	100 injured	crushing
Port Vale	1964	1 dead, 2 injured	fall/crushing
Roker Park (Sunderland)	1964	80 + injured	crowd crush
Anfield (Liverpool)	1966	31 injured	crowd crush
Leeds	1967	32 injured	crowd crush
Ibrox (Glasgow)	1967	8 injured	crowd crush on Stairway 13
Dunfermline	1968	1 dead, 49 injured	crowd crush
Ibrox (Glasgow)	1969	24 injured	crowd crush on Stairway 13
Ibrox (Glasgow)	1971	66 dead, 145 injured	crowd crush on Stairway 13
Carlisle	1971	5 injured	barrier collapse
Oxford	1971	25 injured	wall collapse
Stoke	1971	46 injured	crowd crush
Wolverhampton	1972	80 injured	barrier collapse
Arsenal	1972	42 injured	crowd crush
Lincoln	1975	4 injured	wall collapse
Leyton Orient	1978	30 injured	barrier/wall collapse
Middlesbrough	1980	2 dead	gate collapse

(continued)

Table 2.1   Disasters and incidents involving United Kingdom stadia or supporters (*continued*)

Venue	Year	Fatalities/injuries	Disaster/incident type
Hillsborough (Sheffield)	1981	38 injured	crowd crush
Walsall	1984	20 injured	wall collapse
Bradford	1985	54 dead	fire
Birmingham	1985	1 dead, 20 injured	disorder/wall collapse
Heysel (Brussels)	1985	38 dead, 400 + injured	disorder/wall collapse
Easter Road (Edinburgh)	1987	150 injured	crowd crush
Hillsborough (Sheffield)	1989	95 dead, 400 + injured	crowd crush
Middlesbrough	1989	19 injured	crowd crush

Incident at rugby league ground.

whilst one, involving supporters of Liverpool football club, was at Heysel in Belgium. The remainder took place in UK football grounds. Evidence of at least twenty-six football disasters outside the UK, derived from the same sources, is set out in Table 2.2. The great majority of these occurred in what might be described as developing countries. This all suggests that British football has a unique history of disaster and disorder. Why should this be?

The particular risks with British football

The answer, as we shall now seek to demonstrate, lies in a combination of social, historical and economic factors and the political response to particular incidents. Simplistic explanations of catastrophe have been put forward by some commentators, for example by Sir Bernard Ingham (Margaret Thatcher's Press Officer 1980–90) who wrote in a 1996 newspaper article 'that the Hillsborough soccer disaster was caused by tanked up yobs who arrived late, determined to force their way into the ground' [12].

That Ingham felt the need to write this some seven years after the tragedy provides an indication of the political importance of the Hillsborough disaster. His comments ignored the conclusions of Lord Justice Taylor who conducted the official inquiry into the incident. Ingham's views however, do reflect a widely held view that somehow if football could rid itself of hooligans then everything would be rosy indeed. As we intend to argue, however, such a view does not reflect the true complexity of the problem and such mindsets have worked to the detriment of

Table 2.2 Disasters in football grounds outside the UK

Venue	Year	Fatalities/injuries	Disaster/incident type
Ibague (Colombia)	1961	11 dead, 15 injured	stand collapse
Santiago (Chile)	1961	5 dead, 300 injured	crowd crush
Lima (Peru)	1964	318 dead, 1000+ injured	riot
Istanbul (Turkey)	1964	70 injured	fire
Kayseri (Turkey)	1967	34 dead	riot
Buenos Aires (Argentina)	1968	74 dead, 150 injured	disorder/stampede
Cairo (Egypt)	1974	49 dead, 50 injured	crowd crush
Port-au-Prince (Haiti)	1978	6 dead	disorder/police shooting
Piraeus (Greece)	1981	21 dead, 54 injured	crush/stampede
San Luis (Brazil)	1982	3 dead, 25 injured	riot/police shooting
Cali (Colombia)	1982	24 dead, 250 injured	crushing/stampede
Algiers (Algeria)	1982	10 dead, 500 injured	roof collapse
Moscow Spartak (Soviet Union)	1982	69+ dead, 100+ injured	crowd crush
Heysel (Belgium)	1985	38 dead, 400+ injured	disorder/wall collapse.
Mexico City (Mexico)	1985	10 dead, 100+ injured	crowd crush
Tripoli (Libya)	1987	20 dead	unknown
Katmandu (Nepal)	1988	100+ dead, 500 injured	hailstorm/stampede
Lagos (Nigeria)	1989	5 dead	crowd crush
Mogadishu (Somalia)	1989	7 dead, 18 injured	riot
Orkney (South Africa)	1991	42 dead, 50 injured	riot/stampede
Nairobi (Kenya)	1991	1 dead, 24 injured	stampede
Rio de Janeiro (Brazil)	1992	50 injured	fence collapse
Bastia (Corsica)	1992	17 dead	temporary stand collapse
Free Town (Sierra Leone)	1995	40 injured	gate collapse
Lusaka (Zambia)	1996	9 dead, 52 injured	crowd crush
Guatemala	1996	80 dead, 150 injured	crowd crush

finding effective solutions to the problems of ensuring crowd safety. Thus in the aftermath of the 1985 Bradford and Heysel disasters Government efforts concentrated upon more rigorous control of spectators through investment in closed circuit television (CCTV), the banning of alcohol at football matches and the failed attempt to introduce the football spectators' membership scheme. This focus reflected the underlying belief that hooliganism was the key issue for football and that strategies for crowd control rather than safety were required. It was to take the deaths of a further ninety-five people to shake this view.

The social importance of football is demonstrated by its immense popularity and its status as the most popular live spectator sport. The game has been described as a symbolic form, representing 'Englishness' or 'Scottishness': through versions of local identity, masculine pride, working-classness both rough and respectable, belief in effort and aversion to fancy ways [13]. The place where the game is played is the object of popular sanctification and place pride [14–16]. And the evolution of football has mirrored the changes in British society [17]. Thus, in Dunning's succinct summary [18]:

> It is clear, in other words, that playing and/or watching football has come to form one of the principal media and foci of collective identification in modern Britain and, for many people, one of the principal sources of enjoyable excitement in their lives. As such, in the context of a society that, for better or worse, has grown increasingly secular over the last 100 years or so, it has come to perform many of the functions that, in earlier times, were performed by church membership and church attendance.

Furthermore, when compared with football, a pop concert crowd may be as large or as exciting, the violence of street gangs as horrifying and the crowd control problems for a demonstration as great. 'But people only associate all these different activities and experiences with one event: football. Football, then, brings together an intriguing combination of special circumstances' [19].

From a historical perspective, the Taylor Reports identified old grounds, poor facilities, alcohol, hooliganism and poor leadership within the sport as the key issues which had brought a blight on British football.

Despite its origins as a medieval folk game, it was not until the formation of the Football League in 1888 that football became established as a spectator as well as participatory sport. Ancient Greece and Rome apart, stadia were almost unheard of until the first British football grounds were constructed at the turn of the century. Reporting in 1987, Inglis [20] noted that sixty-six of the English Football League clubs took up occupation of their grounds before 1910 and the remaining twenty-six moved in between 1910 and 1955. The legacy of this was that football grounds were unsuitably sited for the demands of the late twentieth century, creating congestion for local residents on match days. Close proximity to houses and even, as in the case of Everton, to churches, has acted as a barrier to the extensive redevelopment of many stadia.

Although the grounds were old, there had been substantial redevelopment of many stadia. Some changes might be termed 'modernization', although the most significant alterations arose in response to new legislation or, perhaps more significantly, from developments to contain hooliganism. The supporters remained segregated in steel cages both from each other and from the pitch. Whilst standards of facilities elsewhere in the entertainment industry rose steadily in response to customer expectations, the provision of toilet and refreshment facilities at football grounds notably failed to keep pace. Foul latrines and lukewarm pies were the norm in many stadia. A possible link between poor facilities and unruly behaviour was identified in the Interim Taylor Report. 'At some grounds the toilets are primitive in design, poorly maintained and inadequate in number. This not only denies the spectator an essential facility he is entitled to expect. It directly lowers standards of conduct . . . Thus crowd conduct becomes degraded and other misbehaviour seems less out of place' [21].

Disorder has been associated with sport since before the 'blues' and 'greens' fought each other at chariot races in ancient Rome. But during the 1970s and 1980s, a new trend of disorder as stylized viciousness rather than emotional over-reaction seemed to emerge. Fighting, throwing missiles and obscene and racist chanting became perceived as more commonplace. Drunken groups of rival supporters seemed to be forever running rampage through town centres and on public transport. Although known as the 'English disease', the trend was repeated on the Continent. This 'hooliganism' was countered by an increasingly repressive policing style which removed much of the enjoyment in attending a match, especially for the herded and caged away supporter.

Although measures had been brought in to tackle these various problems, with differing degrees of success, to a large extent the recommendations of previous inquiries had gone unheeded by the football authorities. Indeed, in his report on the Hillsborough disaster, Lord Justice Taylor was forced to comment that, 'It is a depressing and chastening fact that this is the ninth official report covering crowd safety and control at football grounds. After eight previous reports and three editions of the *Green Guide*, it seems astounding that 95 people could die from overcrowding before the very eyes of those controlling the event' [22].

Turning to the economic context, Ian Taylor [23] noted that the Hillsborough disaster occurred in sequence with a series of others in the 1980s. These disasters had common themes including disregard for safety, poor communications, poorly trained and overworked staff and, in particular, dilapidated public facilities. Taylor argued that Britain, since 1979, 'has experienced disastrous breakdowns in public provision on the part of established institutions purporting to provide for . . . the citizenry'. Safety is judged by the amount of money people want to spend. Writing in 1990, Owen Luder reported that, 'the stadia the majority of British football supporters endure every week are, with few exceptions, dangerous, uncomfortable slums, badly located, with minimal spectator facilities' [24].

Although in recent years the advent of satellite broadcasts and the promise of greater income from digital television have seen the fortunes of Premier Division clubs improve dramatically, the period between 1960 and 1990 witnessed a growing problem in football club finances. An *Economist* survey in 1989 suggested that almost all football clubs would be considered insolvent if they were to be judged by the criteria of the Insolvency Act.

This lack of finance, combined with an overemphasis on footballing success, saw a reduction in investment in ground improvements and in the personnel who, nominally, had the role of ensuring crowd safety. As one football club secretary said, 'Ashes to ashes, dust to dust, what the others won't do the Secretary must.' Although many clubs, most notably in the Premier and First Divisions, have invested in administrative infrastructure since 1989, prior to this the club secretary was often responsible for overseeing all activities, from contracts, players' wages, commercial activities and crowd safety. As the Popplewell Reports [25, 26] into the Bradford fire identified, this jack-of-all-trades burden on club secretaries combined with the ineffectiveness of local licensing authorities to limit the implementation of crowd safety mechanisms. Inglis [27] reports that following the Bradford fire, a flurry of regulatory activity led to the closure of stands or terraces at some twenty-seven grounds. A survey by Arnold and Benveniste [28] three years after Bradford (when crowd safety might still be expected to be a major concern) highlighted that ground improvements were a very low priority, cited by only 7 per cent of clubs as one of their top three objectives.

In the case of football grounds, the general climate of recessionary public squalor has been exacerbated by poor attitudes towards supporters. As Rogan Taylor [29, 30] has shown, supporters made enormous financial contributions to the development of grounds, yet were denied any significant involvement in the running of the game. Ian Taylor concluded [31] that, 'the Hillsborough disaster was the product of a quite consistent and ongoing lack of interest on the part of the owners and directors of English league clubs in the comfort, well-being and safety of their paying spectators'. This is partly explained by the widespread historical perception that supporters care little about the facilities anyway, preferring to see the money spent on players. This view was amusingly captured by Ives [32], who wrote that, 'Given the choice between an exceptionally comfortable seat and a centre forward with balance, skill and the ability to shoot with both feet, most of them would answer very quickly. Only some time after their initial decision would they pause to ask, "Is he any good in the air?" '

This perception of spectator priorities is reinforced by the fortunes of those clubs which have, historically, invested in facilities. As Inglis [33] points out, 'the history of ground design is full of clubs who declined rapidly after building a major stand'. Sheffield United, Bristol City and Burnley all built in the 1970s only to soon find themselves in the old Division Four, whilst large stands also caused financial problems for Chelsea, Wolves and Spurs. Even in the post-Hillsborough era, the redevelopments have not all been good news. Millwall, for example, moved into their brand new ground in August 1993, with high hopes of promotion to the Premier League. But the club has struggled both on and off the pitch, and started the 1996–97 season having been relegated into the Football League Division Two.

Having thus set out the social, historical and economic contexts in which the particular risks associated with British football have arisen, let us now turn to an examination of the disasters themselves, and of the official response to them.

An overview of disasters at British football grounds

The chronology of at least forty-one incidents or disasters in British football grounds has already been included in Table 2.1. Crowd pressure, either direct or leading to structural collapses, was the immediate cause of all except the 1985 Bradford and Birmingham tragedies. Accumulated refuse caught fire at Bradford. Significantly, the disorder commonly associated with football was the immediate cause of only the Birmingham disaster. It should, however, be acknowledged that the disorderly behaviour of English supporters was also the immediate cause of the 1985 Heysel Stadium disaster in Belgium, where 38 Italian fans were killed.

Inquiries and the move to 'legislation by crisis'

A total of nine official reports have been commissioned into safety and order at British football grounds. In reviewing the reports and some recent incidents, we are seeking to demonstrate the ineffectiveness of what we have termed the 'legislation by crisis' response to crowd-related disasters.

The 1924 Shortt Report [34] followed the near disaster at Wembley and included recommendations about overall responsibility, ground licensing, stewarding and fire safety. Inattention to the two latter areas were contributory factors at Bradford in 1985. The 1946 Moelwyn Hughes report [35] arose from the Bolton overcrowding disaster. Recommendations about calculating maximum capacities, counting spectators in and central co-ordination of numbers admitted were not pursued. Had they been so, the Hillsborough disaster might have been avoided.

In 1968, Sir Norman Chester [36] reported on the beginnings of increased disorderly behaviour, whilst Harrington [37] developed the study of hooliganism and noted the possibility of more serious disturbances to come. Harrington also reviewed previous reports and noted that their helpful suggestions had often been ignored. He went on to comment on the lack of legislation covering standards of safety and amenity at grounds. Following shortly after Harrington, the 1969 Lang Report [38] included references to the benefits of CCTV and the impact of alcohol on behaviour. The increased focus upon the problem of hooliganism and crowd control was to the detriment of crowd safety.

The 1972 Wheatley Report [39] was prompted by the 1971 Ibrox disaster and resulted in the Safety at Sports Grounds Act, 1975 and the requirement for safety certificates at designated grounds. The first edition of the *Guide to Safety at Sports Grounds* (the *Green Guide*) was also published. It had been fifty years since Shortt first recommended such action. The 1977 McElhorne Report [40] was concerned with spectator misbehaviour in Scotland. Recommendations included legislation to control alcohol, spectator segregation, perimeter fencing, CCTV, improved amenities, stewarding, club membership and club community involvement. Set up following disorder at England matches abroad, the 1984 Department of the Environment Working Group [41] repeated similar recommendations, alcohol control apart, for English clubs, who began to respond slowly to the suggestions about local membership and community involvement schemes. Notwithstanding the Group's recommendation, the Government passed the Sporting Events (Control of Alcohol) Act, 1985.

The 1985 and 1986 Popplewell Reports [42, 43] dealt with the Bradford, Birmingham and Heysel disasters. Many recommendations echoed the 1977 and 1984 reports. The Football Trust funded the installation of CCTV, the *Green Guide* was revised and there was considerable legislative activity. The range of grounds and stands requiring safety certification was increased by the Fire Safety and Safety of Places of Sport Act, 1987. Exclusion orders were introduced by the Public Order Act, 1986 (Part IV), whilst the Football Spectators Act, 1989 allowed for orders restricting foreign travel for convicted hooligans. The 1989 Act also proposed a national membership scheme for fans and provided for the establishment of a national inspectorate and review body.

Hillsborough, Taylor and radical change

Following the fatal crushing of 95 Liverpool supporters early in the FA Cup semi-final at Hillsborough Stadium on 15 April 1989, the 1989 and 1990 reports [44, 45] produced by Lord Justice Taylor's Inquiry into the disaster proved to be the catalyst for radical change in the stadia industry. The headings under which the seventy-six recommendations in the Final Report are arranged indicate their scope:

- All-Seated Accommodation;
- Advisory Design Council;
- National Inspectorate and Review body;
- Maximum Capacities, Filling and Monitoring Terraces;
- Gangways, Fences, Gates and Crush Barriers;
- Safety Certificates;
- Duties of each Football Club;
- Police Planning;
- Communications and Emergency Services Co-ordination;
- First Aid, Medical Facilities and Ambulances;
- Offences and Penalties; and
- *Green Guide* Revision.

Early reaction to the disaster gave Taylor's recommendations the status of criminal law. Speedy implementation of changes in planning, responsibilities, testing and improving the fabric of stadia involved considerable energy and expense for clubs, local authorities, the police and others. Other key areas of change included the revision of the *Green Guide*, the scrapping of the proposed national membership scheme and the establishment of the Football Licensing Authority and Football Stadia Advisory Design Council. New criminal offences of pitch invasion, racist chanting and missile throwing were also created by the Football (Offences) Act, 1991.

The most notable change proposed by Lord Justice Taylor involved the elimination of standing accommodation at all Premier and Football League stadia. This proposal provoked considerable debate among supporters, many of whom desired to maintain the tradition of standing [46, 47], and among clubs concerned at the costs of implementation, notwithstanding the availability of some monies from the Football Trust [48–50].

In respect of the lower Division clubs, the all-seater requirement was relaxed by the Heritage Secretary, David Mellor, who made a parliamentary statement on 10 July 1992 [51] to report that he was 'prepared to allow some standing accommodation to be retained at grounds in the Third and Fourth Divisions providing terracing is safe'. However, the subsequent guidelines produced by the Football Stadia Advisory Design Council [52] suggested that the regulator's perspective of 'safe' terracing would be rather different from most existing terracing.

In a conversation one of the present authors had with academics and members of the Football Licensing Authority at a Wembley seminar in March 1993, three key points emerged. First, the Taylor report's hidden agenda was thought to be to scupper the national membership scheme. The all-seater solution was intended both as a sop to the government and a catalyst to compel stadium reconstruction. Second, safe standing would be so difficult that seating might be a cheaper option, and, third, research showed that, over fifteen years, seventy of the ninety-two clubs would be in either Division One or the Premier League and thus need seating anyway.

Whatever the merits of the seated versus standing debate, the requirement for all seated accommodation gave rise to a massive programme of building works. As Tony Stevens [53] pointed out, there were only 115 designated sports grounds in England and Wales, yet Taylor had given rise to the overnight appearance of a thriving industry offering a diverse range of services and products. By 1993, according to a display board at the 'Making a Stand' exhibition at the Building Centre, over £300 million had been spent on football stadium developments since 1990, one-third of it funded by the Football Trust. By 1996, the estimated costs of implementing the Taylor Report in the football industry alone had been put at £620 million [54]. The impact of the Taylor Reports has extended beyond football, and stadium redevelopments at least partly prompted by the Taylor recommendations have been seen in a variety of other sports, including rugby union, rugby league, horse racing and motor sports.

Continuing problems since Hillsborough

We want to argue that, notwithstanding the post-Hillsborough activity, a comprehensive analysis of club accident records, Football Licensing Authority inspections, police match reports, media reports, anecdote and our own research experiences would reveal a multitude of examples of potential and actual disasters in sporting venues in Britain since 1989. Table 2.1 is not the end of the chronology, but experiences of such near misses are not normally monitored. A few further examples must suffice to make the point.

In 1992, one of the present authors was made aware through his former duties as a police officer of crushing and crowd distress at the conclusion of the England v Ireland rugby match at Twickenham. A perimeter fence was subsequently moved to allow more concourse space. He was also present in the control room at the Newcastle United v Sunderland fixture on 25 April 1993 when Sunderland supporters experienced crushing whilst both queuing at the turnstiles before the match and on leaving the ground afterwards.

In May 1993, the *Daily Mail* reported [55] that several Newcastle United fans were treated on the pitch after crushing problems at a match at Grimsby Town. The same month, after the Arsenal v Sheffield Wednesday FA Cup Final at Wembley Stadium, one of the authors was one of many people crushed in the crowds making their way off the concourse to the underground station. On the following Monday, the *Daily Telegraph* expressed its concerns [56] in a story headed, 'A Disturbing Crush Down Wembley Way'. For Euro '96 matches played at Wembley Stadium, the police employed a team of mounted officers to restrict the free flow of spectators along Wembley Way.

In the world of motor racing, a near disaster resulted from the mass celebratory circuit invasion after Nigel Mansell's victory in the 1992 British Grand Prix at Silverstone, whilst in 1995, the injuries to spectators caused by a motorcycle leaving the circuit during the TT races on the Isle of Man, were widely reported.

Returning to football, the early rounds of the 1993–94 FA Cup saw intense crowd pressure cause structural failure in the pitch perimeter walls at two non-league grounds. The 1994–95 season saw a similar incident at Tiverton Town for their first-round FA Cup match against Leyton Orient.

And we have not mentioned any of the hostile pitch invasions and/or disorderly behaviour seen in the 1990s at grounds such as Fulham, Manchester City, Millwall, Chelsea, Brighton and, perhaps most notably, at Lansdowne Road in Dublin in February 1995. This latter incident, where the throwing of missiles by England supporters caused injury to other spectators and forced the abandonment of the match, clearly illustrates the risks which public disorder poses to public safety. An unrecorded incident that occurred a month earlier during the Ireland v England Rugby Union fixture involved a collapsed barrier with, fortunately, no injuries.

Other public safety scenarios

Although football grounds are most prominently represented in the history of British sports and leisure disasters, there have also been fatalities in at least three other leisure contexts (not including transportation disasters such as Zeebrugge and the Marchioness). In 1973, fifty people died in a fire at the Summerland Leisure Complex on the Isle of Man. In 1988, two people died in a crowding incident during a rock concert in Castle Donington. Subsequently, in 1993, four teenagers drowned in a canoeing accident at an activity centre in Dorset. And if we examine the media reports of other incidents, we can find plenty of examples of near misses too.

The Pavarotti Concert in Hyde Park in 1991 was expected to attract 250 000 people. Sir John Wheeler, MP, wrote to *The Times* on 21 August 1991 to report the absence of proper safety and stewarding arrangements and to suggest that, 'the Government may well have been saved from a Hillsborough disaster by the wet weather which deterred so many people from attending'.

The New Year celebrations at Trafalgar Square have seen fatalities and concerns about annual crushing prompted the police to initiate discussions on improving safety with other interested parties.

During 1993, crushing problems were reported at pop concerts at the Hammersmith Palais, Crystal Palace and Birmingham City Centre, whilst in October 1994, forty people were hurt as a result of the collapse of a stand at a Pink Floyd concert at London's Earls Court Exhibition Centre.

The failure of 'legislation by crisis'

The British stadia disasters we have reviewed show a remarkable degree of similarity in terms of the responses of the regulators involved. The immediate post-crisis incident phase is characterized by a flurry of activity as regulatory agencies enforce regulations more rigidly, as was observed following the Bradford and Hillsborough incidents. In the later stages of the post-crisis incident 'legitimation' phase [57] specific legislative controls were developed to deal with the demands of that particular incident. Consequently, a piecemeal framework of control has developed that has failed to address the fundamental problems associated with managing complex space. As we have shown, much of the attention of regulators has been focused on the technical solutions to complex space problems. This whole approach comes from the unitary perspective of a world organized by rules. Each report has been commissioned to serve the political purpose of being seen to have done something in response to the disaster. This has been achieved by each post-disaster report proposing further rules and prescriptions, ostensibly to prevent further disaster.

Such a fragmented approach brings with it its own inherent problems. It is centrally oriented, remote from the ground and results in piecemeal, generalized and short-term panic measures. Canter et al. [58], for example, are critical of any piecemeal approach to developing safety, arguing that:

> It has all the quality of closing the stable door after the horse has bolted. An accretion of legislation adds in a piecemeal fashion to previous controls. As a consequence there is never any possibility of examining the system of legislation as a whole, of seeing the directions in which it is accumulating or of developing radical solutions that will deal with fundamental problems. A further problem is that rules and principles get built into the legislation in the early years and, provided it cannot be demonstrated that somebody has been injured because of these rules, there is a powerful inertia in the system of controls operating against changing the rules.

An example of this 'inertia' concerns the role of Scion consultants, who provided technical information to the Wheatley Report [59]. Their findings, regarding rules for crowd movement, speeds and passageway widths, were considered preliminary and, therefore, requiring further research. However, these figures have been used extensively, despite the fact that more recent work has shed doubt on their accuracy. In essence, we can see the creation of a technical paradigm which has become virtually impossible to shift [60]. According to Canter et al. [61] once the problem of crowd safety and control is seen as a technical question, then the mindset becomes one of only technical solutions. This culture of technocracy is held to be important in luring organizations into a false sense of security. An example concerns the building guidelines on sightlines developed by the Football Stadia Advisory Design Council [62]. Calculations on viewing lines have been developed for the average man making no adjustment for the presence of women, children and non-average men.

Thus we have occasional major disaster inquiries leading to radical change rather than allowing the lessons from near misses to feed into a continuous process of incremental improvements in guidelines [63]. Technical recommendations quickly assume paradigm status and have proved extremely difficult to change, even when evidence contradicts them.

Consequently, as we have shown, the disasters and near misses have continued to occur. A 1994 television documentary [64] claimed that British football grounds remained 'An Accident Waiting to Happen'. Much of that documentary was mischievous, but the underlying point is, we believe, still true of a number of stadia. At such venues the historical and economic factors we have outlined still hold powerful sway, the culture of safety remains insufficiently established and the administrative structures remain inadequately resourced. We suggest that fundamental change is still required. Even in those clubs where better practice has been observed there is a danger that as memories of the Hillsborough tragedy fades that resources for ensuring crowd safety will be more difficult to acquire. At one Premier League Club, whose transfer dealings amounted to a multimillion pound figure, the chairman was heard to inquire whether the club really needed that number of stewards (paid no more than £20 per match). The result was that a number of stewards were removed from one stand and located out of sight.

It seems clear to us that the stadia industry has something to learn, both from the research that has been carried out by academics in the areas of safety culture and crisis management and also from the best practice developed by practitioners in the field. But, as we have shown, the problems are not confined to stadia. Thus a focus on the experience of football stadia should make it possible to add to knowledge about safety management in the wider context. Lord Justice Taylor was clear [65] that 'all those responsible for certifying, using and supervising sports grounds should take a hard look at their arrangements and keep doing so. Complacency is the enemy of safety'. Safety is important in all sectors of the sports and leisure industry. The complacency which is shattered only by occasional disaster and radical change needs to be replaced by a marked willingness to seek out and adopt best practice, informed by the results of relevant research.

Summary

- For a variety of social, historical and economic reasons, British football grounds are prominently represented in the overall history of crowd-related disasters.
- There is still ample evidence of potential disaster and near misses are regular occurrences.

- The 'legislation by crisis' response to crowd-related disasters has failed.
- Football and other sports have something to learn both from academic research and from the good practice developed by practitioners.
- Ongoing monitoring of 'near misses' is required to highlight weaknesses and promote wider learning within the sports and leisure industry.
- Technical assumptions should be regularly reviewed and challenged, particularly in the light of new knowledge.
- A proper understanding of the immediate and underlying causes of disaster incidents is required to avoid the pitfall of attempting to solve sociotechnical problems with technical solutions.

Acknowledgements

This chapter draws on earlier versions of the authors' work, and is therefore derived from the following publications:

Elliott, D. and Smith, D. (1993). Football stadia disasters in the United Kingdom: Learning from tragedy? *Industrial and Environmental Crisis Quarterly*, **7**(3), 205–229.
Frosdick, S. (1995) Organisational structure, culture and attitudes to risk in the British stadia safety industry. *Journal of Contingencies and Crisis Management*, **3**(1), 43–57.

References

[1] Sime, J. (1985). Movement towards the familiar. *Environment and Behaviour*, **17**(6), 697–724.
[2] Elliott, D. and Smith, D. (1993). Football stadia disasters in the United Kingdom: Learning from tragedy? *Industrial and Environmental Crisis Quarterly*, **7**(3), 205–229.
[3] Inglis, S. (1987). *The Football Grounds of Great Britain* (2nd edn.), p. 28. Collins Willow.
[4] *The Hillsborough Stadium Disaster 15 April 1989 – Inquiry by the Rt. Hon Lord Justice Taylor – Interim Report* (Taylor Report, 1989). HMSO.
[5] *The Hillsborough Stadium Disaster 15 April 1989 – Inquiry by the Rt. Hon Lord Justice Taylor – Final Report* (Taylor Report, 1990). HMSO.
[6] Elliott, D. (1996). *Organisational Learning from Disaster in the Football Industry.* Unpublished PhD Thesis. University of Durham.

[7] McGibbon, E. (1996). *Do Football clubs learn from Disaster: Case Studies in Isomorphic Learning.* Unpublished MA Thesis. University of Leicester.

[8] Inglis, S. (1996). *The Football Grounds of Great Britain* (3rd edn.), p. 9. Harper Collins.

[9] Football Stadia Advisory Design Council (1991). *Football Stadia Bibliography 1980–1990*, pp. 153–157.

[10] Wyllie, R. (1992) Setting the scene. In *Lessons Learned from Crowd-Related Disasters.* Easingwold Papers No. 4. Home Office Emergency Planning College.

[11] Press reports held in the archives of the Football Licensing Authority.

[12] Ingham, B. (1996). *Daily Mail*, 20 June, p. 20.

[13] Critcher, C. (1991). Putting on the style: Recent aspects of English football. In *British Football and Social Change – Getting into Europe* (J. Williams and S. Wagg, eds.), pp. 67–84. Leicester University Press.

[14] Taylor, I. (1991). English football in the 1990s: Taking Hillsborough seriously. In *British Football and Social Change – Getting into Europe* (J. Williams and S. Wagg, eds.), pp. 3–24. Leicester University Press.

[15] Bale, J. (1991). Playing at home: British football and a sense of place. In *British Football and Social Change – Getting into Europe* (J. Williams and S. Wagg, eds.), pp. 130–144. Leicester University Press.

[16] Bale, J. (1993). *Sport, Space and the City.* Routledge.

[17] Walvin, J. (1986). *Football and the Decline of Britain.* Macmillan.

[18] Dunning, E. (1989). The economic and cultural significance of football. In *Football into the 1990's.* Proceedings of a Conference held at the University of Leicester, 29/30 September 1988, pp. 13–17. Sir Norman Chester Centre for Football Research, University of Leicester.

[19] Canter, D., Comber, M. and Uzzell, D. (1989). *Football in its Place – An Environmental Psychology of Football Grounds*, p. 133, Routledge.

[20] Op. cit. 3. p. 10.

[21] Op. cit. 4. p. 5.

[22] Ibid. p. 4.

[23] Op. cit. 14. pp. 10–12.

[24] Luder, O. (1990). Introduction. In *Sports Stadia After Hillsborough* (O. Luder, ed.), pp. 1–4. Royal Institution of British Architects and the Sports Council in association with the Football Trust.

[25] Home Office (1985). *Committee of Inquiry into Crowd Safety and Control at Sports Grounds – Chairman Mr Justice Popplewell – Interim Report.* HMSO.

[26] Home Office (1986). *Committee of Inquiry into Crowd Safety and Control at Sports Grounds – Chairman Mr Justice Popplewell – Final Report.* HMSO.

[27] Op. cit. 3. p. 37.

[28] Arnold, A. and Benveniste, I. (1988). Wealth and poverty in the English football league. *Accounting and Business Research*, **17**(67), 195–203.

[29] Taylor, R. (1991). Walking alone together: Football supporters and their relationship

with the game. In *British Football and Social Change – Getting into Europe* (J. Williams and S. Wagg, eds.), pp. 111–129. Leicester University Press.

[30] Taylor, R. (1992). *Football and its Fans: Supporters and their Relations with the Game, 1885–1985*. Leicester University Press.

[31] Op. cit. 14. p. 12.

[32] Ives, J. (1992). Take your seats. *Leisure Manager*, December/January, pp. 14–18.

[33] Op. cit. 3. p. 23.

[34] Home Office (1924). *Committee of Inquiry into the Arrangements Made to Deal with Abnormally Large Attendances on Special Occasions, Especially at Athletic Grounds – Report by the Rt. Hon. Edward Shortt KC*. HMSO.

[35] Home Office (1946). *Enquiry into the Disaster at the Bolton Wanderers Football Ground on 9 March 1946 – Report by R. Moelwyn Hughes KC*. HMSO.

[36] Department of Education and Science (1968). *Report of the Committee on Football (Chairman D.N. Chester CBE)*. HMSO.

[37] Harrington, J. (1968). *Soccer Hooliganism: A Preliminary Report*. John Wright.

[38] Ministry of Housing and Local Government (1969). *Report of the Working Party on Crowd Behaviour at Football Matches (Chairman John Lang)*. HMSO.

[39] Home Office (1972). *Report of the Inquiry into Crowd Safety at Sports Grounds (by the Rt. Hon. Lord Wheatley)*. HMSO.

[40] Scottish Education Department (1977). *Report of the Working Group on Football Crowd Behaviour*. HMSO.

[41] Department of the Environment (1984). *Report of an Official Working Group on Football Spectator Violence*. HMSO.

[42] Op. cit. 25.

[43] Op. cit. 26.

[44] Op. cit. 4.

[45] Op. cit. 5.

[46] Williams, J., Dunning, E. and Murphy, P. (1989). *Football and Football Supporters After Hillsborough: A National Survey of Members of the Football Supporters Association*, pp. 23–28. Sir Norman Chester Centre for Football Research, University of Leicester.

[47] Op. cit. 16. p. 47.

[48] Anon. (1992). There they go, there they go: Implementing the Taylor Report. *The Economist*, 18 January, pp. 35–36.

[49] Anon. (1992). Row flares over soccer stadia cash plan. *Building*, 6 March, p. 11.

[50] Anon. (1992). Small clubs left out of £50m football stadia grants. *Building*, 13 March, p. 12.

[51] Hansard. 10 July 1992.

[52] Football Stadia Advisory Design Council (1993). *Terraces – Designing for Safe Standing at Football Stadia*. The Sports Council.

[53] Stevens, A. (1991). Stadia of the future – the pros and cons. In *Panstadia: A*

Comprehensive Guide to Stadium Newbuild, pp. 17–19. Executive Publications (Holdings) Ltd.

[54] Op. cit. 8. p. 13.

[55] Radnege, K. (1993). Keegan's title as Newcastle celebrate. *Daily Mail*, 5 May, p. 52.

[56] Anon. (1993). A disturbing crush down Wembley. *Daily Telegraph*, 17 May.

[57] Smith, D. (1990). Beyond contingency planning: Towards a model of crisis management. *Industrial Crisis Quarterly*, **4**(4), 263–275.

[58] Op. cit. 19. p. 92.

[59] Op. cit. 39.

[60] Fischer, F. (1991). Risk assessment and environmental crisis: Towards an integration of science and participation. *Industrial Crisis Quarterly*, **5**(2), 113–132.

[61] Op. cit. 19. p. 97.

[62] Football Stadia Advisory Design Council (1991). *Seating – Sightlines, Conversion of Terracing, Seat Types*.

[63] Canter, D. (1990). Studying the experience of fires. In *Fires and Human Behaviour* (D. Canter, ed.), pp. 3–10. David Fulton Publishers Ltd.

[64] *Dispatches*, Channel 4, 12 October 1994.

[65] Op. cit. 5. p. 5.

PART 2 ACCOUNTABILITY

Overview

Part Two deals with questions of accountability. It examines the concept of risk as a mechanism for attributing blame and, in that context, reviews the emergence of the legal principle of corporate manslaughter liability. It goes on to examine some general issues in liability from the perspective of the police service and concludes by setting out the role of the football industry regulator.

Chapter summaries

In Chapter 3, Steve Frosdick discusses the concept of risk. He describes how the meaning of risk has changed from risk as chance to risk as danger and, more recently to risk as blame or liability. He draws out the different ideas of risk held by natural and social scientists and outlines the difficulties these create for safety managers. He concludes by suggesting that risk as blame or liability means criminal as well as civil accountability for those responsible for failures in safety management.

In Chapter 4, Lynne Walley seeks to address the evolution of criminal liability in two areas of particular relevance to the sporting world and which impact directly on sports management. They are, first, the change in the way that corporate manslaughter is dealt with and, second, the changing nature of criminal liability regarding assault and injury on the field of play.

In Chapter 5, Alan Beckley examines the organizations that are legally liable and responsible for the safety of persons attending public events. The police are responsible as the safety net for all such events and therefore individual police officers should be aware of their responsibility, liability and the possible harm which can befall emergency service workers. The various types of public event and the likely problem areas are examined. Strategies for preventing or mitigating disasters and the negative effects on the individual are discussed.

In Chapter 6, John de Quidt examines the origins, role and impact of the Football Licensing Authority (FLA) against the background of the changes at English football grounds since it was formed in July 1990. The main focus of the chapter is on the FLA's approach to safety, on its advisory work and on its vision for the future.

3 Risk as blame

Steve Frosdick

This chapter discusses the concept of risk. It describes how the meaning of risk has changed from risk as chance to risk as danger and, more recently to risk as blame or liability. It draws out the different ideas of risk held by natural and social scientists and outlines the difficulties these create for safety managers. It concludes by suggesting that risk as blame or liability means criminal as well as civil accountability for those responsible for failures in safety management.

The meaning of risk

Engineers, scientists, academics and others involved in studying the uncertain business of risk employ terminology which is itself marked by some uncertainty. Even, or perhaps especially, the term 'risk' can be the subject of much debate. For such a little word, 'risk' is a very complex concept. Its meaning has evolved over the years and is now the subject of considerable disagreement between natural and social scientists.

The development of the concept of risk from the seventeenth century to date has been outlined by Mary Douglas [1]. The idea of risk originated in the mathematics associated with gambling in the seventeenth century. Risk referred to probability, for example to the chance of throwing a six on a dice, combined with the magnitude of potential gains or losses. In the eighteenth century, the idea of risk was employed in the marine insurance business. Risk was a neutral idea, taking account of both gains and losses. Insurers would work out a premium based on the chance of a ship returning home laden with riches against the chance of it sinking with the loss of all its hands and cargo. In the nineteenth century, ideas of risk emerged in the study of economics. People were considered to be risk averse, therefore entrepreneurs needed special incentives to take the risks involved in investment.

The twentieth century has seen the concept of risk move on to refer only to negative outcomes in engineering and science, with particular reference to the hazards posed by modern technological developments in the offshore, petrochemical and nuclear power industries. The Royal Society Study Group [2, 3] definitions began with risk as 'the probability that a particular adverse event occurs during a stated period of time, or results from a particular challenge' [4]. Acknowledging the needs of engineers and scientists who specialize in risk studies, the Royal Society Report also included definitions from British Standard 4778, which defines risk as 'a combination of the probability, or frequency, of occurrence of a defined hazard and the magnitude of the consequences of the occurrence' [5].

Distinctions also need to be drawn between individual and societal risks, because of the differences in public reaction to which these give rise. The former has been defined by the Health and Safety Executive as 'the risk to any particular individual, either a worker or a member of the public, [that is] anybody living at a defined radius from an establishment, or somebody following a particular pattern of life' [6]. The latter represents the risk to society as a whole and has been similarly defined as 'measured, for example, by the chance of a large accident causing a defined number of deaths' [6].

As Warner points out, 'Scientists and engineers use these definitions because they provide the basis from which they can carry out their practical work' [7], work which is mainly concerned with putting numbers on risk through the calculation of probabilities and the use of databank information on component failures and reliability.

These ideas of risk are not shared by social scientists, for whom 'there are serious difficulties in attempting to view risk as a one-dimensional concept [when] a particular risk or hazard [means] different things to different people in different contexts [and] risk is socially constructed' [8].

Psychological dimensions of risk perception

Some psychologists argue that the layperson views risk not as the product of scientific rationality but as a matter of popular social construction. In other words, the lay view is swayed not by the scientific evidence about probability and consequences, for example about the risk of catching mad cow disease from eating beef, but simply by how they feel about the consequences – scared that they or their children will be harmed. Some consequences are immediately observable and known to those exposed, whilst others are newer and unknown risks, perhaps with delayed and unobservable effects. On another dimension, some risks are controllable, voluntary and not dread, whereas others are catastrophic, uncontrollable and involuntary. Slovic [9] describes these two dimensions or factors as 'dread risk' and 'unknown risk' and demonstrates, through references to his previous studies of individual's evaluations of the riskiness of a variety of hazards, how the more dread and unknown the risk, the more hazardous the risk is perceived to be.

Taking a simple example, if we were to ask four different people to rate the risk of flying in an aeroplane, we might get four different answers, as follows:

- I often fly and it doesn't scare me at all − flying is a low risk activity;
- I often fly but it still scares me − flying is medium risk;
- I rarely fly but it doesn't really scare me − flying is medium risk;
- I rarely fly and the thought of it really scares me − flying is definitely high risk.

Thus risk is seen as a personal perception.

Socio-anthropological dimensions of risk perception

However, within the behavioural sciences themselves there are disagreements. The psychologists' views have been criticized by anthropologists as failing to take account of the cultural dimensions of risk perception. Mary Douglas argues [10] that, 'the profession of psychologists which has grown up to study risk perception takes the culturally innocent approach by treating political dissension as intellectual disagreement'. The Royal Society Study Group lend credibility to these criticisms in their acknowledgement that, 'one of the major challenges to orthodox psychological approaches to risk perception over the past ten years has come from the grid-group "cultural theory" proposed by the anthropologist Mary Douglas and her colleagues' [11].

This 'cultural theory' [12, 13] now more aptly referred to as the theory of cultural complexity, is a method of disaggregated cultural analysis, which argues that there are four different cultural archetypes: individualism, fatalism, hierarchy and egalitarianism. Each of these reflects a cohesive and coherent cluster of attitudes, beliefs and styles of relationships. These four ways of life inform the perceptions of the participants, determine their behaviour and are used by them to justify the validity of their social situations. Thus the anthropological perspective is that risk is a cultural, rather than an individual perception. As Warner puts it, risk for the anthropologist is 'threat or danger whose perception will depend on the prevailing culture in which there are four major groups: hierarchists, egalitarians, fatalists and individualists' [14].

Risk as blame

During the 1980s and 1990s, the concept of risk has moved on from probability and consequences, and from threat or danger, real or perceived, and into the idea of risk as accountability, or risk as blame and liability, even without fault. This view has emerged from the idea that the world is a more individualist place. Previously, the world made rules to protect itself from individuals. Now, individuals need to be protected from the effects of the world. Douglas [15] shows how risk has thus become a tool of the legal system. The reduced influence of the Church has had implications for the ability of sin and taboo to constrain behaviour. When society was more hierarchical, being in sin or breaking taboo meant the individual was out of line with society. In a more individualist global culture, being at risk means that society is out of line with the individual, whose rights are in need of protection. As Douglas puts it, 'A generalized concern for fairness has started us on a new cultural phase. The political pressure is not explicitly against taking risks, but against exposing others to risk' [16].

The implications for safety management

The psychological dimension of risk perception suggests that different people perceive risk in entirely different ways. The socio-anthropological approach suggests, as the Royal Society Study Group point out, 'that people select certain risks for attention to defend their preferred lifestyles and as a forensic resource to place blame on other groups' [17]. Having acknowledged that there is a substantial debate about the idea of risk, I want to adopt a position on risk which not only sides with the social scientists but also advocates the importance of proper safety management.

Acceptance of the social scientists' findings results in a scenario where no one measure of risk can represent the perceptions of the different individuals and the disaggregated cultural types. This would seem to creates problems for the safety manager. Whilst total safety, in other words a total absence of risk, can never be guaranteed, good safety management means reducing the risks as far as is reasonably practicable. But it would seem that there are no right or wrong answers here! If nobody is wrong to perceive a particular issue as a risk, and if any one hazard can be properly evaluated as either low, medium or even high risk, then why should the practitioner even begin to bother with all this?

The answer lies in two realities. First, it is clear that the owners and operators of sports and leisure facilities are unequivocally responsible for the safety of their customers. Second, the climate of risk as blame means that, in the event of a disaster, owners and operators will be called to account for the adequacy of their arrangements for public safety.

Responsibility for safety

The Home Office Guide to Safety at Sports Grounds – commonly referred to as the *Green Guide*, is quite clear that 'the responsibility for the safety of spectators at the ground lies at all times with the ground management' [18]. Many sports facilities are multipurpose, hosting pop concerts and the like as well as sporting events. And the Home Office and Health and Safety Commission *Guide to Health, Safety and Welfare at Pop Concerts and Similar Events* – the *Purple Guide* – tells us that 'anyone who is directly responsible for the undertaking ... will have responsibilities for the health and safety of third parties affected by it, including the audience' [19]. Finally, the *Crowd Safety Guidance* from the Health and Safety Executive includes a statement that, 'ensuring crowd safety is a basic responsibility of venue managers, owners and operators' [20]. The day-to-day responsibility for risk and safety management may well be delegated to a safety practitioner. But the accountability for safety performance and the liability for safety failures stays where the responsibility starts – at the top – with the Chairman and Board of Directors, or their public sector equivalents, of the company or body running the venue concerned.

Accountability and liability

Both Priest and Lowi have linked risk with the law of tort in America and highlighted the increase in both litigation and liability for risk. Priest observes that 'the principal function of modern civil law is to control risk' [21]. Emphasizing the link with accountability, he goes on to argue that 'the more precise statement of the first principle of civil liability today is that a court will hold a party to an injury liable if that party could have taken some action to reduce the risk of the injury at a cost less than the benefit from risk reduction' [22]. The newspapers carry almost daily stories of large payments being awarded in civil damages for injuries sustained. And since many such cases appear to be settled out of court, there is a suspicion that ability to pay is as important an issue as negligence in any pre-trial discussions about liability. Lowi summarizes the development of tort 'from individual responsibility to interdependence, from individual blame to distributional balance, from liability to risk, and from negligence defined as "no liability without fault" to the dropping of negligence altogether in favor of ability to pay, spread through insurance and customer mark-up, toward the concept of "social costs" '[23].

Whilst public liability insurance can provide the requisite ability to pay in actions for negligence, nevertheless, as the next chapter by Lynne Walley makes clear, it is not now just a matter for the civil law. In December 1994, British legal history was made. An outdoor activities company and its managing director were convicted of manslaughter following the deaths of four teenagers during a canoeing trip in Dorset. The managing director was jailed for three years, later reduced on appeal to two years. But he went to jail. And many more companies and individuals could find themselves facing criminal prosecution if the Law Commission's proposals [24] for a new offence of corporate killing are adopted.

The media's love of scapegoating means there is no doubt that, if public safety arrangements fail disastrously in the future, there will be a clamour for the owners and operators concerned to be called to criminal account. The best public liability insurance will not help the chairman or director 'gripping the rails' at the Old Bailey. Owners and operators therefore need to be sure that their safety arrangements are capable of withstanding the closest public scrutiny. They need to understand risk and know how to assess and manage it. This involves understanding risk as a multiplicity of perceptions about the source and level of threat or danger from future events and about the variety of adverse consequences, including legal liability, to which such events may give rise. It does not mean reacting to every perceived risk with measures which are disproportionately expensive or which damage people's legitimate enjoyment of the event or activity. But it does require the exercise of practical management judgement, informed by a sound understanding of risk and risk perception. It means evaluating which risks have not been reduced to an acceptable level, determining what to do about them and doing it. It means owners and operators knowing how to document their actions and decisions so they can produce the evidence to show their insurance company, a Civil Court, the police, a Coroner's inquest or even the jury in a criminal trial, that they did everything that they could reasonably be expected to do.

Summary

- Engineers and natural scientists see risk as a quantifiable expression of probability and consequences.
- Social scientists disagree, seeing risk as a personal or cultural perception of threat or danger.
- Recent writers have shown how risk may also be seen as blame or liability.
- Maximizing safety means minimizing risk. People who are responsible for safety need to understand these different ideas of risk because they will be held accountable − even criminally liable − if things go wrong and disaster strikes.

Acknowledgement

An earlier version of some of the arguments in this chapter was previously published as Frosdick, S. (1996). Risk and responsibility. *Panstadia International Quarterly Report,* **3**(4), 34−36.

References

[1] Douglas, M. (1990). Risk as a forensic resource. *Daedalus,* **119**(4), 1−16.
[2] Royal Society (1983). *Risk Assessment − Report of a Royal Society Study Group.* The Royal Society.
[3] Royal Society (1992). *Risk: Analysis, Perception and Management − Report of a Royal Society Study Group.*
[4] Op. cit. 3. p. 2.
[5] British Standards Institution (1991). *BS 4778 Part 3 Section 3.2.*
[6] Health and Safety Executive (1988). *The Tolerability of Risk from Nuclear Power Stations,* para. 52. HMSO.
[7] Warner, F. (1992). Calculated risks. *Science and Public Affairs,* Winter 1992, 44−49.
[8] Op. cit. 3. p. 7.
[9] Slovic, P. (1991). Beyond numbers: A broader perspective on risk perception and risk communication. In *Acceptable Evidence: Science and Values in Risk Management* (D. Mayo and R. Hollander, eds.), pp. 48−64. Oxford University Press.

[10] Op. cit. 1. p. 9.

[11] Op. cit. 3. p. 112.

[12] Douglas, M. (1978). Cultural bias. Royal Anthropological Institute, Occasional Paper 35. Reprinted in M. Douglas (1982), *In the Active Voice*, pp. 183–254. Routledge and Kegan Paul.

[13] Thompson, M., Ellis, R. and Wildavsky, A. (1990). *Cultural Theory*. Westview Press.

[14] Op. cit. 7.

[15] Op. cit. 1.

[16] Douglas, M. (1992). Risk and blame. In *Risk and Blame: Essays in Cultural Theory*, pp. 3–21. Routledge.

[17] Op. cit. 11.

[18] Home Office and Scottish Office (1990). *Guide to Safety at Sports Grounds*. HMSO.

[19] Health and Safety Commission and Home Office (1993). *Guide to Health, Safety and Welfare at Pop Concerts and Similar Events*. HMSO.

[20] Health and Safety Executive (in press) *Crowd Safety*.

[21] Priest, G. (1990). The new legal structure of risk control. *Daedalus*, **119**(4), 207–228.

[22] Op. cit. 21.

[23] Lowi, T. (1990). Risks and rights in the history of American governments. *Daedalus*, **119**(4), 17–40.

[24] Law Commission (1996). *Legislating the Criminal Code: Involuntary Manslaughter*. HMSO.

4 The changing face of criminal liability

Lynne Walley

This chapter seeks to address the evolution of criminal liability in two areas of particular relevance to the sporting world and which impact directly on sports management. They are, first, the change in the way that corporate manslaughter is dealt with and, second, the changing nature of criminal liability regarding assault and injury on the field of play.

Introduction

The first area to be examined in this chapter is corporate liability manslaughter. The evolution of this legal principle has gathered momentum in the latter part of this century and has run parallel with the equally rapid evolution of the legal principles of nervous shock and causal links. Many of us are now familiar with these principles following the Hillsborough disaster, which still has legal reverberations in 1996. Many of these evolving legal issues are inextricably bound.

The second principle to be looked at in this chapter is one of sporting negligence. Principles here highlight a duty of care being owed to and by players, in a variety of sports, and how actions on the field are increasingly leading to actions in court.

The discussion on the legal evolution of each of these principles will be illustrated by a case study.

The evolution of corporate liability manslaughter

I shall begin with the legal definitions of 'corporation', 'liability' and 'manslaughter', which give some background to the legal evolution of the situation in which we find ourselves at present with regard to corporate manslaughter.

A 'corporation' is defined as 'a distinct legal entity separate from such persons who may be members of it, and having rights, duties and perpetual succession'. We will see how this definition has begun to change in recent years. 'Liability' is defined as 'a legal obligation which can be civil or criminal'. This legal definition is expanding and again we will be looking at the extension of this liability. 'Manslaughter' is defined as where 'death is caused by an unlawful act or culpable negligence without malice aforethought'.

The legal dilemma that we are in at present arises from the fact that corporations have never been viewed as individuals and therefore were considered to be incapable of committing crimes. Companies have always lain outside the criminal law. This well established legal principle has been in existence for hundreds of years; in fact Lord Chief Justice Holt said in 1701 that corporations were not indictable but their members were.

How could a corporation be viewed as a criminal when it could not stand at the bar or have the necessary *'mens rea'* (guilty mind)? However, as a result of the increase in diversity and complexity of operation within companies, legal account-ability in all forms has become a necessity. We all recognize that many sporting clubs have company status and are therefore liable for a number of civil liabilities; however, these liabilities are increasingly extending into the criminal arena.

Mining disasters in the early 1930s and 1940s highlighted severe safety voids and led to the previously well-established principle of the company as a separate legal entity being questioned. Indirect liability has existed for some time in the form of vicarious liability, that is where the employers are legally responsible for the torts (wrongdoings) of their employees.

In 1957 Lord Denning likened a company to a human being saying that it had a brain and nerve centre which controlled it. The people who controlled that 'mind' were the Directors. From that kernel the gap between individual culpability and corporate liability narrowed [1].

The individual entrepreneur began to be replaced by increasingly larger hierarchically structured corporations where chains of liability increased and became more clouded.

A variety of factors have assisted the legal evolution of corporate liability. First, the decline of public confidence in company responsibility and a greater degree of accountability being demanded by the general public. Second, the growing number of regulatory 'crimes', which are breaches in health and safety regulations. We all regularly witness breaches of regulatory crimes in the exposé type documentaries on television. Third, the effect that the media has had on disasters which are beamed into our living rooms. I am thinking specifically of the Bradford, Hillsborough, Heysel and Zeebrugge disasters.

These images are often graphic and disturbing and enable a 'sitting-room jury' to speculate on the likely causes of the disaster. How many of us speculated about the cause of the Zeebrugge disaster long before the official report was released? Through these instant media images we are immediately able to question the cause of the disaster and demand accountability and liability.

A further factor which has assisted the evolution of corporate liability is the publicly declared annual profits of many companies compared to the seemingly disproportionate level of fines for breaches when, and if, a case reaches court. Often, moreover, if companies are fined, these sanctions are rarely reported in the popular press.

The problem in the way that the present criminal justice system deals with such liability is that breaches have not been perceived as being criminal. Traditionally, safety laws have not been seen as moralistic, they have been formulated and enforced by a separate agency (the Health and Safety Executive) and 'policed' by them. As discussed earlier a company could not have the *mens rea* or the *actus reus* (the elements of the offence) to commit a crime.

Health and safety regulations rarely look at the consequences of accidents but more likely at noncompliance, i.e. that obvious harm can be prevented. Often the complex nature of modern-day machinery and materials mean that accidents generate yet more regulations and safety guidance. Again we see the dichotomy of noncompliance set against acts seen as crimes.

Oddly, the public appear to have a clearer view of corporate liability when dealing with food and drug regulations, partly because we are aware that one individual has not produced all the food from the factory, and that the company should take the collective blame.

Sanctions that have previously lain in The Health and Safety at Work etc. Act, 1974 are now proving wholly inadequate for incidents that result from huge numbers of people collected in one place and from the technical advances made at the end of the twentieth century.

In 1993, Celia Wells [2] addressed the development of corporate liability under a number of different headings; however, development to date has been restrained. Nevertheless, proposals in 1996 [3] have moved these issues further towards criminal responsibility.

We have already looked at the point that historically the corporation was not recognized as a legal entity and that they could not realistically 'stand charged at the bar'. However the existing and well-established principle of vicarious liability moves towards a fuller liability.

It has been estimated that over 19 000 deaths [4] have occurred through corporate activities. However, it was not until December 1994 that the first successful prosecution took place [5]. This successful conclusion came at the end of a long period that had seen some of the most horrific national disasters.

1994 was also the year that the Law Commission [6] looked specifically at involuntary manslaughter when, among other things, the Commission said that 'there was a strength of public feeling that acts or omissions of junior employees should not result in the sole blame being placed on them'. The Commission suggested a change in the law to find a company guilty if they 'ought to have reasonably been aware of a significant risk that its conduct could result in death or serious injury', and also that its conduct fell significantly below that which would have reasonably been demanded.

Difficulties arise in the aggregation of fault principle when several directors are each aware of individual risks but no-one has the overall picture of mounting risk. Previous assumptions within large companies have been that no-one individually had the necessary 'controlling mind'; however, those assumptions are now changing.

The Law Commission [6] also looked at gross negligence manslaughter which was defined as 'indifference to an obvious risk to injury and health, where there was an actual foresight of the risk coupled with a determination to run it'. This was the test used in the OLL Ltd case in 1994 which is the first case study in this chapter.

With regard to inquest inquiries, this increasingly archaic form of jury may hear all the facts of an accident and declare a verdict of 'unlawful killing' but may not deal with factors of guilt or order a re-investigation by the Crown Prosecution Service or the police. The jury in the case of the *Marchioness* boating disaster announced a verdict of unlawful killing, and whilst a criminal prosecution ensued, the captain of the vessel which struck the *Marchioness* was later acquitted of failing to keep watch.

When dealing with the aftermath of disasters and the possible attribution of blame the law looks at a range of causal levels. Whilst these levels can often stand alone as sole responsibility, they are often interwoven. Historically the law has looked at acts which are beyond the control of the company. They are, first, 'acts of God' which relate to natural disasters, most notably the Aberfan coal-slide disaster and dam bursts. Second, 'acts of employees' raises questions of liability relating to the actual act of a company's employee(s). Here the courts would ask if and how they have acted negligently set against company policy or individual negligence.

Case study - corporate manslaughter liability

As a result of a dreadful catalogue of errors four teenagers drowned in Lyme Bay in Dorset having been in the sea for some four hours after they had capsized whilst on a canoeing trip from an outward bound centre.

This incident led to the company being the first to be convicted of manslaughter in English legal history. The company was fined £60 000 but, more significantly, the managing director was given an immediate custodial sentence.

On this particular occasion, training for the canoeing session and the inadequate safety procedures at the centre had been grossly negligent. The canoeing tuition had taken place for only one hour in a swimming pool and by unqualified centre staff prior to the trip, which was undertaken on the open sea.

Previous staff, who had subsequently left the centre, had highlighted the lack of safety provisions and the poor quality of sports equipment. In fact, a former instructor gave evidence to the court as to the lack of safety equipment and overall safety standards. However, these and other previous warnings to the managing director had been ignored.

To compound this situation, on the day of the accident the emergency services were not informed when the canoeists failed to reach their destination. This was due to the fact that the trip had no time limits set and therefore the centre was not aware of a start time or proposed finish time. Furthermore, despite the trip being on open sea and some two miles in length the coastguards had not been alerted.

When the group was finally missed by the centre manager, instead of immediately alerting the rescue services, he first went looking for them by car on a coastal road. On alerting the emergency services, he wrongly stated that the party had flares with them.

The centre manager was charged with four counts of manslaughter, the same charge that stood against the managing director. However, the centre manager was acquitted when the jury failed to reach a verdict after lengthy deliberations.

Critics could not fail to comment that the company profits, £242 603 for the previous financial year, were in direct conflict with the level of safety equipment and trained staff at the centre. Commentators have also noted that this particular conviction was made easier by the fact that the company was managed and owned by a small team and therefore direct liability was easier to attribute.

The *Herald of Free Enterprise* disaster and the Purley train disaster would illustrate this category. Third, 'acts of a stranger' relate to a liability that cannot be located, notably in the cases of the Bradford and Kings Cross disasters, where an unknown individual dropped a lighted cigarette and started a fire. Lastly, the courts would look at company policy which may be a causal factor in the disaster. Here the courts will examine the working practices of the company and indeed those of the industry in which it operates to determine negligence.

In the case of company liability, extension of this area of liability can be broken down into three categories:

- an individual's wrongdoing;
- the principle of aggregation; and
- the liability of company structures.

Individual wrongdoing is already covered in law in the form of vicarious liability and direct liability. However, a danger here is of the individual being used as a scapegoat for a subsequent disaster or conversely the company knowingly shielding culpable employees.

Employees who expose crime, fraud or serious malpractices at work have previously had little or no legal protection. However, current proposals for 'whistleblowers' in the form of a Private Members Bill [7], seek to address some element of protection for the many incidents in which employees are aware of malpractice and health and safety risks.

Elements of 'whistle blowing' have been evident in many high profile cases, among them the *Piper Alpha* accident, the Clapham train disaster, the *Herald of Free Enterprise* sinking at Zeebrugge and the Lyme Bay (Dorset) canoeing disaster. In the Lyme Bay case an employee at the outdoor centre highlighted the imminent danger and lack of safety precautions, but these warnings went unheeded.

Under the new proposals an employee may gain protection against dismissal or discrimination. However, they must firstly raise their concerns in a reasonable way internally and, if no action results, then they would be protected by 'going public'. Anyone making malicious claims through bad faith or for financial gain would not be protected by the proposed legislation. Equally no action would result if it was felt that it was not in the public interest to pursue the issues.

The second category is one of aggregation. This is a holistic approach to liability, with prosecution of the individual and the company. This raises a number of issues, not least that the individual may indeed have been reckless but the company had failed to ensure safe systems of work.

The last category of liability is one of company structures. This raises issues of line management responsibilities and reporting. We could ask whether fines are effective to deal with such breaches. On a wider stage, how do the public react to companies being criminalized and the subject of criminal sentences?

These issues have been addressed by a number of leading academics. David Bergman [8] has commented on the acquittal of all the defendants following the sinking of the *Herald of Free Enterprise* in 1987. The estimated costs of the court actions were £10 million and yet the Crown failed to prove the key element of the crime of manslaughter, namely that the Directors, senior managers or ship masters ought to have known that there was an obvious risk of the ship setting sail with its bow doors open.

The acquittals could not detract from the fact that boardroom decisions and failures can, in principle, form the basis of manslaughter liability. The questions to be asked include, what are the company's working practices and who, on the Board, should have known about them? Mr Justice Turner stated during the *Herald of Free Enterprise* case that a company was properly indictable for the crime of manslaughter through the controlling mind of one of its agents.

Subsequently academics have addressed both corporate liability as a 'new crime' [9] and the way in which prosecutorial policy is formed to deal with corporations [10].

Issues of company liability are complex and can be compounded by a number of elements, not least that harm done by a company can often result in the loss of many lives. How then, given the old adage, should 'the punishment fit the crime'?

Gobert has suggested that the burden of proof should rest with the defence and not the prosecution [11] and that the burden would not be discharged merely on proof of certain acts but would also have to deal with the foreseeability of the risk when linked, as mentioned earlier, to the current practices and conventions of the industry.

Current worldwide commercial practices would not want to see repressive commercial law however that must be set against incoming legislation from the European Community (EC) which would ostensibly set all countries on the same level. Therefore United Kingdom status regarding EC legislation and directives would impact on proposals for the social charter and the way in which we operate with regards to health and safety initiatives.

Gary Slapper has commented that the lack of action on the part of the criminal justice system has stemmed from the general public's reluctance to recognize that companies can commit serious crime [12]. The Hungerford disaster, where Michael Ryan shot several people, took place inbetween the Zeebrugge disaster and the Kings Cross disaster and yet no-one would fail to recognize Hungerford as a purely criminal act. The same cannot be said for the former and latter disasters [13].

Statistics provided by Gary Slapper calculated that the majority of prosecutions against companies for commercially caused death were brought before the Magistrates court where the maximum fine is £5000. The same research calculated that of the mere 3 per cent of cases that reached the Crown court the average fine was £2145 [14]. Equally, information given in the Health and Safety Committee Report of 1994/95 stated that the average fine was falling and that 83 per cent of prosecutions resulted in a conviction [15].

The way that companies deal with safety internally has, historically, emphasized notions of 'turning a blind eye' to minor accidents and breaches of safety rules. However, innovative work undertaken by the University of Manchester Institute of Science and Technology (UMIST) has deconstructed safety budgets and records by looking at the behavioural approach to safety. Research undertaken by UMIST at a Courtaulds factory started with a 'safety climate' questionnaire and then set departmental targets and trained certain employees in safety observation. This sixteen-week scheme, supported by workers and the management, saw a fall in accidents for a similar period of 52 per cent [16].

Two notable cases quoted by the Health and Safety Committee Report could easily apply to sports grounds. The first case involved self-employed workers removing external pipework lagged with asbestos which was thrown into an open skip in a car park. The clients who were in control of the site were subsequently fined £15 000 for failing to ensure the health and safety of those not in their employment. The second case involved a safety consultant who was engaged to supervise a site where asbestos piping was being used. The Health and Safety Inspector found an unsafe system of work and the consultant was fined £2000. He subsequently declared himself bankrupt [17].

There is clearly a change in attitude regarding company safety and this is being mirrored by flatter management structures and the growing awareness that safety is the responsibility of every employer and employee. This vanguard of change is also being seen in the legal system and in the attempts to examine company liability.

To end this first part of the chapter I shall refer to the Law Commission paper which was published in March 1996 [18]. This paper, having consulted those concerned with matters of criminal liability in this area, sought to address the liability of those who kill when they do not intend to cause death or serious injury.

For the purposes of this chapter I shall refer to the two Law Commission recommendations which would have implications for the sporting industry, namely, corporate manslaughter and (briefly) the use of independent contractors.

It is particularly timely that the Law Commission looks specifically at corporate manslaughter. The proposed definition is that a person would be liable where their conduct created a risk of causing death or serious injury to another or where they were seriously at fault in failing to be aware of this risk. Of course this test had previously been used in the *Herald of Free Enterprise* case where several officials testified that the risk was not obvious.

Many observers were critical of the ruling in the *Herald* case and it highlighted the notion of 'identification', that is, who are the officers of the company who are the 'embodiment of the company'? Problems arise, as discussed earlier, when there is no clear line management or where no one individual has a vested interest in the safety issues of the company.

The Law Commission examined the pros and cons of extending the current legislation. In favour of doing so was to supplement the seemingly inadequate health and safety regulations and also to clearly define the identification notion, that is, who in the company is responsible for safety issues. The main reason against the proposals for extending legislation was the whole notion of having corporate manslaughter on the statute books.

The Commission discussed the possibility of extending corporate liability. Vicarious liability as operated in the United States incorporates liability as a crime committed by any corporation employee if committed within the scope of his or her employment. To evade liability the company would have to prove that the employee had acted for personal gain or directly against the policies of the company. Again, the provisions that the company had made for safety issues and protocols would be examined.

The Commission accepted the arguments put forward and did not extend the doctrine of identification by introducing aggregation.

The introduction of a new offence would involve the following:

- the defendant's conduct caused the death; and
- the risk of death or serious injury would be obvious to a reasonable person; and
- the conduct fell below what would be reasonably expected.

With regard to the foreseeability of the risk the courts would look at the seriousness of the defendants conduct and how, if at all, that conduct had veered from company policy.

The Commission refers to a 'management failure' by the corporation. This is further clarified by failure being defined as 'the activities managed or organized fails to ensure the health and safety of persons employed in or affected by those activities and such a failure may be regarded as a cause of person's death notwithstanding that the immediate cause is the act or omission of an individual' [19].

With regard to the use of independent contractors a corporation may employ a contractor to carry out work in a variety of situations. A corporation who engages a contractor is not normally liable to others for the negligence of that contractor. However, there are exceptions, notably where the employer fails to co-ordinate the subcontractor or where the employer exercises control over the subcontractors. As we saw earlier in relation to recent health and safety prosecutions, the liability will rest entirely with the subcontractor, given certain criteria.

Extensive work done by Celia Wells from Cardiff Law School on the extension of liability looks to the future and the ways in which we can comprehensively address issues of corporate liability. We need to continue to raise the public awareness of liability placed on companies. We also need to promulgate best practice and inform the public; a task that is largely being done by the Health and Safety Executive and is one of the main aims of this particular book. The currently disjointed legislative forum needs to be consolidated and simplified, as witnessed by the Law Commission proposals, if there is to be an extension of criminality and appropriate, realistic and uniform financial penalties levied against offending corporations.

The evolution of sporting negligence

The second part of this chapter will deal with the evolution of liability on the field of play, and the way in which the courts are dealing with cases which question the basic principles of law.

Many years ago people would have considered sport and the law to be at opposite ends of the playing field. However, the increasing application of legal intervention mean that sports managers have to be aware of judicial decisions. So far the law has impacted on sport in the criminal form of assault, judicial review of sports organizing bodies, the development of contract law for players and EC intervention.

In the United Kingdom the common law duty of care stems from the 1932 case of Donaghue v Stevenson and the principles expounded there have underpinned the application of law ever since. Very briefly the legal principles established in that case, called the 'neighbour principle', and delivered by Lord Aiken set out that:

> You must take reasonable care to avoid acts or omissions which you can reasonably foresee would be likely to injure your neighbour. Who then is my neighbour? The answer seems to be, persons who are so closely and directly affected by my act that I ought reasonably to have them in my contemplation as being so affected when I am directing my mind to the acts or omissions which are called into question [20].

Whilst this principle applies to sports participants, spectators and other members of the public, the commonly held view for some decades after this pronouncement was that those who participated in sport, largely did so with their own consent to some injury.

However, that view is now changing, brought about by a number of factors, which include a growing awareness for the safety of all who participate in sport, calls for higher standards of safety where children are involved in sporting activities and not least the high stakes that many professionals, and amateurs, play for.

Sport is now big business and profits and earnings are such that many people have a vested interest in keeping players fit, whatever the sport, for as long as possible. Players, who may not have alternative careers to turn to, need to ensure that their playing careers are as long and as lucrative as possible. High profile players, if injured, can not only themselves lose money, but can lose money for a number of people, namely clubs and sponsors who have a vested interest in keeping players active. Losses can run into substantial sums of money, and therefore the sports insurance specialists are literally having a field day.

If an accident or mishap befalls a professional which prevents them from realizing their potential then they are likely to find that an insurance policy will be covering them. Such policies can cover clubs, sponsors and even bonus schemes. Premiums are high but a lot is at stake [21].

This is merely one part of the jigsaw which has evolved into the picture we now see. The evolution has often been disaster led, as we saw in the first part of this chapter and the supporting case study. Legal developments in sporting negligence often take place on a much smaller scale but nonetheless are responsible for the extension of well-established principles.

A number of questions have to be examined when we are looking at the whole area of sports negligence. Do spectators watching dangerous sports consent to a lower standard of care? How is liability affected if the participant is a beginner or experienced? What is the responsibility of the club chairman or coaches if they knowingly field a volatile or aggressive player? Is the standard of care owed by players greater if the player is a professional as opposed to an amateur?

It may be argued that the rules of play are no longer sufficient to deter erring players. It is interesting to note that violence on the field is sometimes mirrored by violence off the field. This can all involve players, spectators, the police, referees, homeowners and surrounding shopkeepers. Whilst criminal consequences in the form of fines or imprisonment can be levied, Grayson has shown how further action can be taken by expelling certain clubs from their governing bodies [22].

An increasing number of sports and activities have come under the judicial spotlight. Whilst I shall briefly review some of these cases here, the case study examines the issues in greater detail. Risk assessment has to be called upon in a variety of contexts when organizers are running a sport event and these different aspects will be touched upon in several of the chapters presented in this book.

One of the questions addressed earlier was the liability towards spectators of dangerous sports. This principle has been tested on a number of occasions, notably in the case of Wooldridge v Sumner in 1963 [23]. Here a photographer sitting at the edge of a showjumping arena was injured. On appeal the court examined the acts of the participant and any skills or error of judgement exercised. It was held that the rider had not 'had a reckless disregard' for the spectators and that a horse, by its nature, was more difficult to control than a vehicle. The last point made by the court was that whilst there was no 'reckless disregard' the rider was making every endeavour to win the event. The spectator, an experienced photographer, was aware of the dangers of the sport.

Many of the points raised apply equally to a number of sports, such as rugby touchlines, cricket boundaries, rallycross lines, in fact any sport in which the spectator is allowed to get as close as possible to the action.

A further question was raised as to the liability of a beginner or experienced participant. This point was addressed by a case in 1995, where a parachutist negligently collided on landing with a taxiing plane. It was argued by the defence, first, that as a novice with only thirty jumps a lower standard of care was owed and, second, that the duty of care was modified. The judge rejected both of these submissions and again questioned whether professional sportsmen and women owed a higher duty of care than the less experienced [24].

I shall now look at two football cases, some nine years apart, both of which considered the higher standard of care being owed by professionals. The first case, Condon v Basi in 1985 [25] found for the plaintiff with comments being made by the

Case study – sporting negligence

The facts surrounding this case, believed to be the first brought by a rugby union player against a referee, were that a youth aged seventeen played rugby for the Sutton Coldfield Colts. Two days before county trials he agreed to play for the Colts because they were 'one man short'. During the course of the game against Burton upon Trent he suffered 'a catastrophic injury condemning him to a wheelchair-bound existence for the rest of his days'.

It was alleged that the injury had occurred as a result of a collapsed scrum which, according to the plaintiff, had happened because the referee had not enforced stricter new rules designed to protect younger players. The first defendant was Burton's tight head prop forward. The court heard that the scrum had collapsed a number of times that day, and a linesman had drawn the referee's attention to the fact.

The plaintiff was playing as hooker having replaced a team mate who had left the position after complaining that the collapsing scrums had left him with an aching neck. The plaintiff dislocated his neck when the pack collapsed after a third attempt to form a scrum. He also stated that he believed that the defendant had moved out of position thereby exacerbating his injury.

However, it was determined that the first defendant had not been negligent towards the plaintiff but that the second defendant, the referee, did owe a duty of care in negligence to ensure that scrums did not collapse dangerously. This decision was based on the facts of this particular case, on the fact that it was a colts game, that the risk of injuries to neck and spine were well known and that the rules recently implemented were designed to prevent collapsed scrums.

then Master of the Rolls that he was surprised at the apparent lack of standard of care owed to participants and those governing their conduct. This case, thought to have established a precedent, has not always been followed. In the later case of Elliot v Saunders and Liverpool Football Club [26], although the principle of a higher standard of care amongst professionals was addressed, emphasis was placed on intention. Here it was held that there had been no intention to harm the plaintiff, despite his injuries and the curtailment of his professional career.

Conclusion

It is clear from both parts of this chapter that the law is changing to reflect the changes in society and its attitudes to the standard of care given and received. It is also clear that those involved in the sporting industry must be made increasingly aware of their responsibilities both on and off the field, irrespective of the sport that they are involved in.

Many of the chapters that follow in this book will give a deeper insight into how risk assessment exercises can be undertaken and exactly what factors need to be considered when staging a sporting event. Despite the plethora of legislation relating to sports activities, the law can too often become involved as a result of tragedy.

Summary

- The evolution of liability for corporate manslaughter has advanced rapidly, largely as a result of high profile tragedies during the 1980s and 1990s.
- Factors which have influenced this evolution have included the decline in public confidence regarding company responsibility, the wealth of regulatory 'crimes' and the effect of the media.
- Proposed changes in the criminal code have been put forward by the Law Commission.
- Case law has seen the extension of liability on the sports field with regard to the duty of care owed to players.

References

[1] H. L. Bolton (Engineering) Co. Ltd v T. J. Graham and Sons Ltd [1957] 1QB 159.
[2] Wells, C. (1993). *Corporations and Criminal Responsibility*. Oxford University Press.
[3] Law Commission (1996). *Legislating the Criminal Code: Involuntary Manslaughter*. Paper Number 237. HMSO.
[4] Slapper, G. (1995). PLC – what is your plea? *The Times*, 13 December.

[5] R v OLL Ltd [1994] case unreported.

[6] Law Commission (1994). *Criminal Law: Involuntary Manslaughter*. Consultation Paper Number 135.

[7] Public Interest Disclosure Bill.

[8] Bergman, D. (1990). Recklessness in the boardroom. *New Law Journal*, 26 October.

[9] Gobert, J. (1994). Corporate criminality: New crimes for the times. *Criminal Law Review*, p. 722.

[10] Slapper, G. (1993). Corporate manslaughter: An examination of the determinants of prosecutorial policy. *Social and Legal Studies Journal*, **2**, 423–443.

[11] Op. cit. 9.

[12] Op. cit. 10.

[13] Ibid. p. 436.

[14] Ibid. p. 429.

[15] Heath and Safety Commission (1995). *Annual Report 1994/95*. HMSO.

[16] Arkin, A. (1996). Safer workplaces are no accident. *People Management*, 25 July, pp. 37–38.

[17] Op. cit. 15.

[18] Op. cit. 3.

[19] Ibid. Clause 4(2).

[20] Donaghue v Stevenson [1932] AC 562.

[21] Tyerman, R. (1996). Now sports turns into a field of claims. *Sunday Telegraph*, 11 February.

[22] Grayson, E. (1988). *Sport and the Law*. Butterworths.

[23] Wooldridge v Sumner [1963] 2 QB 43.

[24] Headcorn Parachute Club v Executors of Estate of Pond [1995] case unreported.

[25] Condon v Basi [1985] 1 WLR 866.

[26] Elliot v Saunders and Liverpool Football Club [1994] case unreported.

5 Who is liable? – a police perspective

Alan Beckley

This chapter examines the organizations that are legally liable and responsible for the safety of persons attending public events. The police are responsible as the safety net for all such events and therefore individual police officers should be aware of their responsibility, liability and the possible harm that can befall emergency service workers. The various types of public event and the likely problem areas are examined. Strategies for preventing or mitigating disasters and the negative effects on the individual are discussed.

Public safety

Public safety is an enigma within statutory provisions. Some areas of public safety, such as those relating to football and liquor-licensed premises or 'public houses', are tightly regulated to the point of suffocation. Other areas of public safety, such as events on the public highway, are lax to the point of recklessness. This situation makes it difficult to identify which individual or organization is responsible and, therefore liable, to protect public safety in each individual case.

What is certain is that there is one organization that is the safety net of society and can never abdicate its responsibility to guard the safety of the public regardless of the type or description of the event: the police service.

Certain difficulties afflict the police when trying to fulfill this role. First, unlawful events are held over which police have no control, and can only seek to prevent where possible. Second, there are few powers to prevent lawful events taking place where the police believe that the event could be dangerous to members of the public. An exception to this assertion is the law relating to prevention of raves in the open air [1]. Police have been given powers to enter land where a rave is anticipated, require the persons present to leave and prevent further persons arriving at the location.

It is the prevention of lawful events that should cause police managers the greatest concern, because, despite police objections to events on the grounds of safety, these events can still go ahead; however, the police will continue to have responsibilities in relation to public safety. There have been several examples of this ranging from public firework displays, large-scale carnivals to open-air opera concerts. It is therefore important that police managers realize and understand the risks, liabilities and responsibilities involved and also are in a position of knowledge and strength to take advantage of strategies to mitigate those risks.

Police superintendents – the basic command unit

Police superintendents, as the head of the basic command unit, are the decision-making level of management which determines the strategy for policing public events of a local nature. It is usually at this level where most conflict occurs; as this will be caused by insistence on inclusion of safety features while liaising with organizers of public events. However, it may be a relevant moment to rethink the levels of police authority and responsibility bearing in mind recent developments relating to geographical policing and the devolvement of decision making and responsibility to local commanders mainly of inspector rank. As time goes by therefore, police inspectors will increasingly bear the responsibilities of command.

Whatever the rank of the officer making the decisions, the superintendent will inevitably be directly involved in the strategy of policing operations, either in the planning or execution of the plan. In a basic command unit, the buck stops at the superintendent. Therefore, they should be aware of legal, moral, social and ethical responsibilities and liabilities in addition to what will or should happen if things go wrong.

Football

Football has become a highly regulated public event, but it has taken many disasters and deaths to achieve the co-ordinated response to safety which we experience today. Although the emphasis of the licensing authorities is to place the responsibility for public safety on the management of FA Premier and Football League clubs, and non-League football clubs are also bringing their grounds up to high levels of safety, which they are required to do to achieve League status, there still remain a number of concerns for police.

The first of these concerns is whether the football club management and their staff are capable of managing public safety; many are, but in the lower leagues experience reveals doubts. Second, the police continue to be responsible for public disorder, therefore police attendance, as appropriate to the threat, will still be required at football matches. Third, because of traditional practice, police continue to be heavily involved in safety issues at football matches and are making decisions that should not be theirs to make. All the above issues continue to dilute the direct responsibility of football clubs.

It is essential that police officers are properly trained to take on the task of managing the policing of a football match. Not only do they need to realize the normal policing issues of deployment, briefing and the relevant law; they also need to know about spectator safety, dynamics and policing tactics of large (sometimes intractable or drunk) crowds. Policing tactics cannot be learned quickly and attendance at many football matches is necessary to gain experience. Judicious use of football intelligence and technology (closed circuit television) is needed before the football match commander can successfully 'read' the intentions of the crowd. As crowd safety is being handed over to the football club Safety Officer, these skills should be passed on to avert future tragedies. Conversely, in future, at football matches where public order problems are foreseen, police match commanders will have less experience of managing, directing and controlling events as they will have commanded fewer matches.

The law in relation to sporting events has gone through considerable change in recent years, the most recent developments being in the criminal law and in that of negligence. Injuries at sporting fixtures between participants were generally regarded as 'self inflicted' or incurred with the consent of the players. But where the necessary guilty knowledge of an offence of assault can be established, the case of the footballer Duncan Ferguson, who was sent to prison in February 1996 for headbutting an opponent, indicates that a court will convict. In the same incident, legal precedent was also set that the Scottish Football Association could not sentence the football player involved to suspension from playing when the match referee had failed to punish him.

Another case [2], presented as a case study in Lynne Walley's chapter on criminal liability, (see Chapter 4) set new guidelines for match officials. It was held that a referee who oversaw a colts rugby match owed a duty of care in negligence to ensure that scrummages did not collapse dangerously. A player, who was badly injured by the scrummage, received a substantial settlement in damages.

Another recent development is that of proper qualifications in stewarding techniques. Steve Frosdick and John Sidney report on one type of stewards' training in their later chapter on the evolution of football safety management (Chapter 15). Another type of training is validated as a national vocational qualification (NVQ) in spectator control and establishes many areas of competence in the trainee steward. This is a positive step forward ensuring not only that stewards are sound in body, but also that they are capable of reacting correctly to emergencies, major and minor incidents in a pre-determined, proactive and logical manner. The modular units of the basic (Level 2) NVQ go through health and safety law, support of the safety team, monitoring crowds, response to hazards and customer problems, controlling the entry and flow of people attending the activity and pre-event safety measures. There are also higher levels of training which are appropriate for supervisory stewards (Level 3) and safety officers (Level 4).

During a pilot scheme of the NVQ training at Cambridge, Scunthorpe, Bradford and Leeds, many benefits have been identified for the safety of spectators and their comfort and enjoyment. Local police commanders have been very supportive of the results of training. The ultimate test was the Euro '96 competition, as all of the stewards at the nation's premier football stadium, Wembley, were trained in the NVQ. The stewarding operation was described as a great success by the Wembley management. The professionalism, confidence and competence of the stewards was obvious to all at the matches and viewing the television coverage.

Whether the NVQ or another training scheme, perhaps it is time for police officers in charge of such events, or participating in the multi-agency advisory groups which meet regularly to discuss safety matters, to insist on satisfactory training for stewards before they agree to police them.

Music festivals

Public music and dancing is a highly regulated area of public events [3–5]. Indeed, there is adequate legislation to control most events, if used in a co-ordinated method aggregated with other organizations [6]. However, there have been instances where the police have disagreed with licensing authorities over the safety arrangements for public events. Despite minuted protests over safety issues, the events have still gone ahead, so far without serious consequences. The point is, police are still liable to ensure public safety even though their doubts about safety have been ignored or over-ruled by the organizers of the event.

Because various organizations have powers under many different statutory provisions, it is logical to aggregate these powers to ensure an effective response to musical festivals and pop concerts. It follows that a multi-agency approach by police, local authorities, fire service, ambulance, Health and Safety Executive and any other appropriate body is the appropriate strategy.

Fortunately, there are some very useful advisory documents available on this subject published by the Health and Safety Executive which set out some benchmarks for public safety (and health and safety at work issues) when organizing musical events [7–10]. In relation to potentially unlawful events, the police powers [11] relating to raves apply to prevent or mitigate harm from noise pollution or danger to participants, only where the site in question is in the open air. There are few police powers to prevent unlawful musical events in buildings, such as the 'warehouse parties', which have been fashionable in recent years.

Street events

Although for many street events there appears to be an organizer or organizing committee, these are usually ad hoc arrangements without professional experience, expertise or accident and indemnity insurance. In view of this, the police cannot sit back, watch a disaster happen, and then accuse the organizer. This stance would not be regarded as lawful, nor would it be acceptable either politically or to the media. On the other hand, police must be careful not to take extralegal powers to facilitate easier organization of public events. Powers of search and powers to close roads and divert traffic are particularly revalent in this issue. The Criminal Justice and Public Order Act, 1994 gives police powers in relation to motor vehicles which are heading towards an unlawful rave event or trespassory assembly. Powers may be available under strict circumstances to stop vehicles and turn them back from these specific events. However, there are no general police powers to divert motor vehicles for street events without obtaining special traffic orders.

The police must therefore endeavour to inject some expertise, advice, management and control into the organization of events. This may lead to criticism of being 'killjoys'. Police may also be tempted to resort to extralegal measures to ensure public safety. A policing policy must be decided on this issue; long term safety should not be sacrificed for short-term popularity.

Security incidents

As always, the police are responsible for public safety during security incidents such as bomb threats, and strategy is well developed in locations which have been hardest hit. In the worldwide context of sporting events, 1996 brought the devastation wreaked by a small explosive device at the unsuspecting Atlanta Olympic games, which resulted, miraculously, in only one fatality. There were fewer security incidents in the UK during 1995 and 1996 than in previous years, due to political reasons; however, several devastating explosions indicated that this situation requires constant vigilance and monitoring.

Indeed, despite the reduced number and frequency of such incidents, in April 1996 the UK Government rushed through new powers for the police to 'stop and search'. A total of five new powers under the Prevention of Terrorism Act were enacted authorizing searches of vehicles, persons and non-residential premises. New powers were also introduced authorizing the long-established but extralegal powers used by police of establishing cordons around suspected or actual incidents and imposing temporary parking restrictions.

It is important to remember that liability may result from bad advice or good advice from persons in authority. If good advice is to evacuate a building and a bomb goes off, but occupiers decide to remain or are slow to move to safety, there may be criticism. Alternatively, if bad advice is given to evacuate and there is no bomb, there will be criticism because of loss of business. Also, precautions should be taken to indemnify police before people are allowed into a potentially dangerous or uncleared area. Therefore, it is essential that a policy is formulated which is adhered to so that all parties are aware of, and have agreed to, the relevant issues.

Police contingency planning

Police liability .

Liability for contingency planning is shared between the author of a contingency plan and the operational policing commander. It follows that where the plan is a local one, the basic command unit commander will have the responsibility for ensuring there is a plan, that appropriate planning has been completed, and that plans are current and relevant. If the plan crosses basic command unit borders or demands a Force response, then the responsibility for preparation of the contingency plan rests with the Assistant Chief Constable (Operations), who usually delegates it to the Operations Department or Contingency Planning Department.

The provision of contingency plans is a necessity which brings with it a constant problem of updating and monitoring. However, some general principles apply which may assist in identifying strategies to reduce the burden of preparing plans and give reason and purpose for their compilation.

Primary objective of contingency planning

The pursuit of operational excellence based on knowledge, professional standards and the law should dictate the formulation of policy, training and operational effectiveness in practice. It follows that contingency plans are not for the purpose of liability avoidance; they exist to assist the operational police to respond to set circumstances and fixed locations.

For this reason, it is useless to write contingency plans that are impracticable or list resources that are not immediately available. The scope of contingency plans should be limited to the immediate response to incidents that have been assessed as a likely occurrence. If circumstances escalate towards a major incident or disaster, or continue for a long period of time, then the organization's Emergency Procedures or Major Incident Manual is more appropriate.

Police force policy

When a disaster has occurred, the Force Contingency Plan to prevent that occurrence will be exhibit number one at the Public Enquiry and/or Inquest. That tribunal has every right to expect that the document should be of a high standard, consistent with supporting documentation and procedures, well planned, specific as to individual roles and responsibilities, and, above all, current.

In view of this, every police force should issue guidelines, best practice guides or blueprints on acceptable standards of documentation to officers delegated the task of preparing plans. It is a sensible precaution to pass any such guidance through the Force legal adviser before general release. Contingency planning for football matches should be completed on a multi-agency basis, taking into account the roles, responsibilities and functions of all parties such as all the emergency services, the local authority and the football club. Sound advice on this subject is given in guidance from the Football Licensing Authority [12], who would expect that such planning actually takes place.

Training of police officers

Having discussed the relevant legal issues on the subject of contingency planning, the reader should now realize the importance of staff training. In order that all the appropriate issues are considered by the officer writing contingency plans, and the officer responsible for signing that plan (if different persons), they need to be aware of those factors and establish sufficient information upon which to base the risk assessment and the content of the plan.

Negligent completion of contingency plans could be a problem, and the responsibility would rest with whoever is in charge of the command unit (not necessarily the person who compiled the plan). One police force recently attempted to devolve the responsibility and legal liability of operational orders to the level of police inspector; it was decided that this proposal was not commensurate with the role and responsibilities of that level of management in the police service. In addition, if police officers who compile plans have not been properly trained, this could well be a cause for criticism in the event of a disaster.

As Bryan Drew's chapter on the Euro '96 football championships shows, there were few public disorder problems during the competition, although the media and the police had predicted them with certainty, judging by previous similar events (see Chapter 17). *The Times* headline on 28 June 1996 summed up the situation by saying, 'Skilled policing contained fury of hooligan minority', after incidents in central London. The article concluded that three years' detailed planning had been the key to the undoubted success of the policing operation throughout the competition.

Health and safety at work

Individual responsibilities

Health and safety at work affects everyone. Under the principal legislation, health and safety is not only the responsibility of management; an employee also has general duties to take reasonable care for themself and other persons who may be affected [13]. Employers are also responsible for ensuring the safety of persons other than their employees. Managers may be individually liable for offences committed under this legislation, or may be charged jointly with the organization.

On the face of it, the police manager will therefore be liable to ensure the safety of themselves, subordinates, and members of the public at police-organized events and in police buildings. This has fundamental effects on the responsibility and liability of police officers in charge of public events.

Police – a special case

Although the intention of the government and the European Commission was to include every employee in the country and every organization that employs people (including self-employed persons) in health and safety measures, the unique status of constables as 'office holders' temporarily defeated the legislators. In fact, the main Health and Safety at Work etc. Act, 1974 did not directly apply to police officers, but provisions under other enactments enforced certain responsibilities.

The law on health and safety relating to police officers will be amended in 1997 to include them in the original legislation. Guidance and generic risk assessments relating to general police duties will be available, as risk assessments will be required in all pre-planned police operations. The implementation of this law will necessitate a massive programme of retraining for all police officers. Health and safety at work legislation will be appropriate where all hazardous or dangerous working practices or environments are involved to ensure the provision of safe working practices. Managers may be liable for health and safety offences within their management remit for subordinates, colleagues and other visitors to police buildings, or police-organized events.

Psychological injuries

It is necessary for organizations to provide support and care for emergency service workers and to take into account psychological injuries which could be sustained during events involving public safety. In the interests of the health, safety and welfare of employees, organizations must take precautions to provide support and guidance to ensure their continued psychological health.

In 1996, eight years after the Hillsborough disaster, fourteen police officers who had been on duty at the match were awarded £1.2 million in agreed damages for mental trauma suffered as a result of rescuing football fans. Although there was criticism of the award by relatives of victims of the tragedy, newspaper coverage was generally sympathetic to the undoubted suffering of the police officers involved.

Despite the slow and patchy response to provision of psychological support in the UK, the principle is well established in relation to the increasing number of policing incidents where firearms are discharged. One technique used in psychological care and support following traumatic incidents is critical incident debriefing.

Critical incident debriefing

'Critical incident debriefing' or 'psychological debriefing' or 'critical incident stress debriefing' are all terms to describe the same technique. The debriefing is a group meeting to review the impressions and reactions that survivors, the bereaved or helpers experience during or following critical incidents, accidents and disasters. It is neither an operational debrief, nor for evidence-gathering purposes, nor even a blame-seeking session. The sole reason for holding it is to reduce unnecessary psychological after-effects and to ensure the long-term physical and mental wellbeing of the participants.

Recognition of post-traumatic stress disorder

Post-traumatic Stress Disorder (PTSD) is recognized as a serious psychological disorder, the symptoms of which supervisors, relatives and colleagues can identify if given correct information or training. PTSD may be suffered by a person who has experienced an event that is outside the normal range of usual human experience and that would be markedly distressing to almost anyone. Such events would include serious threat to life or physical integrity, or harm to the individual's children, spouse, or other close relatives and friends. Of particular relevance to emergency service personnel is the inclusion in the list of seeing another person who has recently been, or is being, seriously injured or killed as a result of an accident or physical violence.

As a result of growing awareness of PTSD, recommendations have been made that occupational health units should be established in police forces. Consequently, most forces now have such a facility. In addition, it has been shown that psychological support should be provided to all emergency services workers to ensure that appropriate welfare is available. Psychological injuries sustained in major incidents can result in the civil liability of the employer towards the employee.

A survey (unpublished) in 1996 of 1000 police officers from south-east England revealed that nearly a quarter of police officers suffer severe psychological distress as a result of their everyday policing activities. Overall, the study found that 40 per cent of the force showed significant psychological distress and reported a much higher level of symptoms of post-traumatic stress disorder than the general population.

The future

Having established the problems, the future is not encouraging. Society is becoming more litigious and is expecting ever higher standards of management and expertise from their police without loss of civil liberty or public safety. All police officers should be aware of, and fully appreciate, the responsibilities and liabilities they take on when dealing with public events. There should be proper planning and, if possible, some sort of quasilegal document or 'statement of intent' to outline the various responsibilities of each party organizing public events. The media will not be slow to criticize, quite rightly, if this issue is not addressed.

Table 5.1 is a checklist of points to be addressed by organizations looking to the future.

Table 5.1   Looking to the future

- The police must look around for support in their functions.
- A multidisciplinary approach to planning and execution of policing operations for public events is essential.
- Liaising with other organizations, such as the Health and Safety Executive and the local authority, will pool expertise and offer sound advice to organizers of events.
- Working together will broaden the responsibility for safety and lessen the effect of criticism. Organizations can learn from each other and grow professionally.
- Each event should be individually assessed for the most effective multidisciplinary liaison arrangements.
- The police service should be progressive in being prepared to accept technical advice from the experts, and give up areas where they purport to be effective, but in reality are not so.
- Where the responsibility for public safety is vested in stewards, police should ensure that adequate training and briefing has taken place.

Summary

- Some areas of public safety are tightly regulated and others are lax.
- The police are the organization that is the safety net for safety at public events.
- Football is a highly regulated public event and safety officers and stewards should be well trained in safety techniques.
- Licensed music festivals are highly regulated and guidance is available to organizers.
- There is little statutory control over street carnivals and few police powers.
- Security incidents cause problems when they involve the safety of large numbers of people in public places.
- Contingency planning is essential and police officers should be properly trained to compile them.
- Health and safety factors should be built into contingency plans.

© Alan Beckley 1997. The opinions expressed in his document are those of the author alone, and not necessarily those of West Mercia Constabulary.

References

[1] Criminal Justice and Public Order Act, 1994. Sections 64–67.
[2] Smolden v Whitworth (1996). *Times Law Reports*, 23 April 1996.
[3] Local Government (Miscellaneous Provisions) Act, 1982 (Schedule 1). As amended by Fire Safety and Safety of Places of Sport Act, 1987 (Part IV).
[4] Licensing Act, 1964. As amended by Licensing Act, 1988.
[5] Private Places of Entertainment (Licensing) Act, 1967.
[6] Department of the Environment and the Home Office (1992). *Control of Noisy Parties*. HMSO.
[7] Au, S., Ryan, M., Carey, M. and Whalley, S. (1993). *Managing Crowd Safety in Public Venues: A Study to Generate Guidance for Venue Owners and Enforcing Authority Inspectors* (HSE Contract Research Report 53/93). Health and Safety Executive.
[8] Health and Safety Executive (1993). *Managing Crowds Safely* (Guidance Leaflet). HSE Books.
[9] Health and Safety Executive (in press). *Crowd Safety*.
[10] Health and Safety Commission and Home Office (1993). *Guide to Health, Safety and Welfare at Pop Concerts and Similar Events*. HMSO.
[11] Op. cit. 1.
[12] Football Licensing Authority (1994). *Football Club Contingency Planning*.
[13] Health and Safety at Work Act, 1974. Sections 3, 7 and 37.

6 The origins and role of the Football Licensing Authority

John de Quidt

This chapter examines the origins, role and impact of the Football Licensing Authority against the background of the changes at English football grounds since it was formed in July 1990. The main focus is on its approach to safety, on its advisory work and on its vision for the future.

Introduction

On 15 April 1989 ninety-five supporters were crushed to death on a standing terrace at Hillsborough. English football had reached its nadir. In his subsequent Report [1] Lord Justice Taylor spoke of a general malaise or blight over the game due principally to old grounds, poor facilities, hooliganism, excessive drinking and poor leadership.

Yet in June 1996 England was able to stage the European Football Championships, without any safety problems, in what could by then be described as the most user-friendly football grounds in Europe [2]. A revolution had taken place. It has yet fully to run its course.

Many organizations and individuals have contributed to this revolution. The Football Licensing Authority (FLA), however, has been one of the major catalysts and facilitators. This chapter reflects its perspectives and involvement.

The Football Licensing Authority's origins

Hillsborough was only the latest in the long and depressing list of disasters at British football grounds or involving British fans. The response to each disaster followed a familiar pattern: an inquiry, a report containing strong criticisms of safety failures [3] and, in the more recent cases, legislation, known to the cynics as tombstone legislation, to prevent a repetition. In Chapter 2, Dominic Elliott, Steve Frosdick and Denis Smith have described this process as 'the failure of legislation by crisis'.

This legislation steadily increased the Government's involvement in the affairs of the sport. After the Ibrox disaster of 1971, the Safety of Sports Grounds Act, 1975 [4] introduced safety certification by local authorities. After the 1987 Bradford fire, the Fire Safety and Safety of Places of Sport Act, 1987 [5] extended the 1975 Act and gave these certifying authorities additional powers. After the Heysel disaster, the Football Spectators Act, 1989 [6] created the FLA.

Thus the FLA was not, as is often supposed, a child of Hillsborough. It was originally devised to oversee a football membership scheme. However, when this did not find favour with Lord Justice Taylor [7] the Government decided to scrap the scheme. The FLA would be used instead to implement the recommendations in the Taylor Report, in particular those relating to all-seated grounds [8].

The Football Licensing Authority's functions

The FLA was therefore given the following functions:

- licensing league and international football grounds;
- advising the Government on making grounds all-seated;
- ensuring that any remaining standing accommodation meets the necessary safety standards; and
- keeping under review the discharge by local authorities of their safety certification functions under the Safety of Sports Grounds Act, 1975 [9].

The FLA's best known task has been to enforce the Government's decision that every club in the Premiership and First Division of the Football League should make its ground all-seated by August 1994 or (if later) by three years after its promotion into the First Division. This is done through the licence from which the FLA takes its name.

Nevertheless, the FLA's primary role is and probably always will be the promotion of spectator safety. As will be shown below, this goes much wider than merely keeping under review the work of local authorities.

Safety certification

The functions of the local authority (the county or unitary council) under the 1975 Act are often misunderstood. It is not in fact the task of the local authority to make a ground safe. Rather, the local authority is responsible for determining how many spectators may be admitted to the ground taking into account not merely the physical structure of the ground but also the club's safety systems and procedures. The local authority's mechanism is the safety certificate. This specifies the permitted capacity of each area of the ground provided that the club complies with the terms and conditions set out in the safety certificate. These will normally cover, inter alia:

● responsibility for safety;
● spectator entry and exit;
● stewarding and policing;
● structures, fabric and fittings;
● fire safety;
● medical and first aid facilities; and
● record keeping.

As recommended by Lord Justice Taylor [10], the local authority is assisted in its functions by the police, fire and ambulance services and other relevant bodies gathered together in a Safety Advisory Group. This is designed to ensure that the local authority, police, fire service and other agencies act in concert and do not seek to impose conflicting requirements upon clubs.

The FLA approach to safety

It is within this framework that the FLA keeps the work of the local authority under review. Keeping under review does not involve taking over. Nor does it mean second guessing, provided that the local authority can satisfy the FLA that its procedures are sufficient and appropriate and that the terms and conditions in the safety certificate are those which are necessary to ensure reasonable safety at the ground [11].

On the other hand, keeping under review is more than merely monitoring. It is the active promotion of consistency, which is not the same as uniformity, and best practice. From its inception the FLA has seen its role as being to inform, to encourage, to advise.

The FLA has the power to compel a local authority to insert terms and conditions in a safety certificate [12]. In six years, however, it has never exercised that power. It hopes never to have to. The FLA firmly believes that safety can never satisfactorily be achieved by means of requirements imposed upon the reluctant from outside. Those who are responsible have got to think it through and believe in it for themselves.

One of the great temptations for any safety organization is to continue ratcheting up its requirements to the point where these become disproportionate and unreasonable. The technique of risk assessment, which runs as a central theme throughout this book, must be used to determine what is reasonably necessary. The FLA therefore seeks always to work with a light touch both towards local authorities and towards clubs.

Football Licensing Authority guidance

It was in this spirit that, after thorough consultation with all interested parties, the FLA issued detailed written guidance on safety certification [13]. Further guidance documents have followed, most notably on contingency planning [14] and on producing written safety policies [15]. The FLA has also contributed heavily to the guidance on stewarding and safety management [16], published by the football authorities.

None of this guidance is radically new. What it does is identify, assemble and promulgate best practice both from within the world of football and from elsewhere. The FLA is therefore a resource upon which local authorities and others can draw. One authority may not know what its equivalent is doing elsewhere.

The FLA's impact is provided by its nine full time Inspectors. These were drawn from a variety of backgrounds: the police, the fire service, architecture, civil engineering and building control. During a period of local government reorganization or when there has been considerable staff turnover, the FLA Inspector may be the only person with the knowledge and experience of particular issues.

It is hardly surprising that the FLA is frequently called upon to act as an honest broker. It can help a local authority reconcile and balance the need for safety with the demands of other agencies who may have legitimate concerns, for example for public order.

Although the FLA's formal role extends only to grounds in the Premiership and Football League in England and Wales, its influence inevitably extends much wider. Its written guidance is often equally relevant for other sports. Its views are frequently sought by clubs outside these leagues, by other sports and from outside England and Wales – in particular during the run up to and the aftermath of the 1996 European Championships.

During 1995 to 1996 the FLA also conducted a full scale review and subsequent revision of the Government's *Guide to Safety at Sports Grounds* [17] popularly known as the *Green Guide*. This had first been produced following the 1972 Wheatley Report on the Ibrox disaster [18]. Subsequent revisions had always been disaster or crisis driven and produced under acute time pressure.

For the first time it was now possible to re-examine the *Guide* in detail. It quickly became apparent that much of it had stood the test of time. However, there were many areas that required updating or clarification.

The lessons of the Hillsborough disaster

The FLA believes that there are two fundamental lessons to be drawn from the Hillsborough disaster:

● the needs of safety and security must not get out of balance; and
● there must be no confusion about who is responsible for safety.

In its *Guidance on Safety Certificates* [19] the FLA made it clear that the statutory responsibility for safety at a football ground rests neither with the local authority, nor with the police, nor with the emergency services but with the club. Clubs have got to believe that safety is their business. They have got to develop their own safety culture. An awareness of safety and a willingness to identify and tackle problems before they arise needs to permeate clubs' entire thinking right up to boardroom level.

Before Hillsborough the police had often by default effectively taken charge of safety. There was a safety vacuum; only the police appeared capable of filling it. Thankfully that has changed and there is now widespread acceptance that the police should limit themselves to their primary role of maintaining law and order. As early as February 1991, the House of Commons Home Affairs Committee identified higher profile stewarding supported by lower profile policing as the way forward [20].

The FLA would not advocate a total police withdrawal from football grounds. It would be foolish to move from a culture dominated by security to one where this was undervalued. So long as there is a public order threat, the police will have a role inside grounds. The extent of that role will depend upon the assessment of the risk on each individual occasion.

Clubs and police need therefore to work together as equal partners, each with their own responsibilities. These are identified through what Lord Justice Taylor described as a statement of intent [21]. This is a simple operational document, agreed between the police commander and the club safety officer, which specifies who does what and when.

The management of safety

As will be shown below, the most dramatic changes to come out of the Hillsborough disaster have been to the structures and fabric of the football grounds. Nevertheless, this is but one aspect of safety. However good a facility, it will not be safe if the safety management is inadequate. Moreover, achieving a reasonable standard of safety is not a once and for ever event. It requires continual vigilance. Memories of disasters quickly start to fade. Complacency, identified by Lord Justice Taylor as the enemy of safety [22], starts to creep back in.

For example, locked exit gates have historically been one of the greatest causes of loss of life at leisure facilities. The FLA's *Guidance on Safety Certificates* states unambiguously that no door or gate forming part of an exit route should ever be locked or fastened unless it can easily and immediately be opened in an emergency without the use of a key by those seeking to escape in an emergency [23]. Yet FLA Inspectors still occasionally find locked unstaffed exits at grounds during matches.

Safe capacities

It should come as no surprise, therefore, that the safe capacity of a ground does not merely depend on the number of seats and the size and layout of standing areas. Nor is it just a function of how many spectators can safely use the available entrances and exits within a given time. It is also necessary to ask how many people a club can safely manage at any one time.

Where a club does not habitually attract capacity gates it probably copes without difficulty. The test comes with the big match. Such an event will test its safety procedures, equipment and personnel. Should they be found wanting, the permitted capacity is excessive and must be reduced. The remedy will often lie with the club itself. An improvement in its safety management can in many cases lead to an increase in capacity.

Safety personnel

It should thus come as no surprise that the FLA has devoted considerable time and energy promoting the need for clubs to have a proper safety management structure, contingency plans and written safety policies and be capable of implementing them. It is only by writing down its safety policy that an organization discovers if it actually has one.

One of the key requirements of every safety certificate is that the club shall have a safety officer to take operational responsibility for the safety of spectators. He or she must have a written job description and sufficient status and authority to undertake his or her responsibilities effectively.

The FLA has taken great pleasure in the growing professionalism and expertise of club safety officers. It particularly welcomed the formation of the Football Safety Officers' Association whose meetings it regularly attends. This body provides an invaluable forum where safety officers can share their experiences, learn from each other and foster their own commitment.

A safety officer's main resource is the club's stewards. Formerly often little more than supporters in tabards, 'of limited capacity and reliability' [24], their role and performance has been transformed at many grounds. As their quality and training have improved, so the police have gradually been able to reduce their presence and clubs have become much more masters of their own destiny.

The FLA draws great encouragement from the enthusiastic welcome given by the world of football to the guidance document on stewarding and safety management

[25]. The training package for stewarding at football grounds, discussed by Steve Frosdick and John Sidney in Chapter 15, is a major step forward, the culmination of many years work which encountered much initial scepticism.

Control rooms

As indicated above, the safety officer should work in partnership with the police commander. Often they will jointly occupy the ground control room. Its five main functions were defined by the FLA-led working party which produced the Football Stadia Development Committee report on control rooms [26] as follows:

- to monitor the safety of people inside the stadium and in its immediate vicinity;
- to oversee public order;
- to assist the club or stadium owner in the management of matches or events;
- to co-ordinate responses to specific events or emergencies;
- to provide, if required, a monitoring facility for fire and ambulance services.

A major part of the control room's operation is taken up by closed circuit television (CCTV). Covering both inside the stadia and their immediate environs, the cameras enable the club's safety officer and the police commander to be aware of potential safety problems or disorder. CCTV has a powerful deterrent effect. Along with all-seated grounds and clubs taking back responsibility for safety, the introduction of CCTV has been one of the three most important developments of the last few years.

All-seated grounds

Lord Justice Taylor reported that 'there is no panacea which will achieve total safety and cure all problems of behaviour and crowd control. But I am satisfied that seating does more to achieve these objectives than any other measure' [27]. This has proved to be the case. Where seats have been installed the first aiders are treating far fewer injured spectators.

Seating also makes spectator management easier. Potential troublemakers can be spotted and identified much more quickly, especially with good CCTV cover. Seats also give supporters their own defensible space and help make grounds much more civilized.

Many supporters had a strong emotional attachment to the standing terraces. Initially there was considerable opposition to all-seated grounds. However, recent surveys [28] have shown that supporters actually like being treated as human beings, as part of the club. They appreciate and even look after new facilities. Indeed supporters have started putting pressure on their clubs to match what is being provided by their rivals. Many smaller clubs, which are not required to make their stadia all-seated, have now set themselves this objective. Nearly all the others are seriously examining options for improvements.

The years since the Hillsborough disaster have therefore seen some remarkable strides by many clubs – and not just by the élite. In 1990 at least 50 per cent of most British football grounds consisted of terracing for standing spectators. There were only five senior all-seated football grounds in Great Britain (Wembley plus four in Scotland). Yet by early 1995 there were sixty-one. Between 1990 and 1995 164 new stands were built [29]. How sad that it took the Hillsborough disaster to create the momentum for such change.

Initially many clubs underestimated the magnitude of the task facing them, partly because they had no recent experience of major construction work. Some assumed that they could merely install seats on existing standing terraces. The FLA had to warn them that any new seating which failed to provide an adequate view of the pitch, for example because the rake was too shallow, would not be licensed.

To help clubs implement the Taylor recommendation, the Government, through the Football Trust, made available up to £2 million per club. The FLA encouraged this process by providing advice to clubs on standards, helping local authorities vet schemes and assisting the Football Trust to determine whether they should be grant aided.

Between 1988 and 1996 eight English clubs moved to new grounds. At least six more were due to follow suit by 1998. More would have done so but for planning difficulties, local opposition or lack of funding. The most spectacular was in Huddersfield, the Royal Institution of British Architects' Building of the Year for 1995.

High quality facilities

Along with new stands and stadia, many clubs have taken long overdue steps to provide decent facilities for their supporters. For example, it is not difficult nowadays to provide reasonable quality food and drink quickly, efficiently and in pleasant surroundings. Many clubs have even been able to reintroduce the sale of alcohol to supporters under controlled conditions. Crèches and family areas, better facilities for spectators with disabilities and above all decent toilets can now be found at many grounds. Indeed in the latest guidance on toilets [30] it has been necessary to recommend that clubs provide a higher proportion of toilets for women. At one time, a ratio of 95:5 was quite common, that is if toilets were provided for women at all! Now a ratio of 85:15 is considered necessary.

These measures make economic sense. New and better facilities attract more spectators. Clubs that have moved to new stadia have seen extraordinary increases in attendances even if the football has not improved. However, there is also a safety dimension. The way a club treats its supporters in matters of amenity is symptomatic of how the club is run. Better facilities attract spectators into the ground earlier. This helps ease the traditional, and dangerous, last-minute rush.

Safe standing

The FLA would prefer to see every ground all-seated. However, it recognizes that this might be a bridge too far for some smaller clubs. It was for this very reason that, in July 1992, the Government decided to permit clubs in the Second and Third Divisions to retain some standing accommodation. This, however, should fully accord with 'the high standards of safety which all spectators have a right to expect' [31].

Getting terracing right has had to be done in two stages. The first was to implement the guidance in the report by the Football Stadia Advisory Design Council [32] (commissioned by the FLA) on the calculation of safe capacities. This expanded and clarified the guidance in the previous *Green Guide* [33] which had given rise to some confusion.

The FLA therefore asked the local authorities to review the capacities of all standing accommodation taking into account not just the physical structures but also the clubs' ability to manage them. As a result of this, the capacities of many standing areas had to be reduced. This, however, did not fully resolve the issue. Reducing the number of people permitted to stand on substandard terracing may reduce the risk to spectators. However, if they can still congregate in areas with no barriers, especially if these are right behind the goal, the hazard may still be too great.

The FSADC report set out detailed criteria for all new or refurbished terracing but did not specifically address what work should be done to existing terracing that failed to meet these standards. The FLA had therefore to define a minimum standard, for the layout, spacing and strength of the crush barriers, that terracing should meet by 1999 or else be taken out of use.

Perimeter fences

Perhaps the most potent symbol of the changes that have occurred since the Hillsborough disaster is the disappearance of the hated perimeter fences from the vast majority of grounds. They came down in England and Wales because (and after) the physical structures, the crowd management and safety systems had been brought up to a sufficient standard to make them unnecessary. Their removal was vindicated during the 1996 European Championships.

This has been recognized elsewhere in Europe. The international football authorities technical recommendations [34] recognize that 'Ideally, the playing area of a stadium should not be surrounded by security fences or screens, and although it has to be recognized that there may be places in which it would be imprudent to fail to provide such measures against intrusion, there is little doubt that a more civilized and pleasant atmosphere prevails when there are no unsightly barriers between the spectators and the playing field'. Significantly, the first option given in the recommendations for keeping spectators off the playing area is the presence of police and/or stewards.

Prospects for the future

The next few years will present football in general and the FLA in particular with new challenges. In the aftermath of the Hillsborough disaster, it was necessary to focus mainly on the physical redevelopment of grounds and on tackling major safety weaknesses. Over time, however, the emphasis has shifted steadily towards the positive promotion of safety, in particular to:

● safety awareness, systems and procedures;
● qualifications and training; and
● monitoring and enforcement.

In some ways, the challenge will become harder. Tackling obvious safety failures normally commands ready support. However, the value and importance of apparently 'bureaucratic' systems and procedures may be less immediately apparent to the untutored. The FLA will need to maintain an active and high profile advisory role towards both local authorities and clubs.

Its long-term ambition is to be able to reduce its role in relation to a significant number of individual local authorities and clubs in order to concentrate more on matters of general concern. This process of disengagement cannot be rushed, especially during a period of local government reorganization. Nevertheless, an increasing number of local authorities and indeed clubs are taking more of the initiative on safety improvements themselves and are coming to the FLA for advice and support rather than waiting to be guided or pressured to move forward.

Summary

- The Football Licensing Authority (FLA) was created by the Football Spectators Act, 1989. It was originally conceived as the body that would supervise a national membership scheme.
- Following the Hillsborough disaster, the Government decided to drop the membership scheme and instead to use the FLA to implement the recommendations in Lord Justice Taylor's Final Report.
- The FLA's best known function has been to enforce the Government's decision that every club in the Premiership and First Division of the Football League should make its ground all seated by August 1994 or (if later) three years after its promotion into the First Division. This is done through the licence from which the FLA takes its name.
- The requirement for lower division clubs to go all seated was dropped in July 1992. The Government decided instead to permit the retention of some standing accommodation at these grounds provided that this meets the necessary standards by August 1999. The FLA is charged with ensuring this.
- The FLA's other main task is described as keeping under review the discharge by local authorities of their safety certification functions under the Safety of Sports Grounds Act, 1975. In practice, this goes much wider than ensuring that these authorities set and enforce such terms and conditions as are necessary for the reasonable safety of spectators.

● From its inception, the FLA has believed that safety cannot effectively be imposed upon the unwilling from outside. Accordingly the FLA has promulgated best practice, provided guidance and assistance, and worked towards the creation of a safety culture not merely within local authorities but above all at clubs. It has been able to do this without having to resort to its statutory powers of compulsion.

● The years since the Hillsborough Disaster have seen the substantial redevelopment of many grounds in both the higher and the lower divisions. Several excellent new ones have been completed with more to come. There have also been widespread improvements in facilities for spectators.

● Safety management has improved out of all recognition. Many clubs are committed to safety, have established the good systems, and employ skilled personnel. The challenge for the future is to bring about a permanent safety culture.

Crown Copyright. Reproduced with the permission of the Controller of Her Majesty's Stationery Office. The views expressed are those of the author and do not necessarily reflect the views or policy of the Department of National Heritage, Her Majesty's Stationery Office or any other Government department.

References

[1] *The Hillsborough Stadium Disaster 15 April 1989 – Inquiry by the Rt Hon Lord Justice Taylor – Final Report* (Taylor Report, 1990), p. 5. HMSO.
[2] Inglis, S. (1996). *Football Grounds of Britain*, p. 10. Collins Willow.
[3] Op. cit. 1. p. 4.
[4] Safety of Sports Grounds Act, 1975.
[5] Fire Safety and Safety of Places of Sport Act, 1987, Parts II and III.
[6] Football Spectators Act, 1989. Sections 1 and 8-13.
[7] Op. cit. 1. Chapters 12–18.
[8] Op. cit. 1. Recommendations 1–4.
[9] Op. cit. 6. Section 13.
[10] Op. cit. 1. Recommendation 31.
[11] Op. cit. 4. Section 2(1).
[12] Op. cit. 6. Section 13(2).
[13] Football Licensing Authority (1992). *Guidance on Safety Certificates.*
[14] Football Licensing Authority (1994). *Football Club Contingency Planning.*

[15] Football Licensing Authority (1995). *Guidance Notes for Drawing up a Statement of Safety Policy for Spectators at Football Grounds.*

[16] The Football League, the Football Association, the FA Premier League (1995). *Stewarding and Safety Management at Football Grounds.*

[17] Department of National Heritage and Scottish Office (1997). *Guide to Safety at Sports Grounds.* HMSO.

[18] Rt. Hon Lord Wheatley (1972). *Report of the Inquiry into Crowd Safety at Sports Grounds.* HMSO.

[19] Op. cit. 13.

[20] House of Commons Home Affairs Committee (1991). *Policing Football Hooliganism,* p. xxv. HMSO.

[21] Op. cit. 1. pp. 37–38.

[22] Op. cit. 1. p. 5.

[23] Op. cit. 13. Paragraph 7.3.

[24] Op. cit. 1. p. 36.

[25] Op. cit. 16.

[26] Football Stadia Development Committee (1994). *Stadium Control Rooms – Planning, Personnel, Design and Equipment.* The Sports Council.

[27] Op. cit. 1. p.12.

[28] Sir Norman Chester Centre for Football Research (1995). *The FA Premier League Fan Surveys 1994/95.*

[29] Op. cit. 2. p. 15.

[30] Football Stadia Development Committee (1993). *Toilet Facilities at Stadia.* The Sports Council.

[31] Hansard. 10 July 1992.

[32] Football Stadia Advisory Design Council (1993). *Terraces – Designing for Safe Standing at Football Stadia.* The Sports Council.

[33] Home Office and Scottish Office (1990) *Guide to Safety at Sports Grounds.* HMSO.

[34] Fédération Internationale de Football Association and Union of European Football Associations (1995). *Technical Recommendations and Requirements for the Construction or Modernisation of Football Stadia.*

PART 3 THEORY

Overview

Part Three has a theoretical orientation and reports the results of academic research into sport and safety management. It begins by using crisis management theory to investigate club management attitudes to safety in the British football industry, revealing the difficult context in which safety practitioners have to work. It goes on to use the theory of cultural complexity to explain the tensions which exist between commercialism, safety and order, enjoyment and environmental impact at both the macro level of the British stadia safety industry and the micro level of the individual venue.

Chapter summaries

In Chapter 7, Dominic Elliott and Denis Smith report research findings which suggest that there is an air of complacency within many of the UK football clubs with regard to crisis potential. Despite the disasters of Ibrox, Heysel, Hillsborough and Bradford, many clubs have only complied with legislation. It is argued in this chapter that such a compliance-based approach is indicative of an organizational culture that may prove to be crisis prone. The chapter explores the implications of the data and concludes by identifying a series of actions that need to be taken by the regulatory authorities and the clubs themselves.

In Chapter eight, Steve Frosdick and Gerald Mars introduce the theory which underpins the analysis of safety culture in Chapters 9 and 10. The chapter shows how the theory of cultural complexity (TTOCC) defines cultures as ways of life, each of which is the product of a distinct set of values and attitudes (cultural bias) and a distinct pattern of relationships (social relations). There are four archetypally different ways of life: individualism, fatalism, hierarchy and egalitarianism. These are the only four viable ways of life, and each depends on the other for its own continued existence. The four ways of life give rise to four different ways of perceiving risk and there are, therefore, no right or wrong answers in the risk assessment process.

In Chapter 9, Steve Frosdick argues that, in order to reduce the risk of disasters, there is a need to better understand why the mistakes and misunderstandings leading to such incidents actually occur. He uses the theory of cultural complexity to analyse ethnography from and literature relating to sport and safety management at British sports grounds. The analysis reveals the conflicting risk perceptions of individualist/entrepreneurial clubs, hierarchical regulators, long-suffering fatalist spectators and their more egalitarian colleagues in supporter and local resident pressure groups. These perspectives are narrow and biased. At a strategic level, there is a need for each constituency to acknowledge the validity of the others' points of view. Increased awareness is the key to disaster prevention. The conclusions drawn should be applicable to wider scenarios where a multiplicity of organizations are involved.

In Chapter 10, Steve Frosdick presents findings from research into the management of public safety risks in British sports grounds. The chapter opens by discussing the concept of 'safety culture' and briefly sets out the methodology adopted for the study. Some previous work on 'safety culture' analysis is reviewed, and it is then argued that the theory of cultural complexity offers a powerful framework for disaggregated cultural analysis. The research findings reveal the four contrasting, viable and archetypal models of organizing the cross-organizational collaboration required. The chapter concludes by drawing out some implications for public policy.

7 Waiting for the next one: Management attitudes to safety in the UK football industry

Dominic Elliott and Denis Smith

This chapter reports research findings which suggest that there is an air of complacency within many of the UK football clubs with regard to their crisis potential. Despite the disasters of Ibrox, Heysel, Hillsborough and Bradford, many clubs have only complied with legislation rather than sought to adopt best practice. It is argued in this chapter that such a compliance-based approach is indicative of an organizational culture that may prove to be crisis prone. The chapter reports the results of a series of in-depth interviews with senior representatives of football clubs in the UK with a view to assessing the nature of managerial attitudes towards risk potential.

Introduction

The generation of crises and their escalation from incidents and accidents into major catastrophic events has attracted considerable attention in the academic literature. A series of major events over the last fifteen years have served to focus attention on the range of causal factors that appear to underpin such tragedies. In certain cases, notably the sinking of the *Herald of Free Enterprise* and the Kegworth aircrash, it appears that the complexity of these events resulted from interactions within a family of causal agents that made the official determination of the accidents' root cause, as human error, something of an oversimplification. In both of the cases mentioned, it was clear that there were a number of managerial and systems elements that conspired to result in the accident and that simply blaming operator (or human) error as the root cause failed to address these issues.

Research has pointed to the importance of managerial action in setting the culture of organizations and influencing the strategies in place within them [1, 2]. More recently, research has suggested that the approach of management in dealing with issues relating to regulation may prove to be important in affecting the crisis potential of an organization. Simply complying with existing legislation may not be sufficient for an organization to conform to what should be best practice for crisis management [3–5]. An analysis of crises over time suggests that many occur because management either fail to comply with safety-related legislation or that the legislation in place is simply inadequate to deal with the issues associated with crisis generation [6, 7]. It can be argued that organizations which move beyond a narrow compliance-based approach to dealing with potential crisis issues may develop managerial systems that allow them both to go some way towards preventing crises as well as to respond more effectively to those that may occur [8]. This largely theoretical view has not been adequately tested empirically beyond a series of case study analyses which have indicated that management culture played a major part in the generation of such crises [9–14].

The purpose of the research reported in this chapter was to evaluate managerial attitudes towards issues of crisis potential in the wake of a series of high profile, loss of life events. This work was undertaken in the UK football industry which has suffered a series of major events during the 1970s, 1980s and into the 1990s. These events, which resulted in considerable loss of life at Ibrox, Heysel, Hillsborough and Bradford, illustrated how vulnerable football spectators were at major sporting events. This vulnerability was seen to extend beyond the more traditional issue of hooliganism, which has plagued the British game, to include crowd crushing, fire and structural collapse. In short, the national game was perceived to be a dangerous pastime for spectators. Why had the events of the previous twenty years occurred and, perhaps more importantly, were they indicative of a deep-seated malaise within the industry? Research elsewhere has suggested that organizations may prove to be 'crisis prone' [15] and the key proposition addressed in this paper centres around the view that the UK football industry may display such tendencies.

It is felt that the football industry provides a useful vehicle for examining broader issues relating to crisis management for a number of reasons. First, the industry essentially deals with safe processes and products: watching football has not, to date, been proved to cause degenerative health problems! However, such a complacent view of a process that can bring up to 50 000 people together in a confined space, with limited means of egress in an emergency, may have been a major contributory factor in the development of crisis proneness within the industry.

Second, the industry is readily accessible to a large proportion of the population and is watched by millions of spectators in the UK alone each week. This high profile nature of the industry serves to ensure that any crises which occur receive massive and immediate publicity. The events at Heysel, Hillsborough and Bradford were all being filmed for transmission, and, in the case of the first two, were being transmitted live at the time of the crisis.

Third, the industry has been beset for many years with the problems of hooliganism and crowd disturbances which have served to create a stereotypical view amongst many as to the source of problems within the game. A consequence of this has been a series of managerial interventions which have sought to eradicate one problem, that of hooliganism, and yet which may have served to incubate a series of different problems. For example, the perimeter fences which were introduced to combat the problem of pitch invasions proved to be an important factor at Hillsborough.

Fourth, the industry as a whole is faced with severe financial problems which would have led to bankruptcy had clubs been treated as conventional companies. Outside of an élite group of clubs, the industry is simply starved of the cash needed to invest in substantial ground improvements. Whatever money is available is all too often siphoned off into buying players and paying their wages. As a consequence, the industry has little money to spend on improving ground safety and related issues. Indeed, it might be argued that safety issues could be neglected by some clubs as a result of their poor financial circumstances and this raises issues for the effective regulation of stadia.

Fifth, many grounds have been in existence since before the turn of the century and are often located in built up areas which are now unsuitable venues to cope with the large influx of people that occurs on match days. When these grounds were built, they were often located at the edge of an urban area but with urban drift, have now become subsumed within both housing and industrial estates. In some cases, this creates major problems for the effective policing of crowds coming to and leaving the grounds.

Sixth, it is held that many of the problems faced by the football industry would be indicative of problems found in other sporting activities, notably rugby (union and league).

Finally, football clubs can be considered to be a diverse group which provide for the opportunity to investigate the impact of a range of dependent variables upon the development of a crisis-prone culture. The combination of these factors makes the football industry an important vehicle though which to explore the more generic issues relating to crisis management.

Crisis management: Prevention is better than cure

Interest in crisis management has risen considerably during the last fifteen years and, more recently, there has been a movement away from the early contingency-based approach towards a more holistic and preventative stance, which focuses upon crisis prevention [16]. Of particular importance in this shift has been that research which has sought to address issues relating to the crisis-prone nature of organizations [17–20] and the potential that may exist for creating organizations that display high reliability or, put differently, are crisis prepared [21–27]. What is clear from this body of research is that the whole issue of crisis management is broader than simply developing plans and proposals to deal with particular scenarios. Effective crisis management necessitates that organizations pay attention to their culture, informal methods of operating and the core values and beliefs of senior managers.

Within this context, interest has also been focused upon the nature of crisis incubation [28] and the notion of latent error developed in organizations through both managerial and systems design decisions [29, 30]. The main point to emerge from this body of work is that there is a series of factors that serve to create an environment in which a series of trigger events may expose these incubated, and invariably hidden, factors which can escalate an incident to an accident and then on to a crisis within a short period of time. Perrow [31] has observed that systems display both tight coupling and interactive complexity which combine to ensure that a failure will cause an unforeseen pattern of events which occur at great speed. This interaction serves to beguile management attempts to contain such events and almost ensures that an incident escalates into a major accident in a short period of time. For example, the accident at Hillsborough was not simply caused by a police officer authorizing the opening of the gates at the Leppings Lane end of the ground, in order to prevent a crushing at the gates. This then caused a surge into the ground and a crushing at the perimeter fence. This decision, which was taken for the best of reasons, simply exposed a whole series of latent errors that had arisen over time and which served to incubate the crisis potential of this operation. These include: the design of the ground and the effect of the tunnel in speeding up the flow of people into the Leppings Lane end; the use of fences to contain potential hooligans and prevent pitch invasions; the dominant culture of the police which seemed to assume (in the absence of effective communication) that the crowd movement was an attempted pitch invasion; the culture of the crowd that resulted in the late surge to enter the ground, following a period of time spent in local public houses around the ground; the imbalance in ticket allocations to the clubs involved; the failures of the police contingency plan to cope with the event, along with failures in both command and control and communication; the reluctance of (many) football clubs to invest in ground improvements and the lack of seating provision; and, finally, the poor provision of facilities for the police control base at the ground served to exacerbate the problems.

What is clear from Hillsborough, and indeed from other football disasters, is that it was not a single root error alone which caused the crisis. There is a complex interaction of organizational and human factors along with a range of environmental conditions in which the event is contextualized. What, then, are the lessons that were raised by the Hillsborough accident and to what extent have organizations sought to change their operations in the light of this and other stadia-based accidents? Before seeking to answer this question, it is first necessary to explore the notion of crisis incubation in more detail.

In discussing the nature of latent failures in organizations Reason argues that it is possible to make a number of assertions concerning accident generation. In developing the resident pathogen metaphor Reason suggests that complex systems will have greater potential for playing host to pathogens than more simple systems and the greater the number of pathogens that exist in a system, the greater will be the probability of a failure [32]. He also observes that for simpler systems with fewer defences in depth, fewer pathogens will be required to cause such a failure. The development of such pathogens can be seen, according to Reason, as a function of an individual's position within the organizational hierarchy and their role in decision making. Echoing the work of Pauchant and Mitroff [33], Reason [34] argues that the higher an individual sits within the organization's structure, the greater potential they have for creating resident pathogens. Such a view, reflecting the relative span of control or influence that an individual has, moves us away from the more commonly held view of operator error towards a recognition of managerial error as a factor in determining latent error potential within systems.

A third group of comments made by Reason concerns our ability to identify and predict pathogens in a diagnostic manner, a point that has also been addressed within the management literature [35, 36]. In dealing with this predictive dynamic,

Pauchant and Mitroff [37, 38] argue that there are four key elements which determine an organization's vulnerability to crises: the structure of the organization, its strategy, the assumptions and culture that exist within it and, finally, the core beliefs and values of key decision makers and managers. This model is drawn as an 'onion model' with the most observable elements of strategy and structure at the surface and, at the innermost, core level, the fundamental beliefs that influence the way an organization, or individuals therein, process information collected for decision making. It is argued that the interaction between these elements creates the potential for resident pathogens (that is, crisis incubation) across the organization and it is essential that attention is given to all four elements in order that management can fully understand the nature and extent of organizational capabilities in this regard. This framework of four key elements provides the theoretical basis for this chapter.

In order to test the assumptions inherent in the model, crisis events in the UK's football industry have been assessed [39] and this has formed the basis of a programme of research aimed at assessing the industry's level of crisis preparedness. Whilst it is accepted that there is no effective diagnostic for crisis proneness, the framework used within this research does, it is argued, provide some useful insights into the effects that recent disasters have had upon stadia management.

The national game: Crisis prone or crisis prepared?

In order to test the extent of the football industry's state of crisis preparedness, a series of interviews were undertaken with club secretaries or their nominees [40]. In the interests of confidentiality, each respondent is referred to by a two digit code (P4, T1, etc.). The focus of these interviews was around the lessons of Hillsborough, the requirements of the Taylor Report and the four elements identified by Pauchant and Mitroff. Because of the requirements of the Taylor Report, the study not only included those clubs covered by the report but also those that fell below the Taylor recommendations. The remainder of this chapter deals with the findings of this study and concludes by making a series of recommendations for the football industry with regards to its state of crisis preparedness.

Our analysis indicates the failure of regulation to promote high standards of safety in football stadia. Despite increased regulation the industry appears to have remained prone to crisis. Mitroff and Pauchant's 'onion model' of crisis management, discussed earlier, highlights four key factors that determines the extent to which an organization may be considered crisis prepared or prone. Using data collected from our semistructured interviews, this section examines the responses using the different layers of Mitroff and Pauchant's 'onion model'.

Level one: Individual defence mechanisms

Table 7.1 identifies the seven key defence mechanisms identified by Pauchant and Mitroff [41]. Through our use of grounded theory an eighth defence mechanism was identified to be added to the original list. Displacement was the term used to describe instances where respondents appeared to allocate responsibility to other groups, primarily official or regulatory agencies.

The use of displacement as a defence mechanism was most evident in two respects. The first was in terms of discussions concerning the causes of Hillsborough and the second related to the role of the regulatory agencies in preventing crises. Twelve of the sixteen respondents interviewed for this study indicated that primary responsibility for the Hillsborough tragedy lay with another group(s), from supporters (nine respondents), police (six respondents) to the local authority (one respondent). This contrasts with Bradford where four respondents identified the club as having primary responsibility for the incident. This displacement reflects a key finding of this study, that is, the tendency for clubs to use a variety of means to protect themselves from acknowledging threats.

Level two: Organizational culture

Where level one focused upon the individual, level two deals with the group or corporate level. Of course drawing an absolute distinction between the two levels may be impossible, a weakness acknowledged by Pauchant and Mitroff. This level concentrates on the widely held views within an organization concerning crises and crisis management efforts. These rationalizations are categorized into four groups, namely, properties of the organization, properties of the environment, properties of crises themselves and properties of prior crisis management efforts. To provide a focus for our discussion we shall concentrate on the views on respondents concerning the causes of the Bradford and Hillsborough tragedies and their effect upon the various organizations. Tables 7.2 and 7.3 summarize respondents' views concerning the main causes of the Hillsborough and Bradford tragedies respectively, together with an assessment of who was held to have primary responsibility.

Table 7.1 Level one: Defence mechanisms

Defence mechanism	Explanation	Example
Denial	Expressed refusal to acknowledge a threatening reality or realities	'Hillsborough was horrible but it couldn't happen here' (quoted by Lord Justice Taylor)
Disavowal	Acknowledge a threatening reality but downplay its importance	(Club F1) 'I suppose that when you assess the odds then it won't happen, you know the number of disasters when you consider the number of football matches, it's one of the safest pastimes isn't it, it really is low odds'
Fixation	Rigid commitment to a particular course of action or attitude in dealing with a threatening situation	(a) The emphasis upon technical solutions, physical constraints such as perimeter and radial fencing rather than ensuring the additional use of effective crowd supervision (Club T3) 'Pre Hillsborough there wasn't the emphasis on making sure that the stewards were there, if one didn't turn up then you'd saved yourself a few bob' (b) Focus upon hooliganism and crowd control rather than crowd safety
Grandiosity	The feeling of omnipotence	The misperception observed at Club F1 that stewards were replacement police officers and that their role was to 'get stuck in and sort out any trouble'
Idealization	Ascribing omnipotence to another person	Use of unmonitored private security companies to ensure crowd safety
Intellectualization	The elaboration of an action or thought	The assumption that all-seater stadia will ensure crowd safety

(continued)

Table 7.1 Level one: Defence mechanisms (*continued*)

Defence mechanism	Explanation	Example
Projection	Attributing unacceptable actions or thoughts to others	The view that the root cause of football stadia problems lie with the hooligans; the problem would not be there if it were not for the drunken yobs that disrupt sporting events
Splitting	The extreme isolation of different elements, extreme dichotomization or fragmentation	—
Displacement	Passing responsibility to another person or group	The view, expressed by many respondents, that primary responsibility for crown safety lies with the police, government or regulatory agencies rather than with the stadium owner

Table 7.2 Summary of views of respondents on causes and responsibility for the Hillsborough tragedy

Club	Primary Cause				Primary Responsibility			
	Ground layout	Hooligans	Operational failures	Bad luck	Local authority	Police	All agencies involved	Supporters
P1	***				***			
P2			***					
P3	**		**				***	
P4		***						***
F1		***	*					***
F2		***	*			*		***
F3			***			***		
F4		**	**	**		**		**
S1	**	**	**			**	**	**
S2		***						***
S3	–	–	–	–	–	–	–	–
S4		***						***
T1		**	**			**		**
T2	–	–	–	–	–	–	–	–
T3	*		**			**	**	
T4		**	**			**		**

Cause: *** Sole or primary cause; ** Secondary or one of a number of key factors; * Contributory; Responsibility: *** One group with prime responsibility; ** Balance of responsibility; * Contributory (fleeting mention).

The decision rules used to categorize the responses were based on the assessment offered by respondents. There are clear dangers of including only 'selective' statements that reflect the researcher's bias rather than the respondents' perceptions. To reduce such bias once the table had been first drafted, interview data were re-examined to identify evidence contrary to that included within the table. Few revisions were necessary given the firm, and apparently fixed, views of respondents.

A number of key themes emerged from the data, particularly in respect of the Hillsborough disaster. First, respondents differed in their views of the causes of the tragedy, especially with regard to the complexity or simplicity of those causal agents. For example, P4 and S4 were unequivocal in their identification of supporter

Table 7.3 Summary of views of respondents on causes and responsibility for the Bradford tragedy

Club	Primary Cause				Responsibility			
	Wooden stands/ construction	Locked gates/ exits	Fire!	Poor maintenance and cleanliness	Lack of finances	Freak accident	Smoker	Club
P1	–	–	–	–	–	–	–	–
P2	–	–	–	–	–	–	–	–
P3	**	**			–	–		–
P4	**	**			–	–		–
F1	**	**			–	–		–
F2				***				***
F3		**		**				***
F4			***			***		
S1			***			***		
S2				***				***
S3	–	–	–	–	–	–	–	–
S4					***			*
T1	–	–	–	–	–	–	–	–
T2	–	–	–	–	–	–	–	–
T3	**					*	**	
T4		***		***				***

Cause: *** Sole or primary cause; ** Secondary or one of a number of key factors; * Contributory; Responsibility: *** One group with prime responsibility; ** Balance of responsibility; * Contributory (fleeting mention).

behaviour as the primary cause. Similarly F3 accused the police of breaking the 'cardinal rule' and thus identified a simple explanation for the tragedy. Other respondents cited more complex causes, P3, F4 and T4 for example. Typically, where complex causes were identified more equivocal responses were made. P3 uses 'perhaps', and F4 and T3 begin their statements with 'I think'. Linked to their identification of causes were the allocation of responsibility. For P4 and S4 supporters were to blame, whilst for F3 the police were held to be responsible. P1 placed responsibility with the local authority for not identifying the problem, providing further evidence of 'displacement'. Contrastingly, where respondents identified complex causes responsibility was deemed to be shared between the various agencies and stakeholder groups involved. However, there was one notable omission from all responses – no-one indicated that the owners of the ground, Sheffield Wednesday, contributed to the causes of the disaster or that they had any responsibility for the incident. Even where complex causes were identified responsibility was placed with a combination of police, government, local authority and supporters. Only T3's general statement about the failures of everybody concerned with the match organization might be interpreted as placing some of the responsibility with the stadium owners. Yet in June 1996 the Sheffield Wednesday Football Club, its structural engineers and the South Yorkshire Police settled out of court claims made by police officers who had been at the Hillsborough tragedy.

These reported perceptions of the causes of the two tragedies provide a valuable insight into views relating to the properties of crisis. Using Pauchant and Mitroff's framework a number of observations can be made, first in respect of the perceived properties of the organizations concerning a crisis and, second, concerning the perceived properties of the environment (see Table 7.4).

The most significant change in the industry's environment was reported to concern hooliganism. The risks associated with hosting events attended by large numbers were frequently downplayed by reference to stories of the large numbers that used to attend. S3 for example observed:

> We would all love to see the days when you look back, say at Wembley when they used to have those vast crowds when there were no restrictions and everyone was good and sat quietly at the edge of the pitch and crossed legs, and kids at the front and no cages, no barriers, no anything.

F2 looked back to when the Kop held some 22 000 'safely' compared to only 6000 in 1994. S2 spoke of pressure from the directors who could remember a crowd of 50 000 without any problems and questioned the need to reduce the stadium capacity to below 20 000. P4 remembered a crowd of 51 000 on one terrace with 30 000 the current capacity of the whole ground, but of course 'they were better behaved then'. These rosy reminiscences highlighted an overriding view that much of the blame for stadium incidents could be placed on poor behaviour. It is worth reminding ourselves that there is no suggestion of poor behaviour as a contributory cause of either the 1971 Ibrox disaster or the 1985 Bradford fire. In general there was an inability to consider alternative forms of crises. One exception stood out. P3 commented:

Table 7.4   Rationalizations on the properties of crises

Properties of the organization	
Culture	(P2) 'Funnily enough we are a bit dated now because we were so far ahead with everything and we were right to do it, anyway you look at the ground and you think well they have got nice new stands and we really don't need them'
	(F1) 'We weren't complacent here, we took quite a lot of action after Hillsborough anyway, but not so much, we still had a lot to do after Taylor'
	(F1) 'Why haven't clubs taken the initiative? Basically because no one has been kicking them up the backside'
Properties of the Environment	
	The key change reported by respondents concerned the perceived worsening of spectator behaviour in the last twenty years. Yet the research carried out by Williams, Dunning and Murphy at the University of Leicester identifies that hooliganism has been present for much of this century. Furthermore, our analysis in Chapter 2 of this book indicates a large number of incidents inside football stadia since 1900, very few of which are related to poor behaviour
Properties of Crises	
Technical fixes	(P1) 'We've based everything we've done on the *Green Guide* ... we've used that as a bible really'
Uniqueness	(P3) 'That's what disasters are, that's what accidents are, the unknown happening without warning'
Properties of crisis management efforts	
Training	(P3) 'All I can do is to try and train everybody, including myself, that the majority of things we can do in a major incident scenario would be instinctive'

I'd hate to think that there is any club in the country who will now say, well we've done everything Justice Taylor has recommended and we're OK now, because I don't think you can ever be in that situation ... I mean I don't know at three o'clock or quarter past three on a Saturday afternoon whether a tanker is suddenly going to come along [****] Road and suddenly go through the boundary wall and explode, there are so many outside influences.

This view reflects Toft's [42] isomorphic learning, which identifies general lessons rather than incident specific ones. A prevailing view within the industry was that crises are unique incidents, thereby denying the underlying importance of systemic factors which have been identified as key within the crisis management literature we have reviewed above. Instead there has been a focus upon incident specific learning, based in part as we have seen upon the official regulatory response to issues. Thus, despite citing personal experiences of previous stadium fires, F4 and S1 described the Bradford fire as a freak accident. Explanations offered for the Bradford and Hillsborough disasters frequently revolved around simple cause and effect with a particular focus on the problems on the day, rather than a consideration of how the potential for crisis had developed over a long period before the incidents, as we have shown elsewhere [43].

This evidence supports the view that many key executives within the industry persist in the view that crises are simply chance events' or that they have simple causes. Within the literature [44–47] it has been suggested that such views will lead to a focus on technical solutions to problems rather than a system-wide review.

Level three: Organizational structure

The structure of an organization is held to be a key factor in determining its ability to respond to the demands of a crisis event through the mobilization of crisis management teams and other decision-making bodies. However, it can also be argued that structure is an important dynamic in crisis generation through its influence on formal and informal communications channels and the developing of power relationships within organizations.

For the purpose of this discussion we shall focus upon the relationship between the structure of football clubs and its creation of the context in which individual executives make decisions. A simple observation, that our next section makes clear, is that the development of administration of football clubs has not kept pace with the changes demanded by an increasingly complex environment. Football clubs have been caught in a time warp in which their administrative systems and methods of communication were better suited to a less complex, more stable environment. A fuller discussion of these issues is included in our earlier analysis [48]. For this analysis we shall consider the links between structure and strategy.

Level four: Organizational strategies

Although Pauchant and Mitroff relate the outer skin of their 'onion model' to plans, mechanisms and procedures for crisis management, the routine administration and management of the clubs shall be considered here. The context in which safety management decisions are taken cannot be separated from the day-to-day management of the clubs. As our respondents indicated, clubs do not squander resources on administration and support services. As many safety officers are part time or combine this role, a part of the safety management task will often fall to the senior administrator.

Two key themes emerged in the course of the interviews concerning business practices within football. The first concerned the range of tasks that the Club Secretary had to deal with. The second concerned the extent of the organization's strategic planning. These two themes proved to be closely related as respondents indicated that a heavy workload with wide-ranging responsibilities prevented them from considering the future adequately. This view was supported by the findings of the 1966 PEP Report [49] which identified that the key performance indicators used to assess managerial performance in football were short term, focusing on immediate playing success. 'The manager's position is thus perilous as long term policies, in particular team building and ground improvement, may be sacrificed in favour of the team's current performance' (p. 123).

Such a view was supported by our respondents: P1 for example, commented that the Club was 'better managed now, but before, I didn't have enough time to concentrate on the issues that really mattered because you're bogged down with the day to day issues'. The other Premier League Clubs also indicated significant changes including the appointment of more administrative and support staff and a redistribution of responsibilities allowing the Secretary (or Chief Executive) to devote more time to planning issues. One result of this was that now budgets were prepared on a variety of scenarios from good to bad. For example, P4 reported: 'We have three lots of cashflow each year, and you've got to base scenarios on the worst'. P3 indicated that increasingly those who had the title 'Club Secretary' were legal officers and that many of the duties associated with that post had been reallocated to 'Chief Executives'. The picture that emerged from the lowest two divisions was very different, summed up perhaps by the comments of S1: 'ashes to ashes, dust to dust, what the others won't do the secretary must'. In addition, F4 suggested that a lack of resources for administration combined together with the uncertainty of professional football to prevent proper attention being given to planning:

> Unfortunately football being what it is most people do two or three jobs . . . everybody has more roles than they should have, you just do not have the time, it's not an excuse it's a fact, football clubs can't afford to pay that number of people because the financial structure of clubs is wrong . . . in football it is impossible to do a cash flow for the next month, there are so many unforeseen things that can happen and it is all down to kicking a football on the pitch or drawing a number out of a bag.

T1 told of the difficulties of preparing a plan requested for the Football Licensing Authority regarding ground improvements: 'We didn't do it because it would either have been a blank piece of paper or all fiction so what was the point, last year I didn t know where I'd be next week let alone next year or three years' time. I'm still not sure where I'm going to be.' For T3 planning was limited to the re-signing of their best player to ensure that he could be sold for more at the end of the season. T4's prioritization consisted of:

> You live by the seat of your pants, basically, you just do what you have to get through, whoever shouts the loudest you do that next, there is no other more methodical way of doing it, you learn as you go on and if you're lucky you don't learn too often by your mistakes.

This is a view echoed by S3: 'I've usually got six or eight balls in the air, and I probably should do something about these things and when people shout aloud they do happen'.

The reluctance of Directors to invest more resources in administration and support was noted by two interviewees. S2 indicated a desire to appoint staff in preparation for promotion to the next division, but Directors wanted to wait until they achieved it before committing any resources. Five interviewees used the term 'jack of all trades' to describe their current role.

Our explanation of the reluctance of football clubs to respond to regulation and the problems posed to safety have hitherto focused on a crisis prone safety culture. The study's findings indicate another factor, namely the time pressures upon administrators. Given the lack of resources and the immediacy of problems ranging from preparing for forthcoming events, contractual problems, lotteries, responding to requests for information, dealing with financial matters, the Inland Revenue, ticket sales, etc., it can be seen that, unless rigidly enforced, regulations may be overlooked.

Add to this, the lack of proper job definitions, in practice even if they exist on paper, then 'non-urgent' tasks, however important, may simply be forgotten. In Popplewell's analysis of the causes of the Bradford fire, the dire financial circumstances of that club are posited as key. However, his analysis also shows how the club had received a number of warnings concerning the build-up of combustible waste beneath the main stand. Lack of finances certainly played a part but ironically the replacement of that stand would have begun the following Monday in preparation for the club's newly acquired status as a designated ground. The greater division of labour, facilitated by investment in administrative and commercial staff, was identified as an important development by all Premier and First Division respondents. In the lower divisions it was clear from responses, as well as from personal observations in the course of the interviews, that this greater task specialization was not possible. For example, although interviews lasted for in excess of two hours, no interview with a Premier or First Division club was interrupted by a telephone call. In contrast, with the exception of S1, other interviews were interrupted an average of seven times and a number of other personal callers were either put off or the interview was halted for a few minutes.

Routine business planning also differed between the divisions. Seven of the eight senior clubs identified that they planned between three and five years ahead with projections based on at least three separate scenarios. Only one of the lower division clubs (S1) identified any such planning practice. S3's experience provides a clear example of the perceived problems of the lower division clubs: 'No plans for next season because we might get relegated, so do we do something or don't we, and we can't afford to redevelop the main stand because we don't get the crowds, we don't have the money. But obviously when we are forced to make a decision we will do.'

Despite the uncertainty of either relegation or promotion there can be few industries faced with the certainty of a minimum number of key income-generating events. Fixed income from the league could form a part of any projection and the estimation of likely attendance following promotion or relegation could be estimated relatively easily, given the vast quantities of data concerning attendance.

Conclusions

It appears that the football industry in the UK has learnt little from the disasters that occurred during the latter part of the 1980s and beyond. A number of defence mechanisms are used by senior managers within the industry to legitimize their lack of real action in dealing with the issues raised by the Taylor report. In essence, the industry could be accused of simply complying with the legislation but doing little else to improve safety at grounds. It is clear from the academic literature in accident generation that there are a number of factors that interact together to generate the potential for disaster. A basic conclusion from our analysis is that the football industry remains crisis prone and we are currently 'Waiting for the next one!' We shall confine our conclusions to Mitroff and Pauchant's model and make a series of recommendations from this analysis for those involved with the football industry.

At the level of individual beliefs a simplistic view of the causes of crises was observed. This combined a number of elements. Two were particularly influential. First, was the tendency to apportion blame for past incidents or present problems to a particular group, whether the actions of police officers on a particular day or the behaviour of spectators in general. This displacement of responsibility may act as a barrier to clubs from taking responsibility for ensuring the safety of spectators and create an illusion that safety management is beyond their control. The second, and related, element was the failure of many respondents to grasp that the underlying causes of crises may combine many factors in a complex relationship. As we have shown in our introduction and in our earlier analysis [50], crises have complex causes. Concentration on one or two factors is rarely enough to prevent future incidents, indeed it may increase the risk from other elements. Prevention of crises and improving organizational response requires an understanding of crisis causation and a treatment of all factors. Without this acknowledgement and understanding, attempts to prevent crises or improve organizational responses will be flawed. These 'defence mechanisms' combined with the others that we have identified, will act as a strong barrier to change unless these basic assumptions can be challenged.

As identified earlier, drawing an absolute distinction between levels one (individual defence mechanisms) and two (organizational culture) may be impossible. At an organizational level we have identified a common historical perception of large, well-behaved crowds standing in the sunshine. Implicit in this view is that crowd disasters are a recent phenomena. As we have shown with Steve Frosdick in Chapter 2, this view is false. Throughout this 'golden age of football' spectators lost their lives or suffered serious injuries. This false view has contributed to the assumption that technical fixes can be developed to the particular problems of the present day. The solution, advocated by many respondents, has been to treat the *Green Guide* as 'gospel' and use it as a blue print to ensure crowd safety. A potential danger is that the *Green Guide* is seen as an end point, as the maximum or desired standard rather than a minimum expectation. Only one respondent expressed the view that they sought to learn from the process of planning rather than treating the preparation of an emergency or contingency plan as the key goal.

These two levels prepare the context for the outer layers of Mitroff and Pauchant's 'onion model' with individual beliefs and organizational assumptions shaping structure and strategy. Our main observations were that whilst Premier and First Division clubs had increased investment in their support activities, lower division clubs had largely been unable to. Safety Officers, for example, were often part time and in many cases match-day only. Lack of regular contact with club executives and the Board of Directors acts to prevent the free flow of information from those with the task of crowd and stadium management to those with the ultimate decision making responsibility. Chief executives and club secretaries were charged with a variety of tasks with 'whoever shouts the loudest' influencing the prioritization of tasks. The absence of a proper strategic planning process in all but the better managed clubs prevented the treatment of crowd management issues in any but a piecemeal, short-term way. The responses from the Second and Third Divisions make this point loud and clear.

In summary, our analysis has pinpointed a number of weaknesses in the attitudes, assumptions, structure and strategies of football clubs and their personnel. False assumptions combined with the limited resources provided for non-playing activities have created an environment in which a high potential for further critical incidents exists. Whilst the authors accept that it is never possible to absolutely prevent future incidents it is our view that the probability of such incidents can be further reduced. Such a reduction however, requires actions that deal with weaknesses at each level of the 'onion model'.

At the individual and organizational culture levels, ongoing training and education, for senior executives and Board members, could assist in uncovering faulty assumptions and the presence of defence mechanisms that have acted as barriers to change. Such training programmes should combine analysis of incidents from a range of industries as well as the football industry to facilitate isomorphic learning. Greater understanding of crisis causality and good and bad practice in crisis response is the most powerful means of challenging deeply held beliefs. Given the strength of culture and individual beliefs such training should be ongoing and arguably attendance should form part of the safety certificate process.

For the outer two levels any strategy for improvement should combine ongoing management development training with the reallocation of resources within each club. The lack of planning identified by many clubs was rooted in the lack of time on the part of senior executives and lack of relevant skills. Although there are pressures on clubs to be seen to be investing in the playing side, greater recognition needs to be given to the non-glamorous, but highly important support staff. Lack of resources may lead to a failure on the part of clubs to exploit fully the available commercial opportunities or to manage existing resources efficiently and effectively. At a more dangerous level, from the perspective of human life, failure to invest properly in infrastructure can lead to the loss of life. A lack of skills can be remedied by utilizing one of the many management development programmes available at a number of institutions. A possible role for the Premier, Football and Scottish Football League organizations is that part of the central pool of money that is allocated to clubs to provide a basic income should be earmarked for particular activities, such as improving club administrative infrastructure or in developing the skills of key employees. For the smaller, poorer clubs this is likely to prove the most difficult yet the most important business activity if they are to continue well into the twenty-first century.

A final note for those with responsibility for regulating the industry. As P1 responded to the question concerning the failure of clubs to take the initiative in ground safety, he observed that the reason was, 'basically because no one has been kicking them up the backside'. Given our analysis and the observation that those who shout loudest get heard first, there is an important role for the regulatory agencies to cajole and support change in the industry. For cultural change to occur it is necessary that the *Green Guide* is not seen as the maximum standard but as a basic requirement on which a safety management culture is built. The existence of better managed clubs indicates that dramatic improvement is possible.

Summary

- There has been considerable academic research into the causes of crises in organizations and the reasons why such crises can escalate from incidents and accidents into major disasters.
- Research has shown that there are a series of factors which can create a crisis-prone environment. Trigger events which expose these factors can quickly escalate an incident into an accident and on into a crisis.
- The UK football industry provides a good vehicle for examining some broader

issues relating to crisis management. This chapter reports the outcomes of a study into the extent of the football industry's state of crisis preparedness.

- The analysis is underpinned by an 'onion model' of four key layers which determine an organization's vulnerability to crisis. These four layers or levels, from the inside out, are individual defence mechanisms, organizational culture, organizational structure and organizational strategies.
- At the first level, it was found that football clubs tend to use a variety of means to protect themselves from acknowledging threats.
- At the second level, it was found that clubs persisted in seeing disasters as having simple causes, usually arising from operational problems on the day, rather than appreciating how the potential for crisis had developed over a long period of time.
- At the third level, it was found that the administrative systems and methods of communication within football clubs other than the élite, had not kept pace with the demands of an increasingly complex world.
- At the fourth level, it was found that club personnel had a heavy workload with wide-ranging responsibilities and that this prevented them from adequately considering the future.
- Overall, the analysis pinpoints a number of weaknesses in the attitudes, assumptions, structure and strategies of football clubs and their personnel. It is suggested that these should be addressed through ongoing management development and training, particularly for senior staff, and that there is an important role for regulatory agencies in cajoling and supporting change in the industry. The existence of better managed clubs indicates that dramatic improvement is possible.

References

[1] Pauchant, T. and Mitroff, I (1988). Crisis prone versus crisis avoiding organisations. *Industrial Crisis Quarterly*, **2**(1), 53–63.

[2] Pauchant, T. and Mitroff, I (1992). *Transforming the Crisis Prone Organisation: Preventing Individual, Organizational and Environmental Tragedies*. Jossey Bass.

[3] Turner, B. (1978). *Man Made Disasters*. Wykeham.

[4] Smith, D. and Tombs, S. (1995). Self regulation as a control strategy for major hazards. *Journal of Management Studies*, **32**(5), 619–636.

[5] Tombs, S. and Smith, D. (1995). Corporate responsibility and crisis management: Some

insights from political and social theory. *Journal of Contingencies and Crisis Management*, **3**(3), 135–148.

[6] Op. cit. 3.

[7] Smith, D. (1995). *Bhopal as a Crisis of Ethics: Corporate Responsibility and Crisis Generation*. Crisis Management Working Paper No 3. The Home Office Emergency Planning College and Liverpool Business School.

[8] Smith, D. (1995). The dark side of excellence: Managing strategic failures. In *Handbook of Strategic Management* (J. Thompson, ed.), pp. 161–191. Butterworth-Heinemann.

[9] Shrivastava, P. (1992). *Bhopal: The Anatomy of a Crisis*. Paul Chapman Publishing.

[10] Op. cit. 2.

[11] Elliott, D. and Smith, D. (1993). Football stadia disasters in the United Kingdom: Learning from tragedy. *Industrial and Environmental Crisis Quarterly*, **7**(3), 205–229.

[12] Smith, D. (1992). The Kegworth aircrash – a crisis in three phases? *Disaster Management*, **4**(2), 63–72.

[13] Smith, D. and Sipika, C. (1993). Back from the brink – post-crisis management. *Long Range Planning*, **26**(1), 28–38.

[14] Sipika, C. and Smith, D. (1993). From disaster to crisis: The failed turnaround of Pan American Airlines. *Journal of Contingencies and Crisis Management*, **1**(3), 138–151.

[15] Op. cit. 1.

[16] Smith, D. (1990). Beyond contingency planning – towards a model of crisis management. *Industrial Crisis Quarterly*, **4**(4), 263–275.

[17] Miller, D. (1992). *The Icarus Paradox*. Harper.

[18] Kets de Vries, M. and Miller, D. (1987). *Unstable at the Top: Inside the Troubled Organization*. Mentor.

[19] Op. cit. 2.

[20] Op. cit. 9.

[21] Op. cit. 2.

[22] Roberts, K. (1989). New challenges in organization research: High reliability organizations. *Industrial Crisis Quarterly*, **3**(2), 111–125.

[23] Roberts, K. (1990). Some characteristics of one type of high reliability organization. *Organization Science*, **1**(2), 160–177.

[24] Roberts, K. (1993). Introduction. In *New Challenges to Understanding Organizations* (K. Roberts, ed.), pp. 1–10. Macmillan Publishing Company.

[25] Roberts, K. (1994) Functional and dysfunctional organizational linkages. In *Trends in Organizational Behavior*, Vol. 1 (C. Cooper and D. Rousseau, eds.), pp. 1–11. Wiley.

[26] Roberts, K. and Rousseau, D. (1989). Research in nearly failure-free, high-reliability organizations: Having the bubble. *IEEE Transactions on Engineering Management*, **36**(2), 139.

[27] Rochlin, G. (1993). Defining 'high reliability' organizations: A comparative framework. In *New Challenges to Understanding Organizations* (K. Roberts, ed.), pp. 11–32 Macmillan Publishing Company.

[28] Op. cit. 3.

[29] Reason, J. (1990). *Human Error*. Cambridge University Press.

[30] Reason J. (1990). The contribution of latent human failures to the breakdown of complex systems. *Philosophical Transactions of the Royal Society*, **B**(327), 475–485.

[31] Perrow, C. (1984). *Normal Accidents: Living with High-Risk Technologies*. Basic Books.

[32] Reason, J. (1993). Managing the management risk: New approaches to organisational safety. In *Reliability and Safety in Hazardous Work Systems: Approaches to Analysis and Design* (B. Wilpert and T. Qvale, eds.), pp. 7–22. Lawrence Erlbaum Associates Publishers.

[33] Op. cit. 1.

[34] Op. cit. 32.

[35] Op. cit. 8.

[36] Op. cit. 16.

[37] Op. cit. 1.

[38] Op. cit. 2.

[39] Op. cit. 11.

[40] A modified version of the instrument developed by Pauchant and Mitroff was used in a total of 132 football clubs in England and Scotland. The questionnaire was distributed to club safety officers through the Football Safety Officers Association (FSOA) and some 64 out of the 132 questionnaires were returned completed. In England and Wales the response rate was 62 responses from 92 clubs whereas in Scotland the response rate was two out of 40. It was felt that the reason for this low return in Scotland was a reflection of the low membership of the FSOA, although it does raise some questions concerning the commitment to safety issues in such clubs.

[41] Op. cit. 2.

[42] Toft, B. (1992). The failure of hindsight. *Disaster Prevention and Management*, **1**(3), 48–60.

[43] Op. cit. 11.

[44] Canter, D., Comber, M. and Uzzell, D. (1989). *Football in its Place – An Environmental Psychology of Football Grounds*. Routledge.

[45] Op. cit. 16.

[46] Op. cit. 2.

[47] Op. cit. 42.

[48] Op. cit. 11.

[49] Political and Economic Planning (1996). *English Professional Football*. Planning report B2 XXXII, No. 496. HMSO.

[50] Op. cit 11.

8 Understanding cultural complexity

Steve Frosdick and Gerald Mars

This chapter introduces the theory that underpins the analysis of safety culture in Chapters 9 and 10. It shows how the theory of cultural complexity (TTOCC) defines cultures as ways of life, each of which is the product of a distinct set of values and attitudes (cultural bias) and a distinct pattern of relationships (social relations). There are four archetypally different ways of life: individualism, fatalism, hierarchy and egalitarianism. These are the only four viable ways of life, and each depends on the other for its own continued existence. The four ways of life give rise to four different ways of perceiving risk and there are, therefore, no right or wrong answers in the risk assessment process.

Four ways of life

There has been substantial debate among scholars about the definitions of culture. Rather than getting drawn into this debate, Michael Thompson, Richard Ellis and Aaron Wildavsky have sought to clarify matters by distinguishing between three terms: cultural bias, social relations and way of life. They explain [1] that 'Cultural bias refers to shared values and beliefs. Social relations are defined as patterns of interpersonal relations. When we wish to designate a viable combination of social relations and cultural bias we speak of a way of life.' Their book seeks to identify the viable ways of life and explain how these maintain themselves. Their 'cultural theory' (which is now more aptly called TTOCC), is derived from social anthropology and founded on the work of Professor Mary Douglas. TTOCC has its origins in her argument [2] that there are two dimensions by which all cultures can be classified.

The first is the 'grid' dimension, which has been defined as 'the total body of rules and constraints which a culture imposes on its people in a particular context' [3], and as, 'the degree to which an individual's life is circumscribed by externally imposed prescriptions' [4]. The Hindu caste system is an example of a high grid context, whereas the free and easy lifestyle of the American West Coast represents an instance of low grid. The second dimension, 'group', 'emphasises collectiveness among people who meet face to face' [5]. The group dimension also, 'refers to the extent to which an individual is morally coerced by others, through being a member of a bounded face-to-face unit' [6], and describes, 'the experience of a bounded social unit' [7]. Living in a total institution such as an army barracks represents high group, whereas being housebound alone in a tower block is an example of low group.

Considering the two dimensions together produces a fourfold typology of ways of life, each reflecting a cohesive and coherent cluster of attitudes, beliefs and styles of relationships. Thus each way of life is the product of a value system (the cultural bias) and a pattern of social relations, classified by reference to the relative strength of grid and group. These ways of life inform the perceptions of the participants, determine their behaviour and are used by them to justify the validity of their social situations.

The four ways of life can be depicted on a simple matrix (Figure 8.1). Where both dimensions are weak, we find an individualist way of life. Where both are strong we

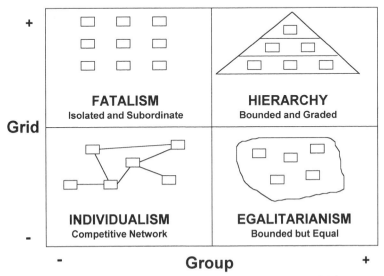

Figure 8.1   The theory of cultural complexity: four ways of life.

have a hierarchical one. These two types represent the conventional economic duality of the free entrepreneurial market at one extreme and the highly regulated Weberian bureaucracy at the other. TTOCC introduces a more disaggregated view of the world since there are two further ways of life to consider: egalitarianism (weak grid/strong group) and the more passive fatalism (strong grid/weak group). These categories can be brought to life through examples which illustrate features of each of the ways of life. Mars, for example, has used grid/group to set out a classification of occupations and their associated deviance [8], whilst Thompson et al. [9] give outline vignettes of a Hindu villager, a communard, a self-made manufacturer and a ununionized weaver.

Thompson et al. introduce the possibility of a fifth way of life, that of the hermit, who withdraws altogether from social life. The hermit avoids both dimensions, refusing either to be controlled by others or to engage in any groupings with others. Since this chapter is aimed at underpinning the practical application of TTOCC in a social world from which hermits are absent, their existence may for present purposes be properly regarded as a theoretical distraction and we will move on.

The impossibility theorem: Four viable archetypal ways of life

We have seen how the grid/group typology gives rise to four ways of life, each the product of a distinct combination of cultural bias and social relations. It is possible to conceive of other alternative ways of life. However, according to TTOCC, these four (ignoring the hermit) are the only four viable archetypal ways of life. That is, it is only these four ways of life that are able to sustain themselves so that they endure over time. This idea that there are only four viable ways of life is what Thompson et al. refer to as the 'impossibility theorem'.

They set out to substantiate this theorem in a number of ways. Summarizing very briefly, the assertion is first grounded in the fact that the grid/group framework meets the logical requirements of classification, namely that the four types produced are both mutually exclusive and jointly exhaustive. The argument is then developed through a complex analysis of the social construction of nature, that is, what models do different people use to explain both physical nature and human nature. The argument then builds by examining the ways in which people manage their needs and resources in order to make ends meet, and the way in which adherents derive their preferences from their chosen way of life, including their preferred perception of risk.

The requisite variety condition: All must be present for each to survive

The impossibility theorem does not of course mean that the four archetypes are necessarily found in their pure form. Most social situations are found to comprise 'regimes' – combinations of these archetypes. Whilst there are only four viable ways of life, according to TTOCC they cannot exist independently of each other. The idea that each depends upon the survival of the others for its own continued existence is what Thompson et al. call the 'requisite variety condition'.

Implicit in this is the recognition that ways of life are inherently political [10, 11], that is they are concerned to control resources, manipulate rhetoric and influence events. They are mutually competitive and define themselves not only by the distinctiveness of their coherent value structures (what we are) but also by their opposition to other ways of life (what we are not) [12]. As Thompson et al. put it [13], 'it is only the presence in the world of people who are different from them that enables adherents of each way of life to be the way they are'. This conclusion is argued through Thompson et al.'s analysis of surprises, that is, the way in which adherents look for an alternative way of life when they find a lack of satisfying fit between the world as they perceive it and the world as they actually find it. Whilst the world as a whole may be stable and coherent, its constituent parts are unstable, evolving and changing in response to surprises.

But the adherents to each of the four ways of life do not recognize the existence of this requisite variety condition. As far as they are concerned, and until they are otherwise 'surprised', their own view of the world is the only right view. This ethnocentricity makes it difficult for adherents to perceive the reality and validity of the other three points of view.

TTOCC and attitudes to risk

Thompson, Ellis and Wildavsky have argued [14] that, 'the test of any theory is its effectiveness: does it explain better than alternatives? A glance at the bibliography [that they append to their book] will confirm that many practitioners ... are convinced that it does'. But the value of TTOCC may appear questionable to the practicing manager. How can such a theory be used to understand more about reducing or managing risk? The answer, as we shall now seek to demonstrate, is that

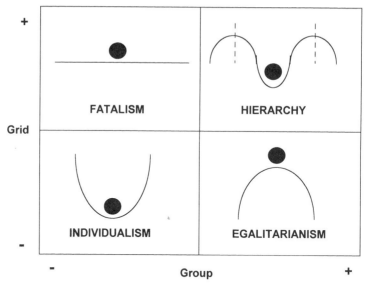

Figure 8.2   Four different ways of perceiving risk.

it is important for practitioners to acknowledge that, given the demonstrable existence of four viable ways of life, it follows that there are four different ways of perceiving risk.

In their review of rival theories of risk perception, cultural theorists Wildavsky and Dake [15] conclude that 'cultural biases best predict risk perception findings', and that 'individuals choose what to fear (and how to fear it), in order to support their way of life'. To develop the analysis, let us draw on TTOCC's four views of nature [16] each of which can be graphically represented by a ball in a landscape, as shown in Figure 8.2.

For the individualist entrepreneur, nature is benign. The ball will never come out of the cupped landscape and so there is an almost wilful disregard of risk in pursuit of short-term advantage. Disaster 'will never happen here'. If it does, the cause is either attributed to competitively induced treachery or else shrugged off as a random chance event. For the fatalist, nature is capricious and the ball thus rolls where it will. The fatalist may well be exposed to risk, but there is nothing he or she can do about it. Disasters are accepted as acts of God. For the hierarch, nature is perverse/tolerant. The ball will stay inside the cupped landscape only if it is not pushed beyond known limits. Risk is perceived as coming about if those limits are exceeded, usually by someone breaking the rules. Disasters are therefore blamed on deviance and rule breaking. Since nature is ephemeral, the egalitarian is concerned that the ball is precariously balanced on the landscape. Risk and potential disaster are an ever present threat from forces in 'the system' beyond the boundary.

The implications for risk assessment

As Steve Frosdick has mentioned in his chapter on risk as blame (Chapter 3), the Royal Society report on risk [17], whilst failing to agree a cohesive approach, made the point that TTOCC could well have revolutionary implications for risk assessment and perception, since no one measure of risk can represent the perceptions of the disaggregated cultural types. What this means in practice is that the risk analyst needs to recognize that different people perceive risk in entirely different ways. There are, therefore, no right or wrong answers and nobody is wrong to perceive a particular issue as a risk. It is important to ensure that a broad range of perspectives are adequately represented in any risk assessment exercise. This is best accomplished by identifying representatives of each of the four constituencies, all of which we know will be present somewhere, and inviting them to participate in the exercise. Most significantly, this means inviting those who oppose you to join in the exercise – they won't hesitate to articulate the risks you would prefer not to hear.

Summary

- The theory of cultural complexity (TTOCC) holds that there are four different ways of life: individualism, fatalism, hierarchy and egalitarianism.
- There are, therefore, four different ways of perceiving risk: as a random chance event, as an act of God, as rule-breaking or as an external force.
- Nobody is wrong to perceive risk differently from somebody else.
- It is important to ensure that a broad range of perspectives are represented in any risk analysis.

Acknowledgement

This account of the theory of cultural complexity has also been included in: Mars, G. and Fosdick, S. (1977) Operationalising the theory of cultural complexity, *International Journal of Risk, Security and Crime Prevention*, **2** (2), 115–129.

References

[1] Thompson, M., Ellis, R. and Wildavsky, A. (1990). *Cultural Theory*, p. 1. Westview Press.

[2] Douglas, M. (1978). Cultural bias. Royal Anthropological Institute, Occasional Paper 35. Reprinted in M. Douglas (1982) *In the Active Voice*, pp. 183–254. Routledge & Kegan Paul.

[3] Mars, G. and Nicod, M. (1983). *The World of Waiters*, p. 124. Allen and Unwin.

[4] Op. cit. 1. p. 5.

[5] Mars, G. (1994). *Cheats at Work: An Anthropology of Workplace Crime* (2nd edn.), p. 24. Dartmouth.

[6] Op. cit. 3. p. 125.

[7] Op. cit. 2. p. viii.

[8] Op. cit. 5.

[9] Op. cit. 1. p. 7.

[10] Douglas, M. and Wildavsky, A. (1982). *Risk and Culture: An Essay on the Selection of Technological and Environmental Danger*. University of California Press.

[11] Douglas, M. (1992). Risk and blame. In *Risk and Blame: Essays in Cultural Theory*, pp. 3–21. Routledge.

[12] Mars, G. and Mars, V. (1993). Two studies of dining. In *Food Culture and History* (G. Mars and V. Mars, eds.), pp. 49–60. London Food Seminar.

[13] Op. cit. 1. p. 96.

[14] Ibid, p. 14.

[15] Wildavsky, A. and Dake, K. (1990). Theories of risk perception: Who fears what and why. *Daedalus*, **119**(4), 41–60.

[16] Op. cit. 1. pp. 26-9.

[17] Royal Society (1992). *Risk: Analysis, Perception and Management – Report of a Royal Society Study Group.*

9 Cultural complexity in the British stadia safety industry

Steve Frosdick

The history of 'regulation by crisis' in the British stadia safety industry has failed to prevent successive disasters and continued near misses. To reduce the risks, there is a need to better understand why the mistakes and misunderstandings leading to such incidents actually occur. Such understanding can be informed by applying the theory of cultural complexity (TTOCC), a method of cultural classification using 'grid/group' analysis and derived from social anthropology. This chapter uses TTOCC to analyse ethnography from and literature relating to sport and safety management at British sports grounds. The analysis reveals the conflicting risk perceptions of individualist/entrepreneurial clubs, hierarchical regulators, long-suffering fatalist spectators and their more egalitarian colleagues in supporter and local resident pressure groups. These perspectives are narrow and biased. At a strategic level, there is a need for each constituency to acknowledge the validity of the others' points of view. Increased awareness is the key to disaster prevention. The conclusions drawn should be applicable to wider scenarios where a multiplicity of organizations are involved.

Introduction

In Chapter 2, Dominic Elliott, Steve Frosdick and Denis Smith have shown how the disaster–inquiry–legislation approach has failed to prevent a succession of disasters, major accidents and near misses in British stadia, particularly British football grounds. According to Turner [1], 'disaster equals energy plus misinformation', whilst Toft [2] concludes that 'the evidence also suggests that accidents are not the product of divine caprice, nor of a set of random chance events which are not likely to recur, but that they are incidents, created by people'. Similarly, Cox and Tait [3] argue that, 'the majority of accidents are, in some measure, attributable to human as well as procedural and technological failure'. There is therefore a multicausality of failures. Like other disasters, stadia disasters arise from people's mistakes and misjudgements. This chapter argues that these may arise from clashes in the value systems and attitudes to risk to be found between the different cultural constituencies in the stadia safety industry. The analysis is underpinned by the theory of cultural complexity (TTOCC), which is set out in the previous chapter by Steve Frosdick and Gerald Mars.

The organizational structure of the British stadia safety industry is extraordinarily complex, incorporating all those people and organizations who have variously been involved in:

- design and building of stadia and spectator stands;
- ownership and operation of stadium facilities;
- safety regulation of stadium operations;
- performing in, or spectating at, stadium events; and
- representing views on stadia safety-related issues.

The industry includes at least all the separate bodies listed in Table 9.1.

Attempting to chart the relationships between these organizations produces an overloaded picture such as Figure 9.1.

To try and bring some order to the chaos, I want to show how TTOCC can be applied to analyse the various organizations, categorizing them under the four archetypal headings of hierarchy, individualism, egalitarianism and fatalism. The analysis will draw out aspects of 'grid' and 'group' and reveal the differences in attitudes to risk and disaster.

Hierarchy

Let me begin by seeking to demonstrate that the industry is dominated by high grid high group regulatory organizations for whom safety means compliance with rules. The individual rules imposed by one organization may conflict with those of another.

Table 9.1   Organizations involved in the British stadia safety industry

Fédération Internationale de Football Association (FIFA)
Union of European Football Associations (UEFA)
The Football Association (FA)
Scottish Football Association (SFA)
Welsh Football Association (WFA)
FA Premier League Ltd
The Football League Ltd
Scottish Football League
BBC, ITV, BSkyB and other television companies
Association of Premier and Football League Referees and Linesmen (APFLRL)
Football Licensing Authority (FLA)
The Football Trust
Football Stadia Advisory Design Council (FSADC) (defunct)
Football Stadia Development Committee (FSDC)
Building Research Establishment
Architects, Engineers and Construction Companies
Football pools companies
Parliamentary bodies
   House of Commons Home Affairs Committee
   House of Commons All-Party Football Committee
Government bodies
   Department of the Environment
   Department of National Heritage
   Home Office
Local authority organizations:
   Fire Brigade
   Building Control Departments
   Planning Departments
   Environmental Health Departments
Medical organizations
   Local Health Authority Ambulance Services
   Voluntary Ambulance Services (St Johns, Red Cross)
Police services:
   Football Sub-Committee of the Association of Chief Police Officers (ACPO)
   National Criminal Intelligence Service Football Unit
   Police forces
   Local police divisions
Football Safety Officers' Association (FSOA)

(continued)

Table 9.1   Organizations involved in the British stadia safety industry (*cont.*)

Contracted-out stewarding companies
British Security Industry Association (BSIA)
International Professional Security Association (IPSA)
Public safety consultants
Professional Footballers Association (PFA)
Institute of Football Management and Administration (IFMAA)
National Federation of Football Supporters Clubs (NFFSC)
Football Supporters Association (FSA)
Fanzines and fanzine editors
Federation of Stadium Communities (FSC)
Football Family Forum
Football Joint Executive

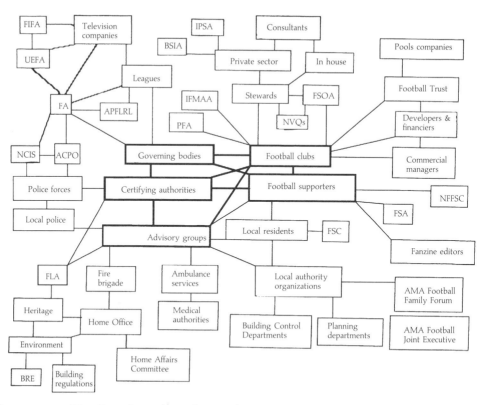

Figure 9.1   The British stadia safety industry.

Football organizations

Football is governed by international (FIFA), European (UEFA), and national football associations, together with the various leagues operating under their jurisdiction. These governing bodies conduct their business through unwieldy management structures comprising large councils with numerous committees and subcommittees. Each body issues its own wide-ranging criteria and technical requirements for stadia features and crowd management. These rules vary enormously and have been summarized by the Football Stadia Advisory Design Council [4].

Match officials

Senior English and Welsh officials are represented by the Association of Premier and Football League Referees and Linesmen (APFLRL). The laws of football provide that the referee is the sole judge of whether conditions are safe for the game to take place. Where there is to be a crowd however, the situation is more complicated. The referee's primary concern is with the playing surface. The pitch may be fit but the safety certificate holder may report that the terraces are too icy and dangerous to admit spectators. Conversely, the police may fear disorder if the game were to be called off after the crowd had been admitted. This conflict in rules is illustrated by the Newcastle United v Sunderland match on Sunday 25 April 1993. It had rained solidly all morning and the pitch was badly flooded. But this was the traditionally volatile derby match and it was inconceivable that it might be called off. As the police commander put it in his briefing, 'I don't care if the waves are eight feet high out there, this game is on'. I am in no doubt the referee was put under pressure to play the game.

Television companies

The circumstances in which football is played are increasingly high grid and prescribed by television. As *When Saturday Comes* magazine argued in their November 1994 editorial:

> Some teams now find themselves having to play three times in less than one week in order to fulfil the demands of television contracts ... Television now determines the names of old competitions – it's the audience reach that pulls in the sponsor. It determines the format of new competitions – the Champions

League, for instance. It determines what day they are played, forcing the people who actually go to games to adjust to Monday night and Sunday teatime kick-offs. And now it's affecting, if not actually determining, the results of these games.

The Football Licensing Authority

The Football Licensing Authority (FLA) is a regulatory body. As Chapter 6 by John De Quidt shows, it has four main roles – licensing grounds, advising Government on all-seater accommodation, ensuring the safety of any remaining terracing, and reviewing certifying authorities' performance. The FLA have issued guidelines on safety certificates [5] and indicated that seating with a restricted view that encourages standing up may not be licensed [6]. They were very involved in producing the FSADC views on safe terracing [7] and have vetted applications for exemption from the deadlines for all-seater accommodation.

The certifying authorities

Certification and annual inspection of designated sports grounds and designated stands is carried out by the appropriate London Borough, Metropolitan District, County Council or Unitary Authority. These responsibilities have been variously delegated to the Fire Service, Trading Standards, Legal Services and other departments such as Building Control. All certifying authorities are advised by safety advisory groups of varying nomenclature and membership. And no two stadia are identical. As Inglis [8] describes it, 'so many different approaches, so many different shapes and sizes'. Given these wide-ranging structural differences in both organization and design, the safety requirements of the certifying authorities are, unsurprisingly, locally different.

The government

At government level, there is a messy sharing of responsibility. Building regulations for new stadia are the province of the Department of the Environment, who are advised by the Building Research Establishment (BRE). Fire safety and policing fall under the Home Office, which also used to publish the *Green Guide* to safety at sports grounds [9]. Safety certification legislation, revision of the *Green Guide* and the FLA are the responsibility of the Department of National Heritage.

The police

National guidelines come from an Association of Chief Police Officers (ACPO) Sub-Committee. Individual police forces have their own policy guidelines on such matters as Sunday kick-offs, all-ticket matches, match categorization etc. At operational level, local police divisions liaise with clubs and other agencies both directly and through the safety advisory groups. Intelligence on hooligans is provided to local police by the Football Unit of the National Criminal Intelligence Service, whose work is described in Chapter 17 by Bryan Drew.

Safety officers and stewards

Like night-club bouncers or swimming pool attendants, stewards enforce venue regulations and implement management policies for safety and order. Operationally, stewards are commanded by stadium safety officers, who are represented nationally by the Football Safety Officers' Association (FSOA). Some clubs operate in-house stewarding schemes, whilst others have contracted out to private security companies. These may be members of a trade body such as the British Security Industry Association (BSIA), who have published their own guidelines on stewarding [10].

Stadium designers

Chapter 2 on legislation by crisis and Chapter 11 on designing for safe stadia show how much post-Hillsborough stadium design has been constrained by the inflexible application of quantified (although largely unsubstantiated) technical rules. However, 'the engineering simplicity of these calculations does not bear psychological examination' [11]. As Cox [12] points out, 'some of the assumptions concerning human movement, ingress and egress and escape times need to be revised on the basis of existing research findings as well as refined through further research'. The lessons from such research have been widely ignored because untidiness is 'anathema to an engineer' [13].

Reports by other agencies

Following in Lord Justice Taylor's wake and subsequently, several other agencies have commissioned their own reports into managing public safety and order both at football grounds and in the wider context. These include the Institution of Structural Engineers [14], the Home Affairs Committee of the House of Commons [15 - 16], the local authority associations [17], the Health and Safety Commission [18], the Sound and Communications Industries Association [19] and the Health and Safety Executive [20, 21]. All these well-intentioned reports have contained a host of recommendations for rules, some complementary, some contradictory, and much lost in the deluge of proposed regulation replacing past laxity and neglect.

Applying TTOCC: The hierarchical risk perspective

What we have here is a morass of rules, regulations and guidelines emanating from a large number of individual professions, regulatory bodies and their national umbrella organizations. In terms of TTOCC, this is all very high grid. All these high grid organizations have strong corporate identities and structures to enable members to meet frequently and do business face to face. Each is therefore also high group. Since these organizations are in the majority, we can see that the industry is dominated by hierarchical organizations. These, in turn, are dominated by hierarchical perceptions of risk and disaster.

Since the hierarch would blame disaster on deviance and rule breaking, hierarchical risk perception is informed by an emphasis on rules, history, tradition and deference to authority. There are problems with potential risk blindness here. In the first place, the hierarch's ethnocentricity inhibits awareness of the equally valid risk perceptions of the other cultural categories. Second, since information in hierarchies does not flow up anywhere near as well as down, senior managers make their plans without asking the advice of the more junior staff who actually know what the problems are. Third, a reliance on local historical experience generates only a limited risk awareness, informed by hindsight and the parochialism of individual hierarchies. Thus the police are preoccupied with public order risks, the ambulance service with illness or injury, the fire service with fire risks and the engineers with structural and mechanical failure risks.

The failures of hindsight have been well reviewed by Toft [22]. Organizations fail to turn passive learning from near misses into the active learning needed to prevent repetitions. Since any learning is confined to similar system types, the opportunities for isomorphic learning are lost. Moreover, hindsight cannot predict the new risks that have never happened before.

Entrepreneurial individualism

I now want to move on to draw out the weak grid weak group cultural bias, diametrically opposed to hierarchy, of those involved in owning football clubs, developing stadia and playing the game itself. I shall then illustrate the problems that can arise from the cultural clash between hierarchy and individualism.

Players and managers

These are represented by the Professional Footballers' Association (PFA) and the Institute of Football Management and Administration (IFMA). Although the former Millwall player, Eamon Dunphy, has argued [23] that, 'I've never believed that terrace violence has anything to do with what happens on the field', the evidence suggests that spectator safety is affected by the behaviour of players and managers. Murphy et al. [24] point out that, even before 1915, the largest category of spectator disorder, 'resulted from anger at the decisions of the referee or the attitudes of opposing players'. Scovell [25] drew attention to incidents at Burnley and Southend when inflammatory gestures by players resulted in crush injuries and the outbreak of disorder.

Football is a team game, yet there is 'no true club ethos in pro football' [26]. Players are maximizing income from a very short career. The newspapers carry daily stories of players unsettled because they 'can't agree terms' with their club. Contracts are individually negotiated. Poor performance means the sack for the manager and the transfer list for the player. Scandals abound about tax evasion, massive cash payments and corrupt transfer dealings involving illegal use of players' agents.

Football clubs and stadium owners

Many European stadia were built and are owned by the municipalities. For many years, however, British stadia were privately owned and run by local benefactors. As Walvin [27] points out, 'until the 1980s, it was virtually impossible to break into the local team's boardroom simply by financial clout'. In the 1990s, whilst a handful of clubs, for example Manchester United, have become hugely successful public companies and one or two, for example Leeds United, have sold their grounds to the local authority, the majority of football found itself in a deep financial crisis

[28, 29]. The clubs' financial incompetence was compounded by both the slump and the cost demands of the Taylor Report, only a small portion of which could be met through grants from the Football Trust [30].

Furthermore, the increasing gulf between the few rich clubs and the impoverished remainder in a climate of media-led globalization has been well documented [31, 32]. In Murphy et al.'s succinct summary [33], 'these concentrations have been facilitated by a series of processes, among them the abolition of the maximum wage, freedom of contract for players, retention of all the gate money for League matches by the home club and the increasingly skewed distribution of TV money'. Benefaction has had to give way to making the business pay. This has led to an enormous growth in marketing and commercial sponsorship of sporting events. Clubs are in commercial competition with each other.

Stadia design and redevelopment

Improvement grants are made by the Football Trust, which is funded from a levy on football pool betting duty. The 'bottom line' philosophy has had a major impact on approaches to stadia design and redevelopment. The FSADC was disbanded in March 1993 after the football authorities declined to fund the £30 000 – one star player's monthly wages – it needed for 1992 to 1993. Why should this be? According to Robert Chase, former chairman of Norwich City and of an FA Premiership committee on safety and standards, the FSADC, 'threw the *Green Guide* out of the window and simply said, how can we design a nice new stand? ... Anyone can do that. What we wanted from them was to say, here's the ground rules, I'm going to show you how to achieve the best possible value for money within those ground rules' (transcript of an interview tape recorded on 15 April 1993).

This issue of design with insufficient regard for cost is illustrated by British envy towards the 'stirring contexts and breathtaking design' [34] of the Italian stadia built for the 1990 World Cup. Indeed, an entire television documentary was devoted to contrasting the Italian stadia with our own (Channel 4, *Without Walls* – 'Et in Stadia Ego', 10 November 1992). Simon Inglis has exhorted designers to make a stylish and locality enhancing architectural statement [35]. Yet harsh financial realities have led to new grounds at Scunthorpe and Walsall being described by Brewster [36] as 'more resembling edge-of-town industrial units than cathedrals of football'.

There have been appalling examples of good terraces becoming poor seating where spectators have to stand up to get a view, because 'the conversion of football grounds ... is being undertaken with cost rather than quality as the overriding imperative' [37]. The exceptions have tended to be confined to the super-rich clubs.

Policing costs

Policing costs are a further factor affecting the bottom line. Clubs had traditionally been part charged only for the police resources deployed inside the ground. Following pressure from the Audit Commission [38], police forces increasingly sought to recover the full costs of all their services to football clubs. As Steve Frosdick and John Sidney show in their chapter on the evolution of safety management (Chapter 15), this trend was accompanied by a change in philosophy about responsibility for safety. Clubs were required by certifying authorities to appoint ground safety officers and the House of Commons Home Affairs Committee expounded the principle that 'higher profile stewarding, supported by lower profile policing is the way forward' [39]. Thus questions of principle and increased police charges encouraged clubs improve their own stewarding schemes or else to look at the cost-effective alternatives offered by the private sector [40].

Applying TTOCC: The individualist/entrepreneurial risk perspective

As Murphy et al. [41] point out, 'professional soccer in England and Wales is loosely organised. Notwithstanding the existence of a central administration, the predominant forces are centrifugal ones ... The League consists of ninety-two self-governing entities: the clubs'. These forces, taken with a bottom line philosophy, commercial competitiveness, individual contracts, frequent staff changes, lack of club ethos and public blame shuttling through the daily washing of football club dirty linen in the pages of the tabloids, all point clearly to a weak grid and weak group macro football club culture of individualist, competitive, entrepreneuriality.

Since nature is regarded as benign, rule breaking is considered fine if short-term advantage results. Disaster is seen as caused by random chance events or treachery. Perceptions of risk are more commercial than safety related. Responsibility for safety can be discharged through provision of the cheapest functional security permitted by the minimum necessary insurance cover. Risk management is otherwise all about revenue protection. This point is particularly well illustrated by the security arrangements adopted by Silverstone Circuit for the 1993 British Grand Prix. The external perimeter fence was heavily patrolled and access points well controlled to ensure only those who had paid got into the circuit. Grandstand attendants' duties were more concerned with ticket control than staffing fire exit gates, some of which were locked. Private security patrols were brought in for cash handling and to seize pirate merchandise and touted tickets. Although excellent arrangements had been made to prevent spectators getting onto the circuit, the crowded terraces and viewing slopes were virtually unsupervised and blocked with deck chairs, cool boxes and even smouldering barbecues! There were no gangways for emergency access, few railings to stop people toppling backwards off the slopes and constant unexpected changes in levels underfoot.

Cultural conflict: Safety v commercialism

Three examples drawn from my own experience show how financial considerations can create a conflict between the commercial priorities of the marketing industry and the safety priorities of the regulators. At Newcastle United v Sunderland in April 1993, disorder broke out as a result of stewards and the police attempting to remove a Sunderland banner draped over a sponsor's advertising hoarding. The commercial manager had deployed the stewards without asking the safety officer and the police got involved to support the stewards. Two officers snatched the banner and a fight broke out. I was watching from the control room with the safety officer. He was furious.

A second example comes from 1995 from a football ground in the north-west of England. Part-way through briefing the senior stewards, the safety officer was called away to speak urgently to the commercial manager. The latter told him there was a fire in a hospitality suite and requested his immediate attendance. The commercial manager was teasing − 'I thought that would get you here quick'. In fact he wanted the pitch covers to be moved from where they had been folded up because they were preventing the advertising hoardings being seen. He had thought nothing of disrupting the essential briefing for the senior stewards, which had to be curtailed. What would any subsequent inquiry into a real fire have made of the disruption and the irresponsible lie?

The third illustration of this cultural conflict comes from the Glasgow Rangers v CSK Moscow European Champions Cup match in April 1993. The Ibrox stadium has a retractable tunnel, shaped and coloured like a giant McEwans lager can, to protect the players entering and leaving the pitch. Since McEwans were not one of the official sponsors, UEFA marketing personnel directed the club and police not to use the tunnel. Similarly, the police officers normally placed in front of the stands to watch for signs of crowd distress had to be withdrawn from the three sides of the ground where they would have obstructed the cameras' view of perimeter advertising hoardings.

Egalitarianism and fatalism

Having dealt with the individualist/hierarchical axis within TTOCC, I now want to show how the egalitarian/fatalist axis is occupied by stadium communities and football supporters. These two constituencies have differing views of risk both from each other and from the two already examined. Thus the full complexity of conflicts in risk perception will be revealed.

Stadium communities

The Federation of Stadium Communities (FSC) aims to improve relationships between clubs and their local communities. As Bale [42] has shown, football grounds can be landscapes of topophobia – fear and nuisance – for those who live around them. In general, there is passive acceptance of the nuisance, which in many cases, given the age of most grounds, the residents knew was there before they moved in. However, there is evidence of successful activism by ad hoc local resident pressure groups against extensions of activities at grounds [43, 44]. Furthermore, 'the most opposition appears to come from the threat of potential football grounds coming to the backyards of residents' [45].

Supporter groups

There are two main national supporter groups. Traditional supporters' clubs are represented by the National Federation of Football Supporters Clubs (NFFSC). These are more hierarchical and deferential to authority. As their deputy chair put it, 'I've been rather worried about the anti-police attitude from some sections of supporters' [46]. The Liverpool-based Football Supporters Association (FSA), has been acknowledged to be unrepresentative of the general characteristics of football crowds and 'best understood as a tenacious, committed and highly vocal pressure group which is growing in influence, rather than as a mass movement' [47]. The essential difference between the National Federation and the FSA was explained by the latter's chair in evidence to the House of Commons Home Affairs Committee. The FSA, 'provides a structure for policy making and consultation ... We are primarily a campaigning organisation seeking to achieve certain objectives. Now the Federation of Supporters Clubs is just that [a federation]' [48].

Campaigning against proposed bond schemes to finance stadium reconstruction led to the formation of Independent Supporters Associations at West Ham and Arsenal. These and other groups came together to form Independent Fans United. In the typical egalitarian style of organizational fission, 'the IFU found it difficult to create a national network of their own, however, probably because in many places independent supporter organisations were inextricably linked to local FSA branches, in fact in some places there were virtually the same group of people. In response to their initiative, the FSA has reconstituted itself' [49].

Indeed, the literature purporting to represent supporter perspectives betrays a distinctly egalitarian bias. Change is opposed unless there is extensive consultation with supporters and everyone agrees. The most prominent writer, Rogan Taylor [50, 51], is himself a former chair of the FSA. The emergence of the alternative popular culture 'fanzine' movement represents a similar growth in egalitarian perspectives. The 'fanzine' publisher, Martin Lacey has described them as follows: 'fanzines instantly struck a chord. Fans wanted coverage of their team that was intelligent and knowledgeable but also biased, committed, outspoken and irreverent. It reflected themselves. The pioneers ... had a lot in common. They were loosely left in outlook, campaigned vigorously and had a firm idea of the line between making fun of other clubs and pointless abuse' [52].

The fatalist majority

But most supporters do not belong to any organization. Notwithstanding poor facilities, the threat of hooliganism or crushing and the increasingly high grid territorialization of football, these low group individual supporters come to football because of what Bale [53], referring to Tuan [54], describes as topophilia − the coupling of positive feelings with a sense of place. The stadium represents a focus of local pride and collective identification, a sacred place, 'home', an attractive scenic space and a source of local heritage.

Unsurprisingly, the fatalist perspective is not well represented in the literature. The available evidence, however, does support my analysis of the majority of football supporters as passive fatalists. Dunning et al. have shown that football hooliganism is largely the preserve of young males from the rough working class [55]. Moral panic can lead to an assumption that the football crowd as a whole is dominated by young working-class males. Yet in a discussion of the Sports Council's 1988 Report, *The Next Ten Years*, Dunning [56] notes that, 'a significant minority – 17% – of adult spectators are women'. A review of other estimates by Dunning's Leicester colleagues [57] suggests a figure of 5–17 per cent for female fans. Dunning [58] goes on to report the Sports Council's view that 'there is some emphasis on younger adults, but all other age groups ... are fully represented'.

The question of social class is a matter of some debate. On the one hand, Dunning [59] concludes that 'both the playing and watching of football in this country are primarily a preserve of skilled blue collar and routine white collar workers'. Phillips, however, reports [60] that 'I have never failed to get a disbelieving gasp from a Marketing Director with preconceived views on the football market when he sees the percentage of ABs. It is here that I disagree with Professor Dunning.' Both, however, agree that, 'the commonly held belief that football is mainly followed by the unwashed, unloved and unprofitable D/E market can be quickly dispelled' [61].

Notwithstanding the profusion of black players and the composition of the communities in which clubs are set, very few football spectators are of Afro-Caribbean or Asian origin. Racial abuse has been a key feature here [62, 63], and has led to the formation of an Advisory Group Against Racism and Intimidation (AGARI) and campaigns to 'Kick Racism out of Football'.

Thus whilst the football crowd is not a complete cross-section of the community, since ethnic minorities and women are under-represented, the range of age groups and percentage of female fans does refute the assumption of a predominantly young male crowd. There has been disagreement about the proportion of upper-class and upper middle-class fans. However, these are likely to dominate the executive and hospitality boxes whose glass frontages segregate them from the rest of the crowd. The majority of entrepreneurial club directors are also likely to be drawn from their ranks. Notwithstanding the increasing gentrification of the audience at Premier League matches [64] this all still supports Dunning's analysis that the majority of football spectators seem likely to be drawn from the respectable working class and lower middle class. I have termed these the 'fatalist majority' because, as Dunning [65] succinctly summarizes their position:

> The section of the population from which the majority of soccer supporters come tend on the one hand to be the relatively passive recipients of decisions taken by people above them in the social scale, people whose expertise lies primarily in some area of business rather than in football per se ... On the other hand, the 'respectable majority' suffer both from the actions of the football hooligans who

come below them on the social scale and from the effects of decisions taken in an attempt to rid the game of the 'hooligan scourge'.

Thus, supporters and stadium communities occupy the fatalist/egalitarian axis. In the interests of a specific cause or campaign, fatalist supporters or local residents are ripe for recruiting to more egalitarian pressure groups. These add a third dimension to the cultural battle for primacy between hierarchy and individualism.

Applying TTOCC: The egalitarian and fatalist risk perspectives

Since nature is ephemeral, the egalitarian is forever conscious of the need for precautions against disasters, which are blamed on 'the system', on the intrusion of the authorities beyond the sect's own boundaries. Risk perception is dominated by environmental considerations. For the disaffected local resident, this means the impact of noise, litter, traffic, vandalism and disorder on the quality of their lives. For the supporter, aware of the risks, it means being left alone to choose whether and where to stand or sit and to watch the match without being commercially exploited or having one's enjoyment intruded upon by bureaucratic regulation.

For the long-suffering spectator or passive local resident, disasters are acts of God. As far as risk is concerned, the topophilia outweighs the topophobia, and there is thus a resigned acceptance of whatever indignities or annoyances are to be endured. The terrace chant, 'Que sera sera, whatever will be, will be', typifies the fatalist position.

Conclusions

The organization of responsibility for public safety in the British stadia industry is extraordinarily complicated. The range of bodies involved and the dominance of hierarchical regulators is such that at least one Football League Club Secretary (Roy Whalley of Walsall FC, speaking at the Institute of Local Government Studies on 4 May 1993) has expressed concern about the mechanisms for communication within the overall structure and the lack of appreciation of the cost implications of regulatory requirements.

Analysis of the industry has revealed the different cultural biases and attitudes to risk of the four constituencies within TTOCC. Hierarchical perceptions of risk as rule breaking are predominant, and a plethora of hierarchical agencies are variously involved in safety management. Entrepreneurial clubs give priority to commercial rather than safety risks, resulting in operational conflicts between safety and commercialism. Egalitarian supporter and residents pressure groups are more concerned with environmental risks and quality of life, whilst for the majority of fatalist spectators, the pleasure they derive from football outweighs the risks and restrictive control measures they endure as a result of hooliganism and regulation.

The cultural and organizational complexity which my analysis has revealed seems likely to be archetypal of the complicated structures to be found in other public safety scenarios, including other major sporting events, pop concerts and unregulated events such as the New Year festivities in London's Trafalgar Square. TTOCC offers a toolkit for disaggregated analysis in these contexts. A cultural audit of the organizational structures seems to offer the opportunity for all parties to confront the existing culture and be aware of its implications for overall attitudes to risk. Such awareness should encourage an appreciation of the validity of alternative points of view and thus enable each party to manage the interactions between themselves and other agencies in a more constructive and enlightened way.

Inductive engineering risk identification techniques such as Hazard and Operability Studies (HAZOPS), carried out using multidisciplinary and culturally disaggregated teams, may have a great deal to offer in this context. Carrying out such exercises could assist in resolving potential operating difficulties both during the design phase of stadium renovation and newbuild projects, as well as during the contingency planning phase of major event management. Looking to the wider context of project management and the strategic management of major organizational change, for example the installation of a major new technological system or relocation to a new building, the same kind of cultural audit would seem to be an important component of strategic analysis. Asking 'where are we now?' involves not only environmental scanning and a focus on the key internal competencies of the business, but also a clear understanding of the internal culture. The operationalization of TTOCC in the ways I have demonstrated suggests a method of adapting the existing models to undertake such cultural audits in a new and revealing way.

Summary

- Like other disasters, stadia disasters arise from people's mistakes and misjudgements.

- These may arise from clashes in the value systems and attitudes to risk to be found between the different cultural constituencies in the stadia safety industry.
- The organizational structure of the British stadia safety industry is extremely complex.
- Applying the theory of cultural complexity to an analysis of the industry reveals the conflicting cultural biases and attitudes to risk of four different constituencies.
- Hierarchical perceptions of risk as rule breaking are predominant, and a plethora of hierarchical agencies are variously involved in safety management.
- Entrepreneurial clubs give priority to commercial rather than safety risks, resulting in operational conflicts between safety and commercialism.
- Egalitarian supporter and residents pressure groups are more concerned with environmental risks and quality of life.
- For the majority of fatalist spectators, the pleasure they derive from football outweighs the risks and restrictive control measures they endure as a result of hooliganism and regulation.
- An awareness of cultural complexity encourages an appreciation of alternative points of view, including differing perspectives on risk.
- Such awareness should enable the interactions between different organizations to be managed in a more constructive and enlightened way.

Acknowledgement

An earlier version of this chapter was previously published as Frosdick, S. (1995). Organisational structure, culture and attitudes to risk in the British stadia safety industry. *Journal of Contingencies and Crisis Management*, **3**(1), pp. 43–57.

References

[1] Turner, B. (1978). *Man-Made Disasters*, p. 189. Wykeham.
[2] Toft, B. (1992). The failure of hindsight. *Disaster Prevention and Management: An International Journal*, **1**(3), 48–59.
[3] Cox, S. and Tait, N. (1991). *Reliability, Safety and Risk Management (An Integrated Approach)*, p. 93. Butterworth-Heinemann.

[4] Football Stadia Advisory Design Council (1992). *Digest of Stadia Criteria.* The Sports Council.

[5] Football Licensing Authority (1992). *Guidance on Safety Certificates.*

[6] Football Licensing Authority (1991). *Consultation Paper Number 1 – Seating with a Restricted View.*

[7] Football Stadia Advisory Design Council (1993). *Terraces – Designing for Safe Standing at Football Stadia.* The Sports Council.

[8] Inglis, S. (1987). *The Football Grounds of Great Britain*, p. 7. Collins Willow.

[9] Home Office and Scottish Office (1990). *Guide to Safety at Sports Grounds.* HMSO.

[10] British Security Industry Association (1993). *Guidelines for the Surveying, Planning and Operation of Stewarding Services in Stadia and Sporting Venues.*

[11] Canter, D., Comber, M. and Uzzell D. (1989). *Football in its Place – An Environmental Psychology of Football Grounds*, p. 96. Routledge.

[12] Cox, S. (1992). *Building Regulation and Safety*, p. 98. Report to the Building Research Establishment.

[13] Op. cit. 11. p. 95.

[14] Institution of Structural Engineers (1991). *Appraisal of Sports Grounds.*

[15] House of Commons Home Affairs Committee (1991). *Policing Football Hooliganism*, Vol. 1: *Report Together with the Proceedings of the Committee.* HMSO.

[16] House of Commons Home Affairs Committee (1991). *Policing Football Hooliganism*, Vol. 2: *Memoranda of Evidence, Minutes of Evidence and Appendices.* HMSO.

[17] Joint Working Party on Ground Safety and Public Order (1991). *Ground Safety and Public Order.* Report Number One of the Joint Executive on Football Safety. Association of County Councils Publications.

[18] Health and Safety Commission (1993). *Guide to Health, Safety and Welfare at Pop Concerts and Other Similar Events.* HMSO.

[19] Sound and Communication Industries Federation (1992). *Code of Practice for the Assessment, Specification, Maintenance and Operation of Sound Systems for Emergency Purposes at Sports Grounds and Stadia in Pursuit of Approval by Licensing Authorities.*

[20] Au, S., Ryan, M., Carey, M. and Whalley S. (1993). *Managing Crowd Safety in Public Venues: A Study to Generate Guidance for Venue Owners and Enforcing Authority Inspectors. Health and Safety Executive Contract Research Report 53/93.* HSE Books.

[21] Health and Safety Executive (in press). *Crowd Safety.*

[22] Op. cit. 2.

[23] Dunphy, E. (1986). *Only a Game? The Diary of a Professional Footballer* (2nd edn.), p. 55. Viking.

[24] Murphy, P., Williams, J. and Dunning, E. (1990). *Football on Trial – Spectator Violence and Development in the Football World*, p. 42. Routledge.

[25] Scovell, B. (1993). Rethink at FA as gestures get out of hand. *Daily Mail*, 15 January, p. 58.

[26] Op. cit. 23. p. 20.

[27] Walvin, J. (1986). *Football and the Decline of Britain*, p. 28. Macmillan.

[28] Ibid. pp. 17–30.

[29] Op. cit. 24. pp. 216–217.

[30] Anon. (1992). There they go, there they go: Implementing the Taylor Report. *The Economist*, 18 January, pp. 35–36.

[31] Arnold, T. (1991). Rich man, poor man: Economic arrangements in the football league. In *British Football and Social Change – Getting into Europe* (J. Williams and S. Wagg, eds.), pp. 48–66. Leicester University Press.

[32] Goldberg, A. and Wagg, S. (1991). It's not a knockout: English football and globalisation. In *British Football and Social Change – Getting into Europe* (J. Williams and S. Wagg, eds.), pp. 239–253. Leicester University Press.

[33] Op. cit. 24. p. 216.

[34] Luder, O. (1990). *Sports Stadia After Hillsborough*. Paper presented at the Sports Council and Royal Institute of British Architects Seminar, p. 1. RIBA and the Sports Council in association with the Football Trust.

[35] Inglis, S. (1990). Grounds for complaint. *New Civil Engineer*, 7 June, pp. 24–26.

[36] Brewster, B. (1992). Architecture and morality. *When Saturday Comes*, November, pp. 20–22.

[37] Pettipher, M. (1992). Seated areas miss goal. *New Builder*, 6 February, p. 5.

[38] Home Office (1991). *Charges for Policing Football Matches* (Home Office Circular 36/1991).

[39] Op. cit. 15. p. xxv.

[40] Ford, A. (1994). Crossing the thin blue line. *Football Management*, 11 April, pp. 16–17.

[41] Op. cit. 24. p. 214.

[42] Bale, J. (1990). In the shadow of the stadium: Football grounds as urban nuisances. *Geography*, **75**(329), pp. 325–334.

[43] Ibid.

[44] Mason, C. and Robins, R. (1991). The spatial externality fields of football stadiums: The effects of football and non-football uses at Kenilworth Road, Luton. *Applied Geography*, **11**(4), 251–266.

[45] Bale, J. (1993). *Sport, Space and the City*, p. 132. Routledge.

[46] *Football into the 1990s* (1989). Proceedings of a Conference held at the University of Leicester, 29–30 September 1988, p. 118. Sir Norman Chester Centre for Football Research, University of Leicester.

[47] Williams, J., Dunning, E. and Murphy, P. (1989). *Football and Football Supporters After Hillsborough: A National Survey of Members of the Football Supporters Association*, p. 6. Sir Norman Chester Centre for Football Research, University of Leicester.

[48] Op. cit. 16. p. 134.

[49] Brewin, C. (1992). Support for all. *When Saturday Comes*, December, pp. 20–21.

[50] Taylor, R. (1991). Walking alone together: Football supporters and their relationship

with the game. In *British Football and Social Change – Getting into Europe* (J. Williams and S. Wagg, eds.), pp. 111-129, Leicester University Press.

[51] Taylor, R. (1992). *Football and its Fans – Supporters and their Relations with the Game, 1885–1985*. Leicester University Press

[52] Lacey, M. (1992). The end of something small and the start of something big. In *We'll Support You Evermore: Keeping Faith in Football* (D. Bull, ed.), pp. 87–96. Duckworth.

[53] Op. cit. 45, and Bale, J. (1991). Playing at home: British football and a sense of place. In *British Football and Social Change – Getting into Europe* (J. Williams and S. Wagg, eds.), pp. 130–144. Leicester University Press.

[54] Tuan, Y.-F. (1974). *Topophilia*. Prentice-Hall.

[55] Dunning, E. Murphy, P. and Williams, J. (1988). *The Roots of Football Hooliganism – An Historical and Sociological Study*. Routledge & Kegan Paul.

[56] Dunning, E. (1989). The economic and cultural significance of football. In *Football into the 1990s*. Proceedings of a Conference held at the University of Leicester, 29–30 September 1988, pp. 13–17. Sir Norman Chester Centre for Football Research, University of Leicester.

[57] Op. cit. 47. p. 9.

[58] Op. cit. 56.

[59] Ibid.

[60] Phillips, T. (1989). Selling professional football. In *Football into the 1990s*. Proceedings of a Conference held at the University of Leicester, 29–30 September 1988, pp. 33–35. Sir Norman Chester Centre for Football Research, University of Leicester.

[61] Ibid.

[62] Holland, B. (1993). Colour field. *When Saturday Comes*, February, pp. 16–17.

[63] Anon. (1993). Football and race. *When Saturday Comes*, October, pp. 8–10.

[64] Williams, J. (1995). *FA Premier League Fan Survey*. Sir Norman Chester Centre for Football Research, University of Leicester.

[65] Op. cit. 56.

10 Safety cultures in British sports grounds

Steve Frosdick

This chapter presents findings from research into the management of public safety risks in British sports grounds. It opens by discussing the concept of 'safety culture' and briefly sets out the methodology adopted for the study. Some previous work on 'safety culture' analysis is reviewed, and then the theory of cultural complexity is introduced as offering a powerful framework for disaggregated cultural analysis. The research findings reveal the four contrasting, viable and archetypal models of organizing the cross-organizational collaboration required. The chapter concludes by drawing out some implications for public policy.

'Safety culture'

Inquiries into disasters such as the Kings Cross station fire [1] have emphasized the need for organizations to adopt a 'safety culture' to work to prevent future disasters. But what is meant by 'safety culture'? General understanding seems based on an engineering and hierarchical view of the world. It implies rigid compliance with the rules and regulations which follow each inquiry. It implies a bureaucratic structure of meetings and inspections to ensure co-operation and consultation between the various agencies involved. In the sports ground context, 'safety culture' seems to comprise the collective effort and interactions between venue management, contractors, regulatory bodies and the police, fire and ambulance services.

But is there just one hierarchical model for such 'safety cultures', or are there other viable and different ways of organizing the cross-organizational collaboration required? Can the theory of cultural complexity (TTOCC), set out in Chapter 8 by Steve Frosdick and Gerald Mars, offer a new way of explaining how individual organizations provide the subcultures which interact to create the overall 'safety culture' at a particular venue? If it can, what might be the implications of the findings for public policy?

The study

In an attempt to probe these questions, I wanted to investigate how TTOCC might be used to propose the indicators for a fourfold categorization of 'safety cultures'. I wanted to examine the four types in order to help policy makers better understand the implications of their chosen ways of organizing for safety. Between 1992 and 1994, I carried out participant observation activities at a quota sample of thirty-five football matches and eight other sporting and leisure events at twenty-seven separate venues throughout Great Britain. The football matches were purposively sampled to include emotionally charged 'derby' and cup matches, all-ticket and likely capacity crowd fixtures, games being played at stadia under redevelopment and matches at ten football grounds identified [2] as places where supporters felt threatened. The eight other events were an accidental sample which included a test match at Lords cricket ground and the 1993 British Formula One Grand Prix at Silverstone Circuits. Approaches ranged from single visits, through more involved case studies, to detailed ethnographies. In addition, extensive networking resulted in meetings and discussions with over 100 informants from all levels of involvement in the safety at sports grounds industry.

Cultural analysis

Canter et al. [3] have linked the football phenomenon with crowd psychology and a sense of 'place'. Bale's recent work [4] develops the 'place' concept, drawing together a variety of perspectives on the stadium as a source of both pleasure and nuisance. Sense of 'place' is created by a combination of the atmosphere, which is generated by both design features and by the crowd, and of the organization and style of management employed. 'Place' is therefore synonymous with 'culture'. Each venue has a unique sense of place and thus a unique culture. The agencies comprising the local safety management system have a unique 'safety culture'.

Cultural analysis has an important role to play in the study of management in general, including the management of public safety and order. Several writers have proposed models as frameworks for such cultural analysis. Partly due to the popularity of their work as a set text for MBA students, the most familiar and enduring tool is probably Johnson and Scholes [5] 'cultural web of factors within an organisation which preserve and sustain commonly held core beliefs – the recipe'. In the context of cultural analysis, Elliott and Smith [6] have outlined the need for stadium mangers to reconcile the demands of profit maximization, staging a credible event and safety. Referring to Johnson and Scholes, they argue that, 'in order to deal with this problem, we have to look closely at the "cultural web" of the various organisations concerned and assess how this interacts with the crisis recipe that is in place'.

The (crisis) recipe or paradigm is the set of subconscious basic assumptions and beliefs, shared by everyone in the organization, which define the 'way we do things around here'. The paradigm is difficult to change because, 'it is hedged about and protected by a web of cultural artifacts' [7]. The six factors in this surrounding 'cultural web' are: stories and myths, symbols, power structures, organizational structures, control systems and routines and rituals. The 'cultural web' is used as an heuristic device to enable managers to confront the culture of their own organization. Using the web is an exercise 'to allow managers to "discover" the nature of their organisation in cultural terms, the way it impacts on the strategy they are following, and the difficulty of changing it' [8].

For the would-be objective analyst there is a problem here. The cultural web accepts a definition of organizational culture which is biased both because it is top-heavy – only managers have participated in the definition – and because it looks on the organisation as a bounded entity rather than considering the social context in which it is set. Furthermore, because the web surrounds the core values – the paradigm – it cannot actually nail those values in to concrete forms of organizational structure. Whilst use of the web allows members of an organization to consider aspects of culture and assign value to them, perhaps through the relative sizes of the circles, it does not allow them to relate those aspects of culture to the structure of the organization. Thus the web is descriptive rather than analytical.

Elliott and Smith's approach clearly shows the importance of understanding the cultural interaction of organizations in order to learn more about disaster prevention and safety management. But what is needed is a model to disaggregate the different types of (crisis) paradigm to be found within the web. My argument is that TTOCC offers such a model.

Factors for cultural analysis

The organizations shown in Table 10.1 are most closely involved in constituting a local safety management system. Each of these component organizations and their representatives may have different internal structures and cultural biases. But what I want to examine here is the way they all interact with each other as constituent parts of the safety management organization for a particular stadium or sporting venue.

Cox and Tait have emphasized the growing trend towards a more integrated approach towards health and safety, bringing together engineering systems ('hardware'), management systems ('software') and a practical understanding of people ('liveware'). They suggest [9] that, 'One powerful argument in favour of integrating these different areas of concern is the common observation that the majority of accidents are, in some measure, attributable to human as well as procedural and technological failure'. Table 10.2 sets out the indicators of how this interaction takes place, across the three dimensions of 'hardware', 'software' and 'liveware'.

These three dimensions of 'safety culture' may now be analysed using the TTOCC framework shown in Figure 10.1 (derived from the published work [10] and unpublished research of Gerald Mars). The relative strength of the grid aspect is determined from an analysis of the use of space, time, objects, resources and labour; aspects of group are considered under the headings of frequency, mutuality, scope and boundary. These key indicators of the relative strengths of grid and group are set out in Tables 10.3 and 10.4. Following TTOCC, these indicators provide the framework for hypothesizing the four archetypes of 'safety culture'.

Table 10.1   Organizations typically comprising a sports ground 'safety culture'

Football club stewards and other personnel
Agency stewards from the private security industry
The police service
Ambulance services and medical staff
The fire brigade
Local authority officers
Representatives from governing bodies
Representatives from regulatory Inspectorates

Table 10.2   Indicators of cross-organizational collaboration

Dimension	Indicator

'Hardware'	Co-ordination and control of technological life safety systems for:
	    access control
	    surveillance and monitoring
	    communications
	    emergency warnings
	    means of escape

'Software'	Management structures Safety certificates and licences Statements of intent General procedures and operating instructions Handbooks, manuals and instruction cards Police operation orders and deployment schedules Contingency and emergency plans Briefings and debriefings Training programmes and emergency exercises
'Liveware'	Safety group membership/nomenclature/operation Individual attitudes of personnel Individual behaviours of personnel Human error Ergonomics Information rejection Deviance and rule breaking Disagreement and blame

A fourfold typology of 'safety cultures'

The competitive low interaction model

This is the weak grid and weak group way of organizing corresponding to the individualist way of life within TTOCC.

Attitudes towards space are relaxed. Within broad limits, spectators are likely to be allowed to sit or stand where they like. The selling of tickets for specific seats and the designation of events as all-ticket will be confined only to those events that are absolutely certain to be sold out. Segregation is likely to be minimal.

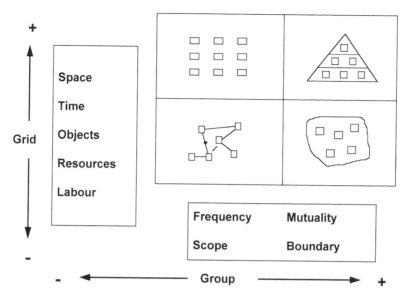

Figure 10.1   Framework for cultural analysis.

The timing of occurrences such as the opening of the turnstiles or of the exit gates at the end of the event will be by default – 'The ground always opens at 1.30 pm' – unless one agency sees a reason to ask for a delay.

Since the emphasis is on functionality with lowest possible cost, there may be a low emphasis on collective technological aids, although the individual agencies may use gadgets to compete with each other in the fashion stakes.

Stewards are more likely to be provided with a tabard or arm band than an expensive high visibility jacket. There will probably be no stewards' dress code. Instructions to staff will be couched in general rather than specific terms. Staff to spectator ratios will be low and staff will be posted to a general area rather than to a specific post. The ratio of supervisors to staff will also be low.

Each agency may have its own control room and its own contingency plans, which may compete and conflict with those of other agencies. Collective emergency planning may be more about establishing who is in charge rather than planning any actual activity.

There is unlikely to be continuity in key personnel from event to event. Functional separation is likely to be strict and staff are unlikely to interact or actively co-operate at front-line levels. When things go wrong, each agency is likely to perceive the fault as lying with others. Blaming and bickering may be overt.

Table 10.3   Aspects concerned with the 'grid' dimension

Aspect of grid	Indicators
Space	Territorialization of viewing areas
	all-ticket matches
	tickets for designated seats
	unrestricted seating/standing
	segregation of different viewing areas
	Means of segregation from the playing area
	high or low fences/walls
	permanent or contingency perimeter track cordons
	Policies for dealing with pitch incursions/invasions
	Attitudes to breaking rules about space
	infiltration of segregated areas
	admission of nonticket holders
	Sectorization for operational command purposes
	Control room
	extent of restrictions on access
	'police' or 'ground' control room
	open plan or designated pods/booths
Time	Ritual or 'as it happens' opening of the venue
	Time rituals
	the '10 minute walk' (Glasgow Rangers)
	'three-quarters time' (Everton)
	'phase one' (Norwich City)
	Enforcement of liquor licensing laws
	Procedures for opening the exit gates
	Departure of 'away' supporters
Objects	Separate, conflicting or joint contingency plans
	Extent of reliance on technology
	Access to/control of technological and life safety systems
	Use of separate radio command channel
	Issue of handbooks and instruction cards
	Insignia of rank/grade
Resources	Prescribed emergency roles or broad framework
	Control of all resources by one lead agency
	Or, competition for resource control/decision making
	Staff to spectator ratios
	Post-specific or general instructions
	Posting staff to functions or to areas

(continued)

Table 10.3   Aspects concerned with the 'grid' dimension (*cont.*)

Aspect of group	Indicators
Labour	Division of responsibilities in statement of intent
	Posting requirements in safety certificate
	Detailed identification of specific postings
	Mechanism for crisis co-ordinating committee
	'Personality' leaders
	Ranks/grades involved in planning and debriefings
	Level of radio traffic
	Freedom to act without reference to control room
	Number of supervisory layers in command structure
	Distinct functional separation at operational level

Table 10.4   Aspects concerned with the 'group' dimension

Aspect of group	Indicators
Frequency	of safety advisory group meetings
	repeated or irregular events at the same venue
	continuity of personnel in key posts
Mutuality	attendance at safety advisory group meetings
	sense of collective responsibility/accountability
	consultation on key operational decisions
	attendance at/input to other agency briefings
	interdisciplinary teams of staff
	isolation or co-operation in front-line operations
	separate control rooms for each agency
Scope	range of different event types held at venue
	extent of joint training and exercising
	all agencies inputting to training programmes
Boundary	blame absorption at safety group meetings
	overt blaming/bickering at safety group meetings
	safety group decisions by consensus or voting
	pre-event meetings between agencies
	post-event debriefings between agencies
	control room nomenclature
	open plan or separate control rooms
	joint contingency plans
	'crisis co-ordinating committee'
	difficult access for visitors
	visitor access through one agency
	control room as focal point of activity

Risk perception is likely to be biased towards commercial risks which pose a threat to revenue. The emphasis may therefore be on access and ticketing control, pirate merchandise and protecting the interests of accredited sponsors.

This model is most likely to be found where individual organizations come together for one-off or irregular events at a venue.

The 'barons and fiefdoms' or 'silo management' model

This is the strong grid and weak group way of organizing corresponding to the fatalist way of life within TTOCC.

There are two key features in this model. First is the presence of a 'personality' leader – the baron – at the head of each agency – the fiefdom. Second is the absence of significant forward planning, based on a 'fire-fighting' approach to risk and problem solving.

One agency, almost certainly the police, will clearly perceive itself and be perceived by others to be in charge of events. This perception may be driven by a strong sense of responsibility and accountability.

Leaders may be particularly charismatic, and the majority of interagency interaction will take place at their level, or involving inadequately briefed deputies of senior rank. Lower grade staff may operate in 'silos', with strict functional separation and low interaction on the ground.

The main control room may be called the 'Police Control Room' and those of the subservient agencies may be separate from it, yet perceive the need to refer the most minor matters to it. What limited planning has taken place, particularly in respect of spatial and timing issues, may often have been at short notice and even then may be thwarted in practice.

Emerging risks and problems will take everybody by surprise, be blamed by each agency on the poor performance of others and be responded to with higher grid solutions, for example, increasing territorialization or staff to spectator ratios. Thus safety strategies will evolve incrementally in response to crises. Contingency plans will have been separately prepared without consultation. Where contradictions exist, the need to reconcile the differences may not be perceived until after a problem has arisen.

The safety certificate may be highly prescriptive about the locations to which stewards are to be posted and in what numbers.

This model is most likely to be found at venues where the range of events is limited and the lead agency does not have confidence in the venue management's ability to properly manage its responsibilities for safety.

The bureaucratic high interaction model

This is the strong grid and strong group way of organising corresponding to the hierarchical way of life within TTOCC.

The nomenclature of the control facility, for example the 'Melchester Rovers Ground Safety Management Centre', may reflect a strong sense of collective responsibility. The control room may be large and open plan, allowing everybody access to all the equipment. The room may be a focal point where staff drop by and visitors gather.

Joint briefings may be held, particularly for police and stewards. Alternatively, each agency may send a representative to give an input at other agency briefings.

Risk perception will be heavily influenced by historical experience at the venue at the views of the senior personnel. Briefings will be very full and every perceived eventuality covered by rules.

Bureaucracy is evident in mechanistic planning. Police operation orders and steward handbooks will be full and procedures set out in some detail. The safety certificate may prescribe the precise posts to be occupied. For each of these, the club and police may have prepared detailed post-specific instruction cards prescribing the postholders duties in both normal and emergency operating conditions. Joint exercising and training may be regularly undertaken.

Rank is important in this model. Each agency may have several internal supervisory grades. The most senior may each have their own 'command' radio channels. Collectively, one agency is always 'in charge' in any given scenario. For example, the club may control all routine activity, the ambulance services all medical emergencies, and the police any outbreaks of serious disorder. There may be competition to be 'in charge' overall, but this is a game played within the rules laid down by the safety certificate and statements of intent.

When staff encounter incidents for which they have not been briefed or which are not covered by their instruction cards, they are likely to initiate a process of reporting up the line to the control room, where a decision will be taken by the appropriate 'in charge' agency and eventually communicated back down the line.

Territorialization for spectators is likely to be high, with supporters occupying designated seats, well segregated both from each other and from the pitch.

Time rituals are important. For example, stewards may walk up and down the gangways every ten minutes on the dot and exit gates may always be opened at three-quarters time.

This model is most likely to be found at venues where a variety of events are regularly held and where there is continuity in the personnel occupying the key posts.

The 'middle out' consensus driven model

This is the weak grid and strong group way of organizing corresponding to the egalitarian way of life within TTOCC.

The key feature of this model is the strong desire for management through consensus, arising from a sense of collective responsibility and, more importantly, a sense of collective accountability if disaster strikes. Safety advisory group meetings may also be consensus driven, with change being approved only if everybody agrees.

Management structures are likely to be relatively flat, with fewer grades and wider spans of command than in hierarchy. Since delay may be perceived as a cause of potential disaster, all staff will be encouraged to intervene in situations on their own initiative, without seeking approval from control. There is likely to be continuity in staff at all levels, certainly in key posts, and staff may operate in interdisciplinary teams deployed to geographical areas rather than to function specific posts.

An open plan multi-agency control room is likely. Since staff are familiar with the venue and acting on their own initiative, radio traffic may be light. Where control room intervention in operational decision making is needed, this may be preceded by consultation between agency representatives. For serious emergencies, there may be plans for a multi-agency 'Crisis Co-ordinating Committee' to assemble to manage the consequences.

The egalitarian view of nature as ephemeral may create a fear of impending doom if the most careful precautions are not followed. This suggests a wide awareness of possible risks and extensive collective contingency planning. However, this is likely to be in broad rather than detailed mechanistic terms.

In order to be ready for any eventuality, considerable resources may be available and staff to spectator ratios may therefore be high. However, these resources may be more held in reserve than deployed since the need for territorialization of spectators may not be so keenly felt.

Important timing issues such as the opening of the ground may happen only after consultation has determined that everybody is ready.

This model is most likely to be found at venues which have experienced a serious incident, from which all the agencies involved perceived a need for increased communication and co-operation to avoid a recurrence.

Ethnographic examples

My fieldwork has provided me with examples of different safety cultures. Whilst none of them conform exactly to one of the four hypothetical types I have proposed, my argument is that each of them has a specific bias towards one of the four models and thus a bias towards one of four different ways of perceiving and managing risk. Like all organizations, all my examples have been dynamic; adapting and evolving themselves. As a result, some may now be substantially different, even in cultural bias, from when I studied them. This does not detract from their value as ethnographic examples. The four vignettes which follow most closely exemplify the key features of the four hypothetical models.

Silverstone Circuits

Overall weak group was reflected in poor communications, separate agency control rooms and competition for primacy between the racing authorities and the emergency services. The management of the whole venue was compartmentalized. In emergency exercises, all the agencies turned up and gave individual situation reports on individual radio systems to individual control rooms. In exercise debriefings, blame for things not going well was overtly expressed rather than absorbed.

The Unified Emergency Action Plan contained no plans at all but was a political document establishing a co-ordinating framework in the event of a disaster. There were no contingency plans. There was a view that plans cannot cover every contingency and therefore there was no point being prescriptive about what to do if an emergency happened. Security personnel were deployed to tackle revenue protection risks and, although there had been some increase in territorialization of spectators, the majority of spectator activity was unregulated. Motor racing is about danger and excitement and spectators shared in this by abnormal risk-taking behaviour. This indicated that grid was also weak.

Goodison Park – Everton FC

The police, under the command of a highly charismatic leader, were very clearly in charge of the event and their operation was highly planned and resourced, almost to the point of rendering the club's involvement superfluous. This was strong grid.

Since the various agencies involved did not communicate with each other very well, and interaction at lower levels was low, overall group was weak. This lack of communication between the different agencies gave rise to a variety of surprises, for example the blocking of an access route by a temporary structure, which could only be addressed through last-minute crisis management.

When several medical and public order emergencies occurred together, the safety management system was unable to cope. In the police debriefing, the system failure was largely blamed on the stewards.

Selhurst Park Stadium – Crystal Palace and Wimbledon FCs

The police and stewarding operations were individually and collectively highly planned and organized. The police were clearly in charge, although they were preparing to hand over and let the club take command. Planned territorialization of spectators was high. This was all strong grid.

The control room was shared by several agencies. There was continuity in key posts and front line co-operation between staff was evident. Relations between all parties within the Safety Advisory Group were good. Selhurst Park stadium was shared by Crystal Palace FC and their tenants Wimbledon FC. The staging of twice as many matches as at most other stadia reinforced the frequency element of group, which was also strong.

The Sheffield clubs - Wednesday and United

The shadow of the Hillsborough disaster hung heavy over the police and other agencies involved in managing safety in South Yorkshire. There was collective risk aversion and a strong sense of collective responsibility and accountability among all parties here.

The Safety Advisory Group had supervised the evolution of higher profile stewarding and lower profile policing at Sheffield United FC through a cautious, incremental and consensual approach to change. At Sheffield Wednesday, the police spoke warmly of the good relations between them and the club and pre-event consultation was evident. This indicated a bias towards strong group.

The delegation to individuals at low levels of the authority to take action on their own initiative and the remarkably low level of radio communication between individuals and the control room suggested that grid was relatively weak.

Implications for policy

Each of the four archetypes has both strengths and weaknesses. Awareness for policy makers will be more enhanced by discussion of weaknesses than a more comfortable focus on strengths. The weaknesses have already begun to be indicated in the models set out above. What I want to do here is emphasize the main points and suggest the possible implications of these pathologies for the crowd.

The competitive low interaction model

Weak group and competition suggests the likelihood of poor communication between the various agencies and duplication of effort. What communication there is may not be trusted. Each agency may send its own representative to every incident to find out what is 'really' going on and whether there is 'anything for us' at the scene.

Weak 'grid' suggests that overall control and co-ordination in routine situations may be poor. A view of nature as benign and emphasis on commercial risks may lead to blindness to potential safety risks. Liability for safety may in any event be discharged through insurance cover rather than the deployment of adequate resources.

This 'safety culture' may create a *laissez-faire* environment which encourages risk-taking behaviour by spectators. Minor accidents may be more frequent, yet go unreported because spectators will shrug them off as part of the experience.

The 'barons and fiefdoms' or 'silo management' model

One agency may have taken all the burden of organization and responsibility on its shoulders. Whilst this may be fine in routine situations, the agency may find itself unable to cope in crises where rapid communication with and assistance from others is required.

Interagency communication is likely to be restricted to the 'barons' at the head of each agency. These may keep important information to themselves, leaving their 'fiefdoms' to operate in isolated ignorance. Frequent minor mistakes in safety management may result.

A lack of effective forward planning may leave this 'safety culture' constantly surprised by events, which have to be addressed through last-minute 'fire-fighting' responses.

This 'safety culture' may create a constrained and confusing environment for spectators, whose general passive acceptance of apparent poor organization may occasionally boil over into frustrated protest.

The bureaucratic high interaction model

Since information flows down better than it does up, and rank and status is afforded more weight than knowledge and experience, plans may be made in ignorance of the operating problems and potential solutions to them known to those actually doing the work.

Although such mechanistic planning ensures that routine operating scenarios work smoothly, with most minor problems referred to and resolved by a central control, this stifles innovation and can result in ineffectual individual performance at operational level.

In emergency situations, the command structure is too cumbersome to respond with sufficient speed and flexibility to provide the support required. The reports of lower grade staff may not be trusted and higher ranks deployed to 'assess the situation' before any response is made.

Bureaucratic regulation and delay in responding to emergencies are inherent features of this model. This can create an environment where spectator enjoyment is spoiled by the unthinking enforcement of petty regulation. When serious problems do occur, the inability to respond quickly may result in disastrous delay.

The 'middle out' consensus driven model

The strong awareness of delay leading to potential disaster may encourage ad hoc low level interventions which are not informed by a strategic awareness of the whole picture. Overall co-ordination and control in routine scenarios may prove difficult to achieve.

A 'just in case' philosophy may lead to excessive staffing and unnecessary costs for the organizers. Many staff may lack a meaningful role in the operation.

The need for consensus in policy issues may require resource intensive and costly debating and consultative procedures. There may be a tendency to concentrate on minor matters on which agreement is easily achieved, deferring the more difficult and contentious decisions.

This may create an environment where the approach to spectator regulation is compliance rather than enforcement oriented, seeking spectator agreement and co-operation with consensually agreed measures. Thus considerable tolerance may be shown towards misbehaviour, with strenuous efforts made to encourage compliance and ejections or arrests being regarded as a last resort.

Conclusion

The application of analytical tools from TTOCC suggests that the agencies within a sports ground safety management system are likely to interact with each other in a way that is biased towards one of four archetypal models of 'safety culture'.

No one model has the monopoly on good practice and there is, therefore, no 'one best way' of organizing the cross-organizational collaboration required for public safety risk management. Equally, no single one of the models represents the 'wrong' way of managing public safety. Since each is derived from local culture and circumstances, each model, in its own environment, is 'right'. However, since culture is dynamic, so 'safety culture' will evolve and change in response to experience and changing local circumstances.

To emphasize again the point made by Johnson [11], the agencies involved in local collaboration for safety at sports grounds need to ' "discover" the nature of their organisation in cultural terms, the way it impacts on the strategy they are following, and the difficulty of changing it'.

Summary

- Official inquiries into disasters such as the Kings Cross fire have emphasized the need for organizational 'safety cultures'. The general understanding of this term is based on an engineering and hierarchical view of the world.
- The theory of cultural complexity can be used to propose a disaggregated model of indicators of 'safety culture'.
- From an analysis of these indicators, a hypothetical fourfold typology of models of 'safety culture' can be developed.
- Examination of the pathology of each model reveals that each has different weaknesses, and different impacts on the crowd environment.
- Ethnographic examples confirm the existence of real life 'safety cultures' with a cultural bias towards one of these four hypothetical models. These ethnographic examples are presented in vignettes of Silverstone Circuits, Goodison Park Stadium, Selhurst Park Stadium and the Sheffield Football Clubs.
- Since there are four viable ways of organizing, and the management system at each venue will have evolved in response to its changing local environment; it follows that there is no 'one best way' of managing safety at sports grounds.

Acknowledgement

An earlier version of this chapter was previously published as Frosdick, S. (1995). 'Safety Cultures' in British Stadia and Sporting Venues: Understanding Cross-Organisational Collaboration for Managing Public Safety in British Sports Grounds. *Disaster Prevention and Management: An International Journal*, **4**(4), 13–21.

References

[1] *Investigation into the Kings Cross Underground Fire* (Fennell Report, 1988). HMSO.
[2] Williams, J., Dunning, E. and Murphy, P. (1989). *The Luton Town Members Scheme: Final Report*. Sir Norman Chester Centre for Football Research, University of Leicester.

[3] Canter, D., Comber, M. and Uzzell D. (1989). *Football in its Place: An Environmental Psychology of Football Grounds*. Routledge.

[4] Bale, J. (1993). *Sport, Space and the City*. Routledge.

[5] Johnson, G. and Scholes, K. (1988). *Exploring Corporate Strategy* (2nd edn.), p. 41. Prentice Hall.

[6] Elliott, D. and Smith, D. (1993). Football stadia disasters in the United Kingdom: Learning from tragedy? *Industrial and Environmental Crisis Quarterly*, **7**(3), 205–229.

[7] Johnson, G. (1992). Managing strategic change: Strategy, culture and action. In *The Challenge of Strategic Management* (D. Faulkner and G. Johnson, eds.), pp. 202–219. Kogan Page.

[8] Ibid.

[9] Cox, S. and Tait, N. (1991). *Reliability, Safety and Risk Management (An Integrated Approach)*, p. 93. Butterworth-Heinemann.

[10] Mars, G. (1994). *Cheats at Work: An Anthropology of Workplace Crime* (2nd edn.). Dartmouth.

[11] Op. cit. 7.

PART 4 PRACTICE

Overview

Notwithstanding the football club management attitudes and overall cultural complexity revealed in Part Three, the practitioners themselves have made considerable progress. Part Four introduces the results of consultancy and best practice in the areas of stadium design, risk assessment, operational safety management and policing. Several of the chapters have been written by leading practitioners, whose perspective and views are rarely captured in the literature.

Chapter summaries

In Chapter 11, Steve Frosdick reviews existing literature and evidence of best practice in safe stadium and sports grounds design. The historical shortage of independent guidance is highlighted and key issues in location, access, egress and segregation are examined. Perceptions of safety risks posed by poor seating and standing terraces are also discussed.

In Chapter 12, Mel Highmore sets out a practitioner perspective on aspects of legislation, principles and practice of health and safety management in stadia and sports grounds. He sets out the context within which the practitioner has to work and outlines the relevant legislation. He goes on to discuss the practical aspects of risk assessment and suggests four requirements for a positive safety culture. He offers advice on a range of measures for controlling safety risks and illustrates the points made with real examples.

In Chapter 13, Clive Warne takes a risk assessment perspective to identify the issues to be addressed by those responsible for crowd management in a stadium. It is a practical approach to operational planning based on a study of crowd composition, personality and anticipated behaviour. Staffing and training in crowd management are highlighted together with other considerations which challenge operational planning and decision making.

In Chapter 14, Glyn Wootton and Peter Mills outline the requirement for risk assessment under health and safety legislation and offer some practical advice to venue managers. There are three key stages to go through and eleven basic parameters to observe in commissioning or carrying out such a risk assessment.

In Chapter 15, Steve Frosdick and John Sidney trace the development of safety management and stewarding at football grounds since the Hillsborough disaster in 1989. The chapter shows how football has become a highly regulated activity. It outlines the lower profile role of the police. It goes on to describe the evolution of the football safety management profession and to highlight the role of the Football Safety Officers' Association. It then provides an overview of higher profile stewarding and introduces the football authorities' training package for stewarding at football grounds. Finally, the chapter refers to the advances made in safety facilities and equipment.

In Chapter 16, Steve Frosdick, Mike Holford and John Sidney present a case study of Nottingham Forest Football Club's safety management experiences during the 1995 to 1996 Union of European Football Associations (UEFA) Cup competition.

In Chapter 17, Bryan Drew notes that the European Football Championships held in England in June 1996 have been widely regarded as a great success. He argues that this success can be attributed not only to the good humour of the many supporters who attended the championships, but also to the extensive and careful planning undertaken by the many agencies involved. This chapter reflects on the security-related aspects of that planning and its outcomes.

11 Designing for safety

Steve Frosdick

This chapter reviews existing literature and evidence of best practice in safe stadium and sports grounds design. The historical shortage of independent guidance is highlighted and key issues in location, access, egress and segregation are examined. Perceptions of safety risks posed by poor seating and standing terraces are also discussed.

Introduction

Designing a new stadium or stand involves a whole range of complex architectural, technical and structural, electrical and fire engineering issues. An overview of the issues could include such topics as the use of ultraviolet stabilizers for colour retention in plastic seat mouldings, the benefits of translucent roofs in reducing shadows for television coverage, or the need for design to allow the wind and sun to grow and dry the grass. But this chapter will focus on the most significant design considerations for managing public safety in the sports grounds environment.

Design guidelines

There are only 117 designated sports grounds in England and Wales, yet Lord Justice Taylor's requirements [1] for all-seated accommodation gave rise to the overnight appearance of a thriving new industry offering a diverse range of products and services [2]. A 1994 conference [3] noted that 'public funds to the tune of £200 million spread over ten years have been made available, via the Football Trust, for a programme that is likely eventually to cost at least three times that amount'.

In this massive programme of redevelopment, many engineers, architects and construction companies were, according to Inglis, 'planning stadiums with little or no experience' [4]. The framework of existing guidance was confined to post-Hillsborough safety engineering documents produced by the Home Office [5] and the Institution of Structural Engineers [6].

Safety engineers have tended to treat people like inanimate objects. According to one engineer, 'crowds behave like water and care must be taken to direct the flow naturally and smoothly' [7]. This perspective has underpinned engineering calculations of crowd flow rates, safe capacities and emergency egress times. As a result, there has been considerable inflexibility in design possibilities, which Canter et al. claimed had become 'so severely controlled by the rigid application of a few key numbers that innovation and variety are very difficult indeed' [8].

The engineering perspective has been criticized for ignoring the findings of psychological research into human behaviour in crowds. Pedestrians do not flow like liquids in pipes. They move unevenly and at different speeds, stop and wait for friends and even move against the flow, for example to retrieve items left under seats [9]. Nor do people begin to move as soon as they receive a cue such as a fire alarm. They either ignore it or investigate its cause. Only once they have interpreted the situation as serious will they take action, which even then may be to go and help rather than to evacuate [10, 11]. And if they do evacuate, people will try and get out the way they came in rather than move to special emergency exits [12]. This all has implications for calculating both egress times and exit network capacities.

The Taylor recommended creation of the Football Stadia Advisory Design Council (FSADC) was intended to provide a source of much needed expertise. Subsequently, the FSADC published useful guidelines dealing with seating and sightlines [13], public address systems [14], stadia criteria [15], stadium roofs [16], and disabled spectators [17]. Perceiving a lack of cost consciousness in the FSADC guidelines, the football authorities declined to continue funding even the paltry £30 000 allocated for the financial year 1992–93. The FSADC was disbanded in March 1993, shortly after publishing guidelines [18] which implied that the majority of existing terracing would need to be replaced.

Although the Sports Council published an updated *Handbook of Sports and Recreational Building Design* [19], the demise of the FSADC resulted in a shortage of independent published guidance available for those building new stands and stadia. The original Panstadia publications [20, 21] sought to fill this gap, however these were sophisticated trade directories rather than substantiated technical guidelines. The same is true of trade magazines such as *Panstadia International Quarterly Report.*

The Department of National Heritage have established a new Football Stadia Development Committee (FSDC); however, in the view of one of my informants, a key figure in the industry, this has been an ineffective forum set up to placate public concern. Nevertheless, further FSDC guidelines have been produced, covering the use of design-build [22], and, importantly, the provision of toilet [23] and control room [24] facilities. Whilst most such amenity issues impact on the quality of the spectator experience, the provision of adequate toilet and control room facilities are also of importance in managing public safety. Lord Justice Taylor found that poor toilets meant that 'crowd conduct becomes degraded and other misbehaviour seems less out of place' [25]. Multi-agency stadium control rooms have slowly replaced the 'police box' as stadium operators have increasingly taken proper responsibility for the safety of their customers.

Stadia redevelopment has been either newbuild, phased rebuilding on site, refurbishment of existing facilities, or a combination of the latter two. The difficulties in providing universal standards for such varied scenarios prompted the 1991 Joint Working Party on Ground Safety and Public Order [26] to recommend that the Home Office *Green Guide* guidelines be revised in two volumes: one for existing grounds, the other linked to Building Regulations for newbuild. It is unfortunate that this recommendation could not be progressed until after so much of the post-Hillsborough rebuilding had taken place. A revised *Green Guide* is nevertheless in the course of preparation. This is proving to be a major undertaking and the new guidelines are expected to be published during 1997. It is likely to be a single document, but will point up where higher standards are recommended for newbuild.

To cater for the incremental development option, an idealized stadium design [27] has been prepared to provide for a six-phased development from a basic 3000 to a fully enclosed 20 000 seats. The design incorporates ramp access and a moat and complies with all requirements for optimum viewing. An award-winning version of the design, with stair rather than ramp access, has been built in Huddersfield. But football clubs are competitive and individualist and this particular approach has not been taken up elsewhere. What club would want a stadium like somebody else's?

Safety design features

Safety zones

For design and safety planning purposes, the stadium can be divided into four safety zones, as shown in Figure 11.1 [28]. The key issues in safety design may therefore be considered with reference to these four zones.

Zone one – the activity area

The most important issue here is preventing spectator invasions of the activity area. The need is illustrated by the well-publicized pitch invasions that have occurred at football grounds such as Millwall and Lansdowne Road in Dublin. The altercation between Manchester United's Eric Cantona and a spectator drew banner headlines across the world. Away from football, the start of the 1993 Aintree Grand National horse race was disrupted by a course invasion by political protesters and the subsequent abandonment of the race was a public relations disaster. The on-court

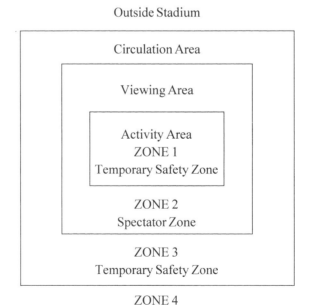

Figure 11.1   Stadium safety zones.

stabbing of tennis star Monica Seles was widely reported and a disaster also nearly resulted from the mass circuit invasion after Nigel Mansell's motor racing victory in the 1992 British Grand Prix (but see the case study for details of the improvements implemented for the 1993 race).

In the light of Hillsborough, where lack of access through the fence was a major factor in the disaster, there is considerable controversy in Britain about the safety risks posed by perimeter fences higher than the standard 1.1 m. The caging of supporters behind high metal fences is a practice still dangerously prevalent at stadia throughout the world. There are, however, a variety of other solutions, and the most successful approaches are those which combine an adequate physical barrier with a variety of other techniques to maximize the message.

Alternative barriers include the dry moat, not yet used in Britain, or the horizontal elastic fence patented by Wembley Stadium. Other measures feature the use of different intensities of police and/or steward perimeter cordons and spectator education tactics such as programme notes reinforced with scoreboard and public address announcements. Unauthorized entry onto the pitch is a criminal offence at designated football grounds [29]. Warning signs to this effect and a rigorous enforcement policy by police and stewards can also be very effective.

Some stadia have only advertising hoardings or a low rail to segregate spectators from the activity area. This is inadequate, and a fence or wall of 1.1 m, incorporating adequate staffed emergency exit gates, in my view represents best practice. This provides a substantial barrier without compromising either viewing quality or emergency egress. The provision of gate stewards allows for public reassurance, crowd monitoring and immediate reinforcement of the barrier where necessary.

Zone two – the viewing area

Seating, roofs and sightlines

The *Green Guide* recommends that 'all spectators should have a clear, unobstructed view of the whole of the playing area. Designs should ensure that sightlines are such that spectators are encouraged to remain seated ... and do not have to strain or stretch to view the playing area' [30]. Many older stadia, with propped roofs, floodlight pylons and shallow rakes, do not meet this goal. To help eliminate restricted views, the FSADC guidelines offer suggestions on roof designs, such as cantilevering and goalpost type construction. They also address seat comfort, durability and the quality of view.

Case study – preventing a circuit invasion

This example illustrates the link between design, management and crowd education in the successful prevention of spectators invading the circuit at the conclusion of the 1993 British Grand Prix.

At the height of 'Mansell mania' in 1992, up to 180 000 people had crowded into the circuit to see the British driver win the British Grand Prix. At the conclusion of the race, whilst racing cars were still going round at over 100 mph, huge numbers of the crowd crawled under the debris fences and invaded the circuit. The authorities considered it fortunate nobody had been killed. A repetition was not to be permitted.

For 1993, the 2 m debris fence between the track and spectators had been reinforced. Gaps had been filled in with gates. Gaps at the bottom of the fence had been filled in with wire mesh or strands. The top of the fence had a new three-stranded wire 'V' shape built onto it. This was a far more substantial barrier. The official event programme contained an article entitled 'spectator safety ', outlining the risks created by the circuit invasion and giving a full explanation of why spectators would find their access to the track and pit lane more restricted this year. In the final few minutes before the Grand Prix itself, the public address announcer began reminding the spectators not to go onto the track at the end of the race. Over several minutes he repeated the message in a number of different ways. During the course of the race, the various stewarding companies received final briefings on their role at the end. As the race was in its final laps, slowly and unobtrusively, these stewards took up positions between the spectators and the debris fence.

There was no hint of a potential circuit invasion. The crowd's mood had been dented by the retirement of the British driver, Damon Hill, and the number and variety of cues given to the crowd had been effective.

In addition to roof obstructions, view quality is affected by three considerations. First is the preferred viewing location [31]. For athletics, this is the side of the stadium where the finishing line is located. For rugby, the touch lines are preferred to the goal lines, whereas with football, the ends are just as popular as the sides. The second consideration is viewing distance [32]. The absolute maximum viewing distance for football is considered to be at a radius of 190 m from each corner. However, the practical maximum is about 150 m radius. An optimum viewing circle can be assumed to be within 90 m of the centre circle for rugby and for football. At several famous stadia, including Wembley, the majority of spectators are beyond the optimum distance and many are beyond the absolute maximum.

The third consideration is the sightline [33]. This is assessed using riser heights, tread depths, angles of rake and thus the 'C' values, which refer to the height distance between one spectator's eyes and the top of the head of the spectator in the row in front. A 'C' value of 150 mm allows for excellent viewing for all events, but the required angles of rake make this impractical, particularly in multitiered stands. At 60 mm spectators will only be able to see between the heads of the people in front. Optimum 'C' values vary with the sport. The optimum for football is 120 mm, but achieving this can be difficult in very large stadia (30 000 or more). Some redevelopments (for example Aston Villa, Blackburn Rovers and Newcastle) have managed an acceptable 90 mm, but there have been other examples where tight sites and/or the club's desire to put in more seats (and so increase revenue) have meant that poorer values have been achieved.

In the view of the Football Licensing Authority, 'any seating which positively encourages spectators to stand constitutes an unacceptable safety hazard and a potential source of disorder which cannot be accepted. It would, furthermore, undermine the purpose of making football grounds all-seater' [34]. Such seating conditions can be created by excessive distances coupled with poor 'C' values on low raked stands. Terrace conversions where seats have been simply bolted onto the existing concrete have created such problems at a number of venues [35]. The case study gives a typical response to poor seating.

Standing terraces

Crowd pressure on standing terraces has been the immediate cause in a high proportion of stadia disasters and is therefore a significant safety risk. The FSADC view of safe standing was that:

Standing spectators should be able to view all elements of play from any part of a properly constructed and designed terrace in such a way that they are not subjected to:

- excessive or undue pressures from crowd surges;
- undue pressure from an excessively high density of spectators;
- forces that cause spectators to lose control of their own movement, so that they step forward in an uncontrolled manner;

Case study – standing up to see

I went to the FA Cup Final between Sheffield Wednesday and Arsenal on 15 May 1993. My £25 ticket entitled me to squat on a low seat with no back in the third row of a very low-raked stand. For the entire match I could only see about half the pitch and even that was obscured by the fence. Fortunately, I had my portable radio tuned into the match commentary. Like everyone else, I repeatedly stood up, even wobbling precariously on the seat, when the radio told me play was developing and I couldn't see what was happening.

- undue physical stresses caused by poorly constructed terracing, such as excessively sloping surfaces, uneven surfaces or broken or damaged terracing;
- obstructed viewing, necessitating frequent changes of position or excessive movement, which might affect other spectators [36].

What emerged from this was that existing terraces would only be acceptable if they complied with the highest standards in the *Green Guide*, were wholly covered or uncovered (to discourage uncontrolled migration in wet or sunny weather) and had adequate safety management procedures in place. Existing terraces which did not meet the *Green Guide* standards, (i.e. most of them) or which had inadequate safety management would only be regarded as acceptable with a reduced spectator capacity. What is more, it seemed clear that new terraces would have to comply with even higher standards than those in the *Green Guide*. They would need to be capable of conversion to seats and therefore have to provide the same sightline 'C' values as seating. In practice, however, most new terracing had for some years already been built to this standard.

Segregation

To minimize the risks of disorder and consequent injury, there is a strong perceived need to segregate opposing football supporters inside the stadium. This need is less keenly felt for other team sports such as rugby league or rugby union, where enjoying a good game is more important to the fans than winning at all costs. It is difficult to judge how far the atmosphere of hate and hostility between groups of segregated supporters is in fact the product of years of such segregation. Having reviewed the evidence from many sides, the House of Commons Home Affairs

Committee recommended that 'gradual but steady progress towards desegregation should be the aim of police and clubs' [37].

Within the stadium, some progress is being made through desegregated family enclosures and the long-term aim is laudable. The experience of the 1996 European football championships has also shown that desegregation can work for the more carnivalesque types of spectator. Nevertheless, my own research experience and media monitoring provide clear evidence of the hostility and disorder which can and does arise. For current design, therefore, I believe the correct approach remains as described in 1990 by the architect, Rod Sheard, who argued that 'I think segregation is here to stay. We may be able to improve it, but any new stadium specifically

---

Case study – the need for segregation

This example illustrates the need for spectator segregation at the European Champions Cup second leg match between Leeds United and Glasgow Rangers at Elland Road, Leeds on 4 November 1992.

Since there was no problem selling the match out, both clubs had agreed to restrict ticket sales for both legs to home supporters only. It was nevertheless anticipated that some 200 Rangers supporters would have managed to buy tickets and be in the ground. The police policy was that such fans would have to take responsibility for their own safety, but if a breach of the peace occurred, the stewards would eject the relevant spectators. Police would support the stewards if required.

Rangers scored a very early goal. There was an almost deathly silence around the ground. Suddenly, the silence was broken by a few cheering Rangers supporters who now revealed themselves around the stadium. The crowd were suddenly angry, looking all about to spot the Rangers supporters, confronting them and even pointing them out to stewards and police. There were supposed to be no Rangers supporters and there was a sense of moral outrage that some had got in. The atmosphere in the stadium had seconds ago been volatile, excited and partisan. Now it was heavy with hatred and hostility. Some fifteen Rangers supporters were ejected, not because they were misbehaving, but, as the police commander later explained in a radio interview, purely for their own safety.

designed for football has to be designed with segregation in mind' [38]. The case study illustrates the need for spectator segregation.

There are various measures currently adopted to segregate supporters within the viewing areas. These include segregation fences, radial rows of seats filled with police or stewards and the leaving of sterile areas between supporter groups. These can be supplemented by stretching a canvas over the empty seats in the sterile area. Particularly effective is the creation of a self-contained 'away' zone or end with entirely segregated entrances, viewing accommodation and facilities.

Zone three – the circulation area

In many existing British stadia, the turnstiles give direct access to the stands and there is no real circulation area. Temporary disruptions and realistic emergency exercises cannot be catered for without requiring everyone to leave the stadium. In newbuild therefore, the circulation area, together with the activity area where appropriate, should be of sufficient capacity to temporarily accommodate all the spectators.

Means of access and egress

Canter et al. have emphasized the importance of design allowing for crowd movement to be free and unidirectional, observing that, 'in many ways the design of all these facilities is really the design of ways into and out of them. They are one vast complex of corridors leading to a circle of seats' [39].

Building Regulations require reasonable provision to be made for disabled people to gain access to use the building. This is an important consideration in designing means of access and egress in both normal and emergency use.

Cox [40] has shown that slips, trips and falls are a major cause of accidents in and around buildings. She concludes that floors and stairways are the main sources of risk, with slipperiness and unevenness the major factors in accidents on a level. Such risks have a greater probability of happening in crowds. Weight of numbers and behavioural inertia mean that when things go wrong, the problems can be large scale.

The extent of awareness at British sporting venues is mixed. Rubber studded flooring has been installed at many new and refurbished stadia. However, at Silverstone motor racing circuit, spectator circulation and viewing was on rough earth embankments. Concrete walkways and terracing at the popular corners contained frequent unexpected changes in level.

The lower probability of accidents and ease of use for the disabled make ramps a preferable design choice to stairs. The American company, Hellmuth, Obata and Kassabaum (HOK), employs over 100 stadium and arena architects worldwide. In their view, stairs are a source of accidents and thus litigation. HOK have advocated the use of ramps in routes that are well signposted, logical, continuous and unidirectional [41]. There are no current British stadia developments where ramps have been used instead of stairs.

Supporting the findings of research into human behaviour in emergencies, they also emphasize the importance of egress routes taking people out of the building the same way they came in. It is clear that people escape by going the way they know. They are far less likely to follow unknown, albeit specially designed, emergency egress routes.

Zone four - outside the stadium

Location and access

Safe access is perceived as involving adequate roads, car parking, public transport and segregated routes for away supporters [42]. For high risk events, the choice of stadium site should, ideally, allow for entry to the outer zone to be restricted to ticket holders only. Whilst this implies locating stadia in places where there is room for such safe access infrastructure, there is considerable debate about the merits of urban, suburban or greenfield locations. All three present planning problems, ranging from 'not in my backyard' residents to greenbelt protection. Local authorities have historically not generally been sympathetic to football clubs seeking to relocate. It is significant that all successful relocations have required strong support from the local authority and/or a development corporation.

In urban locations, parking is often restricted and roads overwhelmed by pedestrian and vehicular traffic. This may need to be significantly disrupted in the interests of pedestrian safety and emergency access. However, the cramped inner-city locations are more likely to be near public transport. More importantly, they have individual and unique character and provide fans with a traditional proximity to the action. Some club chairmen may dream of a new rural all-seated stadium with a docile family audience, but experience suggests the bowl-on-the-bypass may be hard to get to and unpopular with both supporters and the community.

Some of the most successful relocations, for example Huddersfield Town and Millwall, have taken advantage of redundant industrial sites in urban areas close to the site of the original ground. John Bale has shown that, if clubs have to relocate, perceptions of the stadium as a source of pleasure are most likely to be retained if the move is over the shortest possible distance [43]. Bale also refers to St Johnstone's new greenfield location where poor public transport and post-match traffic congestion have created greater negative externality effects than the old town ground.

Segregation

With football supporters, the perceived need for segregation extends beyond the curtilages of the stadium. The days of police phalanxes herding away supporters like cattle to and from their coaches or the station are on the wane, but by no means over. The provision of a supervised rather than segregated away supporter route, monitored by static police patrols, is becoming more common. Similarly, very few clubs routinely require the away supporters to remain behind after the match. Simultaneous desegregated dispersal is the norm, although the police may make exceptions for particularly high risk matches.

Summary

- Delay in revising the *Guide to Safety at Sports Grounds* to reflect the differing circumstances of newbuild, phased rebuilding and refurbishment, coupled with the demise of the Football Stadia Advisory Design Council, means that there is a shortage of independent published guidance available in stadia design.
- The goal of total spectator desegregation in football is unrealistic in the short to medium term. Football grounds should be designed and located bearing in mind the need for opposing supporters to be segregated from each other.
- In all venues, spectators should be properly segregated from the area where the event is being held.
- Spectator circulation routes should be well signposted, logical, level and lead people out the way they came in for both normal and emergency egress. Slips, trips and falls are less likely on ramps than stairs.
- Poor viewing quality from some seating creates safety risks perceived as unacceptable by the licensing authorities. Much terracing is also perceived as unsafe.
- There is considerable debate about the relevant merits of urban and out-of-town locations for stadia.

Acknowledgement

This chapter is derived from a research report prepared by the author for the Building Research Establishment, whose sponsorship is hereby gratefully acknowledged.

References

[1] *The Hillsborough Stadium Disaster 15 April 1989 – Inquiry by the Rt Hon Lord Justice Taylor – Final Report* (Taylor Report, 1990). HMSO.

[2] Stevens, A. (1991). Stadia of the future – the pros and cons! In *Panstadia – A Comprehensive Guide to Stadium Newbuild*, pp. 17–19. Executive Publications (Holdings) Ltd.

[3] *Grounds for Optimism?* (1994). A one-day conference on the football stadium, the city and the future, 24 March, Leicester City Football Club and the Sir Norman Chester Centre for Football Research, University of Leicester.

[4] Inglis, S. (1990). Grounds for complaint. *New Civil Engineer*, 7 June, 26.

[5] Home Office and Scottish Office (1990). *Guide to Safety at Sports Grounds*. HMSO.

[6] Institution of Structural Engineers (1991). *Appraisal of Sports Grounds.*

[7] Thorburn, S. (1990). Ibrox Stadium – a blueprint for the future. In *Sports Stadia After Hillsborough: Papers Presented at the Sports Council and Royal Institute of British Architects Seminar* (O. Luder, ed.), p. 64. RIBA and the Sports Council in association with the Football Trust.

[8] Canter, D., Comber, M. and Uzzell, D. (1989). *Football in its Place – An Environmental Psychology of Football Grounds*, p. 97. Routledge.

[9] Sime, J. (ed.) (1988). *Safety in the Built Environment*, p. xiii. E. & F. N. Spon.

[10] Canter, D. (ed.) (1990). *Fires and Human Behaviour* (2nd edn.). David Fulton Publishers Ltd.

[11] Donald, I. (1992). Crowd behaviour in the Kings Cross Underground Station fire. In *Lessons Learned from Crowd-Related Disasters* (Easingwold Papers No. 4), pp. 30–46. The Emergency Planning College.

[12] Sime, J. and Kimura, M. (1988). The timing of escape: Exit choice behaviour in fires and building evacuations. In *Safety in the Built Environment* (J. Sime, ed.), pp. 48–61. E. & F. N. Spon.

[13] Football Stadia Advisory Design Council (1991). *Seating – Sightlines, Conversion of Terracing, Seat Types*. The Sports Council.

[14] Football Stadia Advisory Design Council (1991). *Stadium Public Address Systems*. The Sports Council.

[15] Football Stadia Advisory Design Council (1992). *Digest of Stadia Criteria*. The Sports Council.

[16] Football Stadia Advisory Design Council (1992). *Stadium Roofs*. The Sports Council.

[17] Football Stadia Advisory Design Council (1992). *Designing for Spectators with Disabilities*. The Sports Council.

[18] Football Stadia Advisory Design Council (1993). *Terraces – Designing for Safe Standing*. The Sports Council.

[19] John, G. and Campbell, K. (1993). *Handbook of Sports and Recreational Building Design, Vol. 1: Outdoor Sports* (2nd edn.). Butterworth Architecture.

[20] Panstadia (1991). *Panstadia – A Comprehensive Guide to Stadium Newbuild*. Executive Publications (Holdings) Ltd.

[21] Panstadia (1992). *Panstadia International – A World-Wide Guide to Stadium Newbuild and Management*. Panstadia International Ltd.

[22] Football Stadia Development Committee (1994). *Design Build – A Good Practice Guide Where Design Build is Used for Stadia Construction*. The Sports Council.

[23] Football Stadia Development Committee (1993). *Toilet Facilities at Stadia*. The Sports Council in association with the Football Trust.

[24] Football Stadia Development Committee (1994). *Stadium Control Rooms – Planning, Personnel, Design and Equipment*. The Sports Council.

[25] Op. cit. 1. p. 5.

[26] Joint Working Party on Ground Safety and Public Order (1991). *Ground Safety and Public Order – Report Number 1 of the Joint Executive on Football Safety*, p. 15. Association of County Councils Publications.

[27] Sports Council, the Lobb Partnership and YRM Anthony Hunt Associates (1990). *A Stadium for the Nineties*. The Sports Council.

[28] Op. cit. 19. p. 77.

[29] Football (Offences) Act, 1991, section 4.

[30] Op. cit. 5. p. 38.

[31] Op. cit. 19. p. 77.

[32] Ibid. pp. 78–80.

[33] Op. cit. 13. pp. 7–9.

[34] Football Licensing Authority (1991). *Consultation Paper Number 1 - Seating With a Restricted View*, pp 2–3.

[35] Pettipher, M. (1992). Seated areas miss goal. *New Builder*, 6 February, p. 5.

[36] Op. cit. 18. p. 7.

[37] House of Commons Home Affairs Committee (1991). *Policing Football Hooliganism, Volume 1: Report together with the Proceedings of the Committee*, p. xv. HMSO.

[38] Taylor, R. and Plumley, E. (Chairpersons) (1990). Question Session, 'Where do we go from here?' In *Sports Stadia After Hillsborough – Papers Presented at the Sports Council and Royal Institute of British Architects Seminar* (O. Luder, ed.), p. 102. RIBA and the Sports Council in association with the Football Trust.

[39] Op. cit. 8. p. 89.

[40] Cox, S. (1990). *Building Regulation and Safety*. Report to the Building Research Establishment.

[41] Frank, C. (1993). The link between good design and management. At *Football Stadia at RECMAN '93*, a Football Stadia Advisory Design Council and Football League Seminar, Wembley Exhibition Centre, 23 March.

[42] Op. cit. 19. pp. 83–85.

[43] Bale, J. (1993). *Sport, Space and the City*, p. 149. Routledge.

12 Safety risks in stadia and sports grounds

Mel Highmore

This chapter sets out a practitioner perspective on aspects of legislation, principles and practice of health and safety management in stadia and sports grounds. Its sets out the context within which the practitioner has to work and outlines the relevant legislation. It goes on to discuss the practical aspects of risk assessment and suggests four requirements for a positive safety culture. It offers advice on a range of measures for controlling safety risks and illustrates the points made with real examples.

Introduction

Ibrox, Burnden Park, Valley Parade and Hillsborough are all stadia with distinguished but sad histories. They are not the only football match venues where spectators have lost their lives and Hillsborough may not be the last. Other spectator sports venues have their records of death and injury to spectators too. How are such tragedies to be avoided or, at least, the potential for harm reduced?

Much has already been done since January 1990, when Lord Justice Taylor completed his report and recommendations. Hundreds of millions of pounds have been spent in stadia reconstruction and rejuvenation, with almost every football stadium in the country being affected.

It is against this background of complex and sometimes frenetic activity, that football safety officers and their stadium manager colleagues have had to come to terms with new health and safety regulations and guidelines. The common thread running through most, if not all, of this legislation is that of risk assessment. This activity forms the heart of every effective action by stadia management to prevent harm to spectators and employees.

Football spectators expect − and should receive − both entertainment and enjoyment. On purchase of a ticket, there is a contractual obligation to present that entertainment in safe and suitable surroundings. Spectators cannot be admitted to a football stadium unless there is in force a licence, issued by the Football Licensing Authority (FLA), and also a general safety certificate, issued by a local authority. It is to the conditions of this certificate that stadia management defer. The signature of a senior official of the club appears in the certificate, and it is that person's responsibility to ensure that all the conditions are met.

Such is the high standard of safety demanded by certifying authorities, that the Health and Safety Commission have ruled that duplication of enforcement should be avoided and the certifying authority, acting under the Safety of Sports Grounds Act 1975, should be the enforcing authority. This means that Sections 3 and 4 of the Health and Safety at Work etc. Act, 1974, are not enforced during the period of the specified event. They do, however, apply at all other times.

Section 3 provides that in addition to their responsibilities to their employees, an employer of five or more persons will also have duties for the protection of other persons, for example members of the public, agency staff or visitors, to premises controlled by their company. Section 4 lays down duties in respect of health and safety on those who are in control of non-domestic premises, where people work who are not their own employees, or where those people use plant or substances provided there for their use.

In this chapter, I am seeking to illustrate many of the features of law, practice and the principles of conducting the safety operation in a modern football stadium. Anyone tasked with safety management or co-ordination has an exacting and onerous responsibility, especially if their name is in the general safety certificate. It is critical that such persons are given the status, authority and full support from chairman, directors and other managers, if criminal law and civil litigation are to be kept at bay, and the stadium is to prosper safely to the benefit of all.

I apologize to the reader who may have other sporting events to manage but, as my safety experience is to do with football, the emphasis of my contribution is bound to reflect that. However, there are matters which will be common to all safety operations involving spectators and the staff who are employed to look after them. I hope that my advice is of some value.

This book is full of references to safety. So I will conclude my introduction by describing what I believe is meant by the word 'safe' in the context of spectator sports. 'Safe' is when a systematic examination and assessment has been carried out by competent (in many cases, qualified) persons; safety hazards identified and committed to written report; and risks eliminated or control measures put in place. It is only when event management is satisfied that identified risks have been evaluated, eliminated or control measures adopted that they should open the venue to spectators.

Principles of risk assessment

It is a requirement of the Management of Health and Safety at Work (MHSW) Regulations, 1992, for employers to carry out a risk assessment of any significant hazards to their staff at work and to any visitors who may be affected by work activities. Self-employed persons have a like responsibility. The main purpose of a risk assessment under these regulations is to assist an employer to meet the statutory requirements under Section 2 of the Health and Safety at Work etc. Act, 1974, which provides that every employer has a duty to ensure that employees at work, so far as is reasonably practicable, enjoy good standards of welfare and their health and safety is assured. It also states that systems of work and for use, handling, storage and transport of articles and substances should not present risks. Employers are required to provide information, instruction, training and supervision as well as providing and maintaining a safe working environment including the means of access and egress.

Where specific assessments are required under any other regulation, such as the Control of Substances Hazardous to Health (COSHH) Regulations, 1994, or the Manual Handling Operations Regulations, 1992, then compliance with that regulation will generally satisfy the requirements of the MHSW regulations. All regulations should be read in consideration of the Health and Safety at Work etc. Act, 1974.

Who is responsible for safety?

It is an inescapable fact that the directors and managers who run a business operation for the entertainment of spectators in stadia, and elsewhere, have prime responsibility for the safety of everyone attending the event. There will be variations in work activities but, whether it is a charity boxing match in a hotel function room attended by just 250 people, or a Wembley Stadium event attracting

80 000, the responsibility for safety of spectators at the event lies at all times with the stadia or event management.

Other authorities

Football Licensing Authority, police, fire and ambulance officers are represented in Safety Advisory Group meetings to advise stadia management in discharging their responsibilities under the general safety certificate and to monitor measures taken by each club to achieve reasonable safety standards. Planning officers and building control officers of the local authority also contribute to the licensing and formal structural matters. The regional inspector, appointed by the FLA, will also monitor safety and ensure that the criteria of the general safety certificate remain relevant in all respects. The FLA licence is valid for one year.

Other relevant legislation

There are two principal acts of Parliament which are directly concerned with safety within stadia. These are:

- the Safety of Sports Grounds Act, 1975; and
- the Fire Safety and Safety of Places of Sport Act, 1987.

It is under this legislation that general safety certificates are issued. However, if a sporting venue is not the subject of a safety certificate, event organizers should still follow the principles of the legislation and enlist professional help as necessary to ensure safe conditions for spectators.

Practicalities of risk assessment and management

Crowd safety at sports grounds is complex and problems may arise which have nothing whatsoever to do with the design or construction of buildings, barriers, exit gates or electrical monitoring systems. So how should safety officers set about their responsibilities to the law and to the well-being and happiness of everyone present?

They have to rely heavily on their training and experience and apply structured, logical thinking to:

- suitable and sufficient assessment of risks associated with staging the event;
- identifying all the hazards associated with activities undertaken by staff or contractors;
- identifying those exposed to the hazards;
- evaluating the risks, taking into consideration any existing controls;
- taking steps (controls) to remove or reduce risks;
- monitoring the effectiveness of control measures; and
- reviewing and revising controls as required;

The case study at the end of this section illustrates these points.

In a particular assessment, all relevant hazards must be addressed with a view to identifying significant risks. These must be recorded. Concentrating on trivial risks may obscure those which require urgent action.

What is a hazard?

A hazard may be defined as 'something with the potential to cause harm.' This could include structural deficiencies and defects, poor security or segregation, forged or duplicated tickets being used to gain entry, excessive numbers attending the event, fire routes blocked, etc.).

What is risk?

Risk may be defined as 'the likelihood that harm will occur, to some extent'. The extent of risk takes account of severity and/or frequency, as well as identifying the person or groups of persons exposed to the risk.

Who is at risk?

Employees

In relation to a football stadium there are differing geographical areas ranging from car parks, turnstiles, the ticket office, pitch and stadium maintenance stores, plant rooms, kitchens, playing areas, etc. In each of these areas, full-time, part-time and temporary employees or agency staff will carry out their preparations for each event as well as being engaged in their various working activities during and after each event. Up to 1000 persons could be employed in some of the larger stadia during an event. Spectators and emergency service personnel may also be at risk.

There is a general understanding that the Health and Safety at Work etc. Act, 1974 was designed to protect employees. Whilst this may be true of Section 2 and other sections of the Act; Section 3 places duties on employers and self-employed persons to conduct their work activities in such a way that persons not employed by them (this includes the public) are not exposed to danger by those activities. Thus anyone and everyone could be 'at risk'.

It may be that programme or lottery ticket sellers are exposed to harm. Hazardous conditions may arise because they are operating in isolation, carrying cash whilst unaccompanied or because their youth or old age makes them an easy target. Only by looking at every aspect of this operation can you quantify the risk. Each risk has to be recognized and steps taken to change the conditions or to remove or minimize the risk.

The law requires a formal assessment of risks associated with all stadia activities. If any staff are exposed to significant risk of injury from any cause, a written assessment must be made and steps taken to remove or control the risks. The only course of effective action for implementing the necessary controls and preventing harm is to properly plan every detail of the stadium operation and to develop a 'safety culture' throughout the management and staff.

Players

It is also important to consider the welfare of the players. How many safety officers have simply accepted pitch-side advertising boards, without making any reference to the hazards the boards might present to players? How many times have we seen examples of poor cable rigging or siting of television cameras, creating hazards for playing staff?

Are players at risk of injury through a poor pre-match 'warm-up' regime? More than ever before, the consequences of failing to follow a structured routine pre-match warm-up are likely to result in a player being unnecessarily injured. Strains and sprains form a very high proportion of injuries, which often require long periods of time to recover. Such injuries can devastate the performance of a team and can be shown as a direct cause of failing to maintain position in a league or, at worst, of relegation. A survey of all such injuries might be difficult but it might reveal what percentage of injuries are so caused and prove how suitable pre-match exercises might afford protection.

Player safety means constant effective monitoring of conditions of the playing surface, and the participation of each player in a structured form of exercise over a reasonable period before taking part in the match proper.

How many times do we actually see a club physiotherapist lead his team onto the pitch a few minutes before kick-off and take them through a series of exercises, to ensure that all participants in the match are properly warmed up and physically capable of taking the knocks and strains associated with the modern football game? Of course, we expect that the players understand the importance of a good warm-up regime. Also, we expect that coaches and physios will have warned the players of the risks.

But it is probably necessary to do more than that. In those clubs where players simply drift out onto the pitch and kick a ball about for a few minutes, it may be necessary to formally assess the risks to their health and to ensure that all concerned are aware of those risks. Controlling the risk will mean players participating in an increasingly vigorous pre-match exercise routine so that their bodies are less likely to succumb to strains.

It may be that carelessly rigged television cables or pitch-side advertising boards represent hazards to playing staff. Looking at the size of some of the Premier League transfer fees, it has to be recognized that these expensive assets cannot be exposed to any risk of injury which might interfere with them playing in the next match or reduce their transfer value.

Spectators

Any hazardous situations likely to affect spectators will need further quantifying, according to the age, level of infirmity or disability of those spectators. Club medical records should reveal any history of hazardous conditions in particular areas or in specific circumstances, such as children trapping their fingers in seats in the Family stand, or scalding incidents in the vicinity of refreshment bars.

Health and safety culture

All personnel, from the chairman down, need to be involved and committed to developing and maintaining the 'safety culture' of the club or organization. So often, all matters relating to safety devolve to one person. In the case of football clubs, this is usually the safety officer, a position which may be full- or part-time work but which will be required as a condition of most safety certificates. To develop the 'safety culture' where it has never before existed, is an uphill task. The safety officer

A winter's tale

Picture a winter's afternoon where all the final preparations are taking place for an evening match. You note that fragments of ice are lying on the concrete apron and on gangways leading up into one of your stands. On looking upward you are horrified to find that ice – the residue of a recent snowfall – has accumulated in the valleys of the roof cladding. It has formed hundreds of three- to four-inch wide bars of ice which during a slight thaw have slid forward, overshooting the gutter. Some sections of the ice are protruding well beyond the gutter and regularly breaking off to fall some forty feet onto five uncovered rows of seats and gangways below.

Clearly, anyone sitting in this part of the stand would be exposed to the risk of injury if ice continued to fall. As more and more people occupied the stand, it was probable that the combined heat from their bodies would ensure that ice on the roof would continue to remain unstable and a danger. Following discussions between the safety officer and police match commander, it was agreed that spectators judged to be at risk would be required to view the match from an unoccupied area in another stand.

Prior to their entry into the stadium, it would have been a very difficult task to identify everyone with a ticket for those particular seats and it fell to stewards and police officers to warn everyone of the danger as they took their seats. Also, an announcement was made via the public address system to inform everyone fully as to why a transfer was necessary. The transfer of 500 fans was largely completed before kick-off.

The transfer removed the threat described from those who had seats in the area of danger. However, there was still a possibility of ice falling onto persons using the gangways. The only other control measure was to post stewards to ensure spectators did not congregate on gangways and to advise the control room if there was any further movement of ice on the roof.

The same night, chunks of ice which had lodged around the light fittings of the two floodlight towers began to drop 130 feet onto the approaches to public refreshment bars and toilets. This hazardous situation was more easily controlled than the first. Club staff climbed the towers and disposed of the residual ice by throwing it down the inside of each tower. This action eliminated the hazard.

Because there had been a significant risk of injury or harm, the safety officer wrote up a risk assessment and looked at ways of eliminating or minimizing the possibility of ice presenting hazards in this way in the future. To prevent ice overshooting the gutter, two-inch galvanized steel panel was riveted to the front of the gutter along its entire length. If ice does slide down the roof cladding in the future, it will come to rest against this panel and melt harmlessly into the gutter. To prevent ice from forming and becoming a hazard around the top of the flood-light towers, a chemical spray (as used by British Airways to prevent ice forming on aircraft) was applied to all steel horizontal sections around the floodlights.

requires the full support of the Chairman, and status and authority within the organization, in order to bring about change.

To attain their goal, the safety officer has to develop the four Cs: competence, control, co-operation and communication.

Competence

Do you have the right level of expertise? You will require training and advisory support. You will also need to assess the skills of others to ensure that all tasks are carried out safely. You will have to provide the means to ensure that all employees, including temporary staff, are adequately instructed and trained. You must ensure that others are trained and have the experience and other qualities to carry out tasks which have been assessed as hazardous or dangerous.

Control

Have you allocated responsibilities for health and safety and risk assessment to specific people? You should lead by example, demonstrate your commitment and provide clear direction to others. You must identify people responsible for particular tasks especially those where the health and safety of others is judged to be at risk. You should ensure that supervisors understand their responsibilities and report regularly to you on any incident or situation requiring your attention. You should ensure that employees know what they must do and how they will be supervised, supported as necessary and held responsible for their acts or omissions.

Co-operation

Do you consult your staff effectively? Consult all staff, being prepared to use their ideas and to meet regularly with any representative they may have selected. Allocate responsibilities and secure commitment. Involve them in planning and reviewing performance, writing down hazards/defects and solving problems.

Communication

Do your staff have sufficient information about the risks they run, and the means of eliminating or controlling them? Provide information about hazards, risks and preventative measures, verbally and in writing. Use notice boards. Discuss health and safety regularly.

Controlling risks

Effective risk management requires firstly that a thorough hazard survey be carried out with a view to identifying how risks can arise. The purpose of risk control is then to either eliminate or else reduce the risk. Some examples are shown in Table 12.1.

The control of risks requires action:

- to eliminate the likelihood of a harmful incident;
- to reduce the likelihood of a harmful incident;
- to reduce the severity of potential harm; and
- to limit the impact of consequential loss;

Table 12.1   Sources and control of risk

How does risk arise?	How is risk controlled?
Poor design	Improve design of buildings, plant, equipment, the organization, management, systems and procedures
Poor systems of work	Improve protection of people, plant, equipment and buildings
Poor selection, training and communication	Safety training of people. Better motivation, communication, supervision and monitoring of their activities

Safety/risk management planning

Do you have a plan to identify and assess risks to the health and safety of your own employees, contractors' employees, club visitors and spectators?

Before any structural, electrical or other contractors start any work in your stadium, do you satisfy yourself that:

- 'competent' persons will be employed?
- the contractor has experience of such work?
- the contractor has access to structural plans and 'as fitted' drawings of the area where they are to carry out work?
- public liability and employee liability insurance cover has been provided to you by the contractor?
- a copy of the company health and safety policy has been provided to you?
- method statements are provided to show how the contractor has assessed risks to their employees and others, how the work will be carried out and the effects on services in the work area(s)?
- the contractor has specified adequate health and safety arrangements, at least to the standards in your own safety policy?
- the work does not fall within the scope of the Construction (Design and Management) Regulations, 1994? If this is the case seek advice from the Health and Safety Executive or local authority environmental health office.

Request a safety method statement. Although not required by law, a written safety method statement is particularly useful for bringing together the assessments of hazards of all tasks under consideration. It may show that 'permits to work' are required, or where only persons with specific qualifications may be employed, or where special lifting equipment or scaffolding or health surveillance is required.

It is very important to understand the seriousness of failing to use the controls listed above. Contractors can play a major part in creating hazards for your own staff and, more importantly, for your spectators. Always check and double-check the work site with the contractor to ensure that work is proceeding to schedule and that there are no hazards before workers leave your site.

Other controls

A Safety Policy – regularly reviewed and revised – is one of your most important control measures. Any organization employing five or more persons is required to have such a document. It should contain the arrangements for public safety as well as employees and visitors to the stadium.

Contingency plans – again regularly reviewed and revised – should be in place for dealing with every possible emergency, including emergency evacuation of all or part of the stadium. Disaster planning is not only vital to the safety of everyone employed at or visiting a stadium, it is also vital to the commercial survival of a football stadium.

- Ensure that you have secure ticket design, i.e. impossible to forge or duplicate. It is also important to have very secure storage for ticket stocks.
- Liaise with certifying authorities, planning and building control departments of your local authority, before any structural or use changes are carried out.
- Advise your insurers of any intended changes before you submit plans to other authorities.
- Ensure regular and effective liaison with the local police to inform them of ticket sales to visiting clubs and to plan each event's arrangements for segregation, searching, etc.
- Extensive pre-event checks should be carried out by competent persons of public address systems, stand-by power, fire detection systems, closed circuit television cameras, emergency communications (including battery-operated loud hailers), turnstiles and exits. Retain records of all such checks and inspections.
- There should be sufficient well-trained and equipped stewards. They should have a proper structure, with more specific training for supervisors and fire stewards, and must be properly briefed before each event. Each steward should have with them written instructions covering their individual responsibilities and how to react to emergency situations.
- Clear signage and public safety information must be set out at all key locations.
- For events which are likely to attract a capacity or near capacity crowd, it is important to designate them as 'ticket only'. Have regard to the actions of ticket touts and refer such matters to the police immediately.
- Ensure that there are sufficient trained and competent first aid staff on hand to deal with medical emergencies and to staff the first aid room(s). Communications with your medical personnel require planning and careful co-ordination. Your local council or NHS Trust ambulance service will also be required to provide resources, depending on the numbers of spectators attending.
- It is my personal opinion that you cannot have safety without security. Ensure that you have the systems and physical controls to keep trespassers and criminals (there is a difference) out of your premises. Only admit people to the stadium on

your terms and conditions. In the current climate of litigation hungry lawyers, even a trespasser can claim negligence of your company if they happen to injure themselves on property you control.

Monitoring of controls

It is a requirement of a general safety certificate issued under the Safety of Sports Grounds Act, that clubs maintain detailed records. These might refer to pre-event checks, mentioned earlier, as well as to medical treatment, incident reports from stewards or supervisors, damage to property and steward attendance numbers, etc. These records are an essential element of stadia safety. They serve to identify trends and any weaknesses in systems, training or equipment. They also might indicate that certain control measures are due for revision.

Conclusion

With the exception of a major catastrophe such as a plane crash, incidents that demand an immediate and full evacuation of the stadium are extremely unlikely. However, any minor incident may escalate very quickly to present a great deal of danger. Unless stewards (and perhaps the police – if present) act quickly and decisively, in accordance with their training and pre-arranged plans, a very serious and harmful situation could occur.

Likewise, unless due diligence and experience is exercised by everyone responsible for stadia management and spectator safety, the probability of any harmful incident occurring is greatly increased. Risk assessment, and the elimination or reduction of hazards giving rise to those risks are the best methods of keeping your event safe.

Summary

● Stadium safety managers have had to come to terms with new health and safety legislation against the background of a massive programme of stadium redevelopments.

- Risk assessment is the common thread running through the legislation.
- 'Safe' means that hazards have been identified and reported, and risks eliminated or acceptably controlled.
- Stadia are complex spaces and a whole variety of people could be at risk from a diverse range of sources. Safety managers need to comprehensively assess the risks involved in the operation of their stadium.
- A positive health and safety culture requires competence, control, co-operation and communication.
- Control of risks requires substantial management action, including safety policy, contingency planning, pre-event checks, proper staffing and security.

13 Crowd risks in sports grounds

Clive Warne

This chapter identifies from a risk assessment perspective the issues to be addressed by those responsible for crowd management in a stadium. It is a practical approach to operational planning based on a study of crowd composition, personality and anticipated behaviour. Staffing and training in crowd management are highlighted together with other considerations which challenge operational planning and decision making.

Introduction

The utmost care, professionalism and finance may be invested in producing a stadium which is structurally safe, well equipped, with design features to facilitate easy crowd flows and with the means to monitor incidents that may justify a response by a management team, but this would still not overcome the need for a professional approach to crowd management, recognizing the frailties and unpredictability of human behaviour.

Experience in dealing with crowds, and particularly football crowds, enables one to anticipate and plan for almost all eventualities thereby removing the likelihood of reactive inappropriate responses. By addressing crowd management issues from a risk assessment perspective, considering foreseeable crowd behaviour and predictable crowd dynamics, it is possible in planning to eliminate, reduce or manage the risks as appropriate.

Assessing the risks in crowd management

Who is the crowd?

For many events the sale of tickets and the nature of the entertainment will determine how many and what type of persons will be attending the venue. In some cases this may restrict certain age groups or attract a particular gender or type of person. The anticipated make-up of the crowd should be a matter for thought and planning by crowd safety managers. Regardless of the event, all large crowds have basic characteristics which create risks, the identification of which should be the starting point in planning for their safety. The crowd can be expected to contain a mix of the following types.

Young/elderly

At all events children from babes in arms can be expected amongst the crowd. Babies may be carried, but the presence of prams and pushchairs may cause other safety problems. It may be felt that it is inappropriate to bring such young children into large crowds, particularly in football stadia, but parents do occasionally insist.

It is not uncommon for people to expect very young children to be allowed free access through turnstiles, the child being passed over the turnstile without it being registered on monitoring equipment. This inaccurate counting could clearly cause problems in all-seater stadia if large numbers of children admitted this way subsequently occupy seats. It also creates a risk of confrontation and dispute for stewards to manage. The risk requires a firm policy, particularly where stadia are expected to reach capacity in any area. Turnstile staff need to know the policy to eliminate the further risk of dispute and congestion at the turnstiles.

The presence of unsupervised young children can be a considerable risk at dangerous events and a minimum age policy may be the most appropriate way to manage the risk, although this presents its own potential for disputes. Stewards should be alert to the problem of children being crushed in large crowds, particularly against barriers and on egress.

The elderly may also need special consideration when assessing crowd risks. Frail, short-sighted, hard of hearing, slow-moving people may be pushed around by a crowd and be at great risk should the need to evacuate arise. Alert stewards should be mindful of the areas of the stadium which may cause difficulties for elderly people, such as steep slopes, stairs and congested walkways.

The disabled, ill and injured people

Stadia should be equipped to cater for disabled people and, in particular, wheelchair users. However, many stadia and venues have not yet fully addressed these issues. Stewards need to be aware of the facilities that exist in order to direct people. They must also be aware of the problems that are likely to be encountered by wheelchair users and be ready to assist if necessary. Most wheelchair users are accompanied by an assistant or helper and they will need to be considered in planning. A procedure must be in place for the evacuation of wheelchair users in emergencies.

Those who are ill or may be taken ill whilst on the premises may require treatment and, therefore, suitably qualified staff should be present to respond. The occurrence is likely to attract the attention of others and staff need to be fully conversant with first aid facilities to transport the injured away quickly and avoid congestion.

Victims of accident or assault

Provision must be made for dealing with those involved in accidents and also the victims of assault. Such incidents often cause crowd reaction and may require quick and effective action. Organizers of events should ensure that staff are aware of the need to record such incidents which may lead to further investigation by other authorities.

Lost persons

A system for dealing with people reported lost and separated from others must be implemented. Staff should be fully conversant with the place identified for re-uniting people. Lost children can result in time-consuming enquiries with excessive messages over public address and radio systems. The commitment to dealing with these cases can detain or remove stewards from their primary responsibilities.

Drunks

Drunken people can cause a number of risks to others. A policy of removal and ejection must be in place where appropriate. Care must be taken where persons appear to be heavily affected by drink and where they may be unconscious. Drunkenness and illness can be confused and it may be appropriate to seek medical assistance. Drunkenness can result in disorder, particularly where drink is sold on the premises and, in this case, supervision of bar areas should assist in identifying potential problems.

Partisans and neutrals

In football stadia, and to some extent now in other sporting venues, a careful analysis of the expected crowd make-up is vital to the preparations and readiness to deal with potential incidents. Football has a uniqueness with its home and away crowds and a level of partisanship which often leaves little room for neutral supporters. This feature obviously becomes a most important part of the planning and assessment of risk. The number of away supporters attending may greatly influence the planning. At smaller clubs they may outnumber the home crowd and this, together with their formidable reputation, can dominate planning to the exclusion of other critical factors which are of equal concern.

Careful consideration must be given to the need to segregate home and away supporters and a firm policy must be agreed on how to deal with incidents that breach the segregation. If the segregation lines are not at natural breaks in the stadium (e.g. the end of a stand or terrace), staff may need to be deployed to enforce the segregation. Usually these decisions are made in conjunction with the local police commander. Policies will need to be in force to deal with supporters who arrive at the event with a ticket for an area of the ground which breaches the segregation arrangements. This is another potential area for confrontation between opposing supporters and between supporters and stewarding staff.

The use of intelligence in assessing risks

When assessing the foreseeable risks to safety posed by the presence of supporters, in addition to the question of segregation, the reputation and history of a particular group must be a key element. This assessment has tended to be based mainly on criminal activity, incidence of public disorder and the number of arrests made in the past. For many years intelligence has been collated about people who attend football matches. Individuals and groups have often gained notoriety from such attention and some groups have been attributed names – often coined by the media – which form the basis of a judgement by the police and crowd manager in their planning. Whilst this information could be invaluable in identifying likely trouble-makers and may contribute to the group personality discussed below, care must be taken not to be distracted by those with a vested interest in promoting these groups.

Group personality

Those experienced in football crowd management identify, in a particular club's supporters, a 'group personality'. When browsing the forthcoming fixture list and planning for the arrival of away supporters an immediate association with this 'group personality' is identified. It immediately conjures up in one's mind the level of attention and planning this group will need.

For example, it may be known that the expected visitors are to come from Manchester, Liverpool or Birmingham, etc., but experience of the individual club's spectators show that a different 'group personality' will be experienced from Manchester United and Manchester City, Liverpool and Everton, Aston Villa and Birmingham City. Take London as the finest example where the 'group personality' of Chelsea or Spurs supporters contrasts with Wimbledon or Crystal Palace. Norwich City supporters are one of a number of groups well known for being exceptionally well-behaved and friendly people.

This 'personality' may be a combination of cultural background – which can be at variance within a city depending from which side of a city a team may draw its support – and the history of the team's success. This varying personality may manifest itself by the group being known to be more aggressive in nature than others; or to be heavier drinkers of alcohol en route to the ground; or they have a record of performing various frauds at turnstiles; or 'jumping' the turnstiles. Some are known for not sitting down; or merely because they come in fancy dress; or because they sing a particular song.

The style of football played by a club and also the highest profile characters associated with the club can also influence the group personality of their supporters. One has only to compare the likely support of a team full of Vinnie Jones's (a well-known 'hard man' of football) playing a team full of Gary Linekers (a well known 'gentleman' of the sport). It is important in planning to be mindful of information about expected groups in order to make informed decisions regarding segregation and staffing levels.

Understanding the crowd – the crowd 'feel'

The unpredictability of crowd behaviour will always be a challenge to those involved in crowd management. Having identified many areas of crowd make-up and behaviour which create risk to safety and for which it is possible to plan, it is important to recognize how features of the event and stadium environment can affect individuals. Being sensitive to how the crowd 'feel' may assist in understanding their resultant behaviour. Because of the nature of football crowds, individuals within them may feel a sense of intrusion and abuse, some examples of which are outlined below.

Controlled, directed and patronized

The level of control over football supporters is in excess of any other crowd. The enforcement of segregation often means that people are not permitted to walk freely inside or outside the stadium and they may well find themselves directed as to which streets they can walk in. This control and restriction of freedom is enforced by the police and stewards often in a patronizing way, stereotyping all football supporters as potential trouble-makers.

Intimidated, threatened and frightened

The presence of aggressive and threatening supporters intimidates many people in football crowds. Some are often frightened to speak their mind or shout in favour of their own team when surrounded by such people. Supporters who find themselves in this position are very often frightened to report aggressive and threatening conduct for fear of immediate retribution. On the day they may be accompanied by a young child, or the event may be sold out leaving nowhere to move to. Season ticket holders regularly occupying the same seats may fear the likelihood of reprisals at subsequent matches.

Vulnerable and claustrophobic

Persons of less fortitude than others may feel very vulnerable in a large volatile crowd. Supporters on a first visit to such an environment may experience feelings of great vulnerability to injury and also claustrophobia in a large packed crowd, both of which are a recipe for panic.

Frustrated and angry

Many things will frustrate people in a football crowd: lack of freedom of movement; restricted viewing behind pillars; perceived bad decisions on the field; disagreement with decisions by police and stewards; football not up to expectations; persistent rain. These frustrations can boil over into anger sometimes directed at the team, the manager, the directors or even the stewards or police.

Excitable, disappointed and emotional

The most natural response to a supporter witnessing his or her team winning well is excitement and conversely a poor performance may bring great disappointment. Scenes of great emotion have been seen when teams lose by narrow margins or when a considerable prize is taken from their grasp. Penalty shoot-outs can be a particularly tense and emotive situation.

Aggravated and abused

The close proximity of supporters in football stadia ensures that verbal and physical contact between them is ongoing for the duration of the event. Supporters, therefore, have to endure the foul language and antisocial behaviour of others nearby to the point of exasperation on occasions. It is not uncommon for football supporters to be spat on and pushed around inducing anger and complaints.

The key elements of stewarding a crowd

Crowd management and control can be challenging issues and require carefully selected staff. Stewards are commonplace now in many types of crowd situation but the standards of their performance can vary considerably. Stewarding a crowd involves two basic elements of contact. First, the 'customer care' aspect, involving mainly verbal interaction, dealing with access, ticketing procedures, seating plans, toilets, refreshments, reports of lost possessions, lost children and assisting with disabled persons, etc. Second, 'safety management', which may require an element of direction and control, particularly where evacuation becomes a necessity. Where action requires a firm and positive approach, and particularly where ejection or intervention in fighting may be required, the contact may go beyond verbal interaction with physical contact unavoidable. Such action clearly requires a very responsible attitude towards training and supervision, and also an awareness of the legal implications.

Training stewards for crowd management

The new national stewards training package (discussed in Chapter 15 by Steve Frosdick and John Sidney) will hopefully introduce a more standardized and consistent approach to the stewarding of crowd management operations. The selection of stewards and their training should produce staff with the following skills and attributes.

Knowledgeable and confident

Basic knowledge to deal with customer care issues will include an intimate knowledge of the stadium and its facilities; the location of the nearest toilets; disabled toilets; first aid points; refreshment outlets, and knowledge of policies relating to lost property, missing persons, etc.

From a safety perspective, stewards will need a knowledge of relevant legislation and regulations particularly where powers to take action are derived from such regulations, etc. Football stewards in particular must know the relevant ground regulations and legislation such as the Football Offences Act, 1991.

It obviously takes time to become entirely confident in one's role but, given the correct training and level of knowledge, together with good supportive management, a confident steward will quickly gain the respect and reciprocated confidence of the crowd. A football crowd will soon identify a new steward who is blatantly lacking in confidence. To place a steward in a highly visible fluorescent jacket, in the centre of a volatile football crowd, when he or she is not fully equipped can be a traumatic experience and managers should take great care not to put anyone into this position.

Awareness and alertness

An awareness of important features of the stadium which may cause crowd management problems is essential. Anticipating areas of possible congestion on steep steps, pinch points on walkways, in the vicinity of toilets and refreshment facilities or any problems caused by extreme weather conditions gives the opportunity for proactive response.

Additionally, an awareness of the crowd make-up and any information on crowd personality as described above and where lines of segregation are planned will assist stewards in prioritizing their attention. Conscientiously maintaining a high level of awareness of their surroundings and activity around them will deter would be trouble makers and reduce the likelihood of being surprised by an incident.

Concentration over a long period of time is difficult in any circumstances but being forever alert is a basic requirement for safety in crowd management. Selecting staff who can show that they do not have a vested interest in the entertainment must be the starting point for ensuring they concentrate their attention on crowd safety matters. The high level of alertness required in staff cannot be overstated. An assumption by a steward that someone is merely coughing in the crowd may overlook the fact that the person may be choking or experiencing a serious angina attack, or worse – someone may have their hands around their throat.

Decisiveness and assertiveness

To be decisive in the face of developing crowd disorder or where there is potential for a serious incident may be crucial to the outcome. However, this may take considerable moral courage on the part of the steward. Having taken the courageous step of making a decision to act he or she will need the tenacity to see the decision through. Staff will need considerable reassurance that they are trusted to make decisions and supportive management must encourage staff in a constructive manner. Where stewards do not have the ability or are not empowered to deal with trivial matters they will refer issues to managers, thus delaying the decision-making process and impeding the operation. Once again staff training and a thorough knowledge of policies will assist those in contact with the crowd in making their own decisions.

There will be times when a steward will need to be assertive and a high level of confidence will be required to impose one's will successfully on a difficult crowd. It is important that stewards are aware of the distinction between assertiveness and aggressiveness. The latter is more likely to incite aggression in the crowd. The most common comparison is where a steward may have cause to advise a spectator – 'Will you please sit in your seat and stop swearing'. The alternative – 'Sit down and shut up' – invariably produces an equally aggressive response.

Whilst staff blessed with the skills listed above will perform to a satisfactory level they will be even more effective if they possess the following qualities which are particularly desirable when dealing with a demanding and challenging football crowd.

Tolerance and discretion

Staff chosen to manage crowds often need to show a very high level of tolerance. Emotions emanating from reactions to the entertainment may often be directed at stewarding staff, recognizable as authority. Stewards at football matches are often expected to tolerate all manner of comment and abuse. For this reason they should be carefully selected as persons with a capacity to cope with this pressure.

The need for managers to identify what will and will not be tolerated in all aspects of the operation, should be part of the pre-planning. Wherever possible this should be incorporated into policies so that all staff can exercise the same levels of tolerance in respect of certain behavioural patterns. The smooth running of an event can hinge entirely on this delicate concept.

In many events today a policy decision is taken to search those entering premises. The reason for search may be a security measure or based on safety, in which case possession of potential missiles or weapons clearly would not be tolerated. This is always a sensitive issue to implement since almost any article could be a potential weapon. Admitting people carrying flag poles into football stadia is always a difficult issue since their principle function is merely to support a flag. This item alone was the subject of considerable discussion in the planning stage of the Euro '96 competition. Searchers need to know what is acceptable so as to be consistent in their approach and clear guidance for spectators is also helpful in avoiding the possible risk of dispute and confrontation.

At football matches certain crowd conduct is tolerated in a way it would not be at other venues. People leaping to their feet and shouting out is tolerated. The use of obscene language, whilst not acceptable in a public place, often has to be ignored in a football stadium unless its use is persistent or to the annoyance of others. To attempt to take action against all offenders would clearly be an impossible task.

To be really effective, staff need to know what will be tolerated and ideally the crowd should know too. Policies agreed in advance can be published on notices or in programmes but the question of degree may still cause uncertainty for the staff and crowd. In these circumstances staff may need to use their discretion. It has already been said that staff should be encouraged to make decisions and the use of discretion is consistent with this. Experienced staff may use their discretion soundly and consistently but the risk is that decisions may be made arbitrarily or capriciously and the resultant inconsistency becomes an issue for confrontation or a breach of security.

Given all the skills so far identified, staff will still only feel confident in using their discretion when a supportive management structure encourages them to do so with the reassurance that decisions taken by them become a corporate responsibility except in the case of blatant negligence.

Tact and diplomacy

It has been identified that large crowds of people can be difficult to handle and, particularly in the case of some football crowds, can present challenges that test all the skills a steward may possess. Stewards working in crowd management operations need to quickly learn when to speak and when not; which comments cause the biggest adverse reactions; and when it is advisable either to act or to withdraw.

The considerable mix of a large crowd at a stadium can in itself lead to confrontation. Differing levels of acceptable behaviour generate complaints to staff seeking resolution. Often the demand is for immediate action which calls upon all the skills and qualities that have been identified.

A classic example in 1996 highlights this need for the utmost tact in dealing with a complainant. A letter of complaint was received from a football supporter regarding the conduct of supporters sitting near her which had caused her to become very frightened. A steward was given the task of dealing with the matter at a subsequent match. He approached the offenders in their seats just before kick-off time. Confidently, he approached the group, and said loudly, 'This is an official warning. I have had a complaint about your foul language from that lady sitting over there.' His less than tactful approach resulted in many of the surrounding supporters verbally abusing the woman when the steward had gone. Her next letter of complaint was worded much more strongly.

The tendency for partisanship in staff is sometimes difficult to avoid in sporting stadia but this can manifest itself in inequitable treatment of visiting supporters. Careful selection of staff is clearly an important consideration but diplomacy in these circumstances must be encouraged throughout training.

Caring and sympathetic

Producing a team of staff who display good 'customer care' skills and a warm sympathetic approach to spectators seeking help and assistance requires a caring ethos throughout the team. This concept should underpin all training topics and be inherent in the behaviour and attitude of all managers and supervisors. The whole atmosphere of an occasion can be adversely affected by the attitude of the staff managing the crowd. An unsympathetic response to a spectator's complaint can escalate into uncomfortable confrontation.

Being proactive by recognizing and responding to spectator problems through the alertness described above will engender good relations between staff and spectator. Complaints about unhelpful stewards and lack of response by them to situations have been particularly common with football crowds. The enhanced status and authority of the steward today hopefully carries a higher level of respect and recognition of their expertise. Achieving the balance between a poor response from a low level of care and intrusion from an overzealous steward motivated to the point of overconfidence should be the target.

Contingency plans for identifiable risks

Clearly stadia should have in place contingency plans for all foreseeable major incidents with clear instructions to all staff informing them of their actions in an emergency. Having completed a full risk assessment from the crowd management perspective, there is no reason why good plans and policies should not be in place for all the anticipated contacts staff will have with the crowd. In a football crowd there is a limited number of activities posing risks, which are repeated at all stadia. Table 13.1 highlights the most common.

Having identified these risks to safety, written policies for dealing with them should be available to all stewarding staff. This will ensure a prompt, effective and consistent response. The agreed policies should be central to any training the

Table 13.1   Common crowd-related risks

Persistent obscene language	Refusing to be searched
Racial abuse	Possessing an offensive weapon
Going onto the pitch or track	Altercations or fighting
Throwing missiles	Entering the stadium while drunk
Standing on or damaging seats	Ticketing issues
Standing on stairways	Allocated seat occupied
Causing a crowd push on the terraces	Segregation issues
Urinating in public	Lost and found persons or property

Table 13.2   Example policy and practice guidelines

These guidelines are provided to assist stewarding staff in maintaining a consistent approach to dealing with spectators. It is not intended that these are rules that must be complied with, but merely guidelines. The use of discretion and common sense will always be encouraged in individual cases. It is also appreciated that because of the circumstances prevailing at the time it may not be possible to achieve the desired action.

Behaviour	Authority	Action
Use of persistent obscene language	Ground Regulations and criminal offence	Advise in first instance If persists – eject Difficulty – call police
Racial abuse	Football (Offences) Act, 1991	Automatic ejection Difficulty - call police
Standing on seats	Ground Regulations	Advise in first instance If persists – eject Difficulty - call police
Refuses search at turnstiles	Ground Regulations	Refuse admission
Person found in stadium drunk	Criminal offence	Automatic ejection Consider safety/welfare Notify police
Away supporter attempts to enter home section	Ground Regulations	If his/her presence is likely to cause problems – refuse entry Difficulty – call police
Spectator wishes to make a complaint about a club employee	Club Policy	Politely advise the person making the complainant to write to the safety officer

stewarding staff are to receive and should become predominant in their responses to any activity they may encounter.

Policies need to be reviewed regularly in the light of experiences and a structure should be in place to communicate and reflect on the effects of policy decisions. This 'checks and balances' approach is not so easily achieved where staff are contracted in for a particular event, where perhaps a lack of ownership and sense of responsibility towards the planning for safety at subsequent events is not paramount in the minds of those so employed. Similarly, stewards who work at a variety of venues may have difficulty addressing policies which may vary from another venue staging the same type of event. For example, inconsistencies exist with football clubs' policies on segregation of supporters. If it is the policy, as it is at some clubs, that segregation should be maintained at all times, and stewards are expected to take action against all away supporters who enter or attempt to enter the home section, the enforcement of the policy may cause more problems than had originally existed. This is particularly pertinent where large numbers of offenders are present, and therefore, some clubs allow discretion to the stewards. This can be very confusing to stewards who work at more than one football ground.

The above example and all other policies need to be clear to the stewards. It is now an acceptable practice to provide stewards with written instructions as to their duties. However, care must be taken to ensure that stewards are not overloaded with information and that written instructions are never a substitute for good training and adequate and effective briefing. The use of *aide-memoire* cards can be very effective in overcoming the problems identified. Policies and practice guidelines for the most common occurrences can be tabulated as a quick reference for stewards. An example of such an *aide-memoire* card is shown in Table 13.2.

Summary

- For all events scheduled to take place in stadia the risk assessment exercise should be extended to include all aspects of the crowd composition, personality and anticipated behaviour.
- Having made these assessments, foreseeable features and activities causing potential risk should be identified and plans prepared for managing them.
- Regular staff members within a stadium, involved in the implementation of the plans, accumulate a wealth of knowledge of crowd dynamics and behaviour relating to that venue. They should be encouraged to contribute to the risk assessment exercise to ensure completeness in the planning and for them a sense of ownership in the success of the operation.
- The training of staff employed on crowd management operations should provide an awareness of all aspects of the crowd make-up and the associated risks.

● Stewards should be encouraged to develop effective people skills supported by a thorough knowledge of all policies and plans for dealing with foreseeable crowd occurrences.

Acknowledgement

An earlier version of this chapter was presented at the *FC Magazine* 'Running Your Stadium' seminar which took place at Liverpool Football Club, Anfield, Liverpool on 15 February 1996.

14 Risky business

Glyn Wootton and Peter Mills

This chapter outlines the requirement for risk assessment under health and safety legislation and offers some advice to venue managers on how to carry out a risk assessment.

Introduction

In Britain, as elsewhere in the world, there has always been a plethora of legislation, regulations, codes of practice as well as regulatory and advisory bodies designed to promote public safety in buildings and at other sites where events take place. The Hillsborough stadium disaster, and the subsequent Taylor Report, has added further to these with the creation of the Football Licensing Authority, the now disbanded Football Stadium Advisory Design Council and the 1997 revision of the *Green Guide* to Safety at Sports Grounds.

Such specific measures to improve safety in our football grounds and stadia facilities, particularly in design and layout, are, of course, to be welcomed and in Britain were very necessary and long overdue. Stewarding and spectator control has, in particular, been an issue. However, it has also tended to overshadow the more fundamental obligations of the Health and Safety Regulations, 1992. These require venue managers to carry out a suitable and sufficient assessment of the risks to the health and safety of their employees to which they are exposed while they are at work, and of the risk to the health and safety of any other person arising out of or in connection with the conduct of their business. Moreover, a great deal of academic debate has arisen about the nature of risk and perceptions of risk and strategic risk management. These have tended to focus on familiar themes like stadium location, seated versus terraced spectator accommodation and hooliganism. Whilst, for the venue manager, risk is more simply determined by the parameters of legal liability as employers, occupiers and to the public at large, damage limitation and insurance costs. The death of a site worker crushed between a lorry and a fork-lift truck at a concert by the pop group Oasis in Scotland in 1996 is one example too many of the importance of this legislation and the emphasis it places on risk management. Yet risk assessment is a part of venue management of which many operators have little understanding and for which they have received little guidance.

All venues will, or should have, procedures in place for controlling health and safety, for example evacuation and emergency procedures. However, the conducting of a formal and documented risk assessment in respect of every aspect of the venue operation will probably be new to many venue managers. It will also test the adequacy of the arrangements that are already in place.

There is no one best way to conduct a risk assessment, although a step-by-step approach will ensure that the principal hazards are fully assessed and that action is taken for safety improvement. The risk assessment should cover every area where there is a danger of health and an identifiable hazard whether arising from work activities or from other factors.

It is sensible for the assessor to concentrate primarily on the hazards with the most serious consequences and trivial risks can normally be ignored, unless there is a possibility that they could be compounded, or they are significant to a particular work activity. However, a comprehensive review of all potential hazards should be undertaken as even minor injuries may be repetitive, troublesome, costly and avoidable.

The risk assessment process

The risk assessment process has three key stages:

1 Identify hazards

Identify hazards associated with the activities that take place in the conduct of the venue's business which includes normal day-to-day work activities, setting up for an event, the event itself and breaking down afterwards. A hazard is something that has the potential to cause harm and is always there, for example a staircase, separating element (fences, parapets, etc.), turf-cutting equipment, athletic equipment, etc.

2   Evaluate the risks

Evaluate the risks from the hazards, taking account of the existing precautions. A risk is the likelihood that the harm a particular hazard can cause will be realized. For example, weed-killing chemicals can be extremely hazardous, but as long as the chemical remains inside a sealed and suitable container and only accessible to authorized personnel qualified in its use, the actual risk remains low. The risk will, however, increase if it is used by ground staff.

To help the assessor prioritize at both the assessment and action plan stages, a simple grading system can be used for hazards, the likelihood of occurrence and the resultant risk. In one system hazards are given a 'potential severity rating' (PSR) which may range from 'negligible injury' to 'catastrophic fatalities'. For example, turf-cutting equipment may, at worst, cause a fatality to the operator and would have a PSR of, say, four, whilst the collapse of a stand could result in catastrophic fatalities, which would have a PSR of six. To assess the PSR value, the assessor must also take into consideration the effects of hazards which may range from cuts and abrasions and broken bones to unconsciousness and asphyxia.

The likelihood of occurrence will depend on two factors. First, the cause of injury, such as tripping, structural or component failure, installation fault, equipment, bad design or layout, user error and so on; and second, on the arrangements in place to control the hazard, such as regular maintenance checks, the existence of completion and inspection certificates, written operating procedures, staff training records, signs, etc. The findings can then be graded on the assessment of the hazard being realized. This is called the 'probable likelihood rating' (PLR) and may range from 'highly improbable' to 'almost a certainty'.

By multiplying the PSR by the PLR for each of the various hazards an overall, or 'risk rating number' (RRN) is obtained. The higher the number, the greater the priority and urgency for action.

3   Report the findings

Produce a report of the findings and an action plan for risk reduction. The regulations require that significant findings are recorded and that those persons affected are identified and informed. The report should contain as a minimum, the significant hazards identified, reference to the control measures in place, identification of those persons affected and a prioritized list of findings. Any serious findings (i.e. those with a relatively high RRN) should be addressed immediately without waiting for production of the report.

At this stage, two further variables should be considered, i.e. the number of people affected and the frequency of occurrence. Although, rather than introduce complicated mathematical formulae, the venue manager should incorporate these when prioritizing the findings. In practice, even in the most conscientious of operations and well-designed venues there will be risks present and all venue managers should have an action plan for reducing the risks by improved control of hazards. Some will say that a de facto risk assessment is done on a daily basis and that good mangers will recognize potential problems in advance. However, apart from the fact that the 1992 Regulations require the risk assessment to be documented, for venue managers to successfully plan, organize, control, monitor and review the health and safety of those affected by their operations, a documented risk assessment provides important information. It is also the first line of defence in damage limitation when a legal action is brought against the venue.

Choosing an assessor

The person responsible for undertaking the risk assessment must be deemed 'competent'. In general, this means that the assessor must have a knowledge and understanding of the work activities and the operating of the venue as well as current health and safety applications. The assessor must be able to apply this in the assessment of the risks and in designing, developing, communicating and implementing the action plan. Competence does not necessarily depend on the possession of particular skills or qualifications. The assessor should be aware of key pieces of legislation and regulations, such as those in respect of the handling of hazardous chemicals, the design and erection of temporary structures, electrical safety, control of explosives for pyrotechnic displays, lighting and special effects, the use of protective equipment, display screen equipment, manual handling, etc. The assessor must also be aware of relevant codes of practice, standards of qualifications and competencies for the activities being examined. A working knowledge of the industry is not essential and, whilst helpful, as long as the assessor has a reasonable combination of skills, they will be credible and more likely to investigate in depth and have their findings accepted.

Having decided on who is going to do the risk assessment, there are some basic parameters and practical issues to observe in carrying it out.

1 Prepare thoroughly

Prepare thoroughly for the risk assessment. This stage will include a desk audit of existing safety documentation and procedures. The desk audit will reveal any obvious weaknesses against good practice or areas for further investigation.

2 Area by area or activity by activity

The most practical way to progress is on an area by area, or activity by activity basis. However, before this, there are a number of general issues that need to be addressed such as emergencies, co-operation with others on site and subcontractors, first aid arrangements, electrical safety, etc. The assessor does not need to be an expert in all of these but needs to assess the adequacy of the measures in place to control the hazards. For example, the assessor does not need to be an installer of temporary seating to check that a seating contractor has measures in place to control the hazard of the seating structure collapsing.

3 Address each site or work activity individually

There is a temptation to generalize. No two venues are the same. Whilst there will be common elements, it is important for the assessor to examine each operation individually and on its merits.

4 Be objective and factual

Objectivity when conducting the assessment can be very difficult to maintain as there will always be a certain amount of judgement based on experience.

5 Understand the service or product

The assessor who has a professional or working knowledge of the activity being audited is more likely to investigate deeper. Whilst not essential, the ability to understand the nature of the site and its operation can often provide a more comprehensive report and action plan.

6   *Independent assessment?*

There is benefit in the assessor being independent of the operation being audited, as a fresh pair of eyes often sees things taken for granted or overlooked. It is not, however, essential to be independent, as long as the assessor remains objective and looks at the operation objectively. If the assessor is independent, a knowledgeable site-based guide should accompany the assessor to provide information and ensure co-operation.

7   *Concentrate on significant risks*

Deciding on what is significant is difficult. However, the assessor must beware of wasting time and effort through relentlessly looking at hazards. Even if a problem is found, after much investigation, the severity of the consequences may be minor. The use of potential severity ratings (PSRs) will assist the assessor.

8   *Plan and time the audit*

As part of the preparation stage, put together an outline plan with times, detailing who you want to speak to; where you want to be, and the sort of questions you want to ask. A timetable will help pace an audit and prevent over-run. Timetables and audit plans should not be adhered to rigidly, especially if a particular key issue comes to light and needs to be investigated further. Audit Plans do provide a useful guide for the assessor and can increase the efficiency of the assessment. For example, the assessor may want to ask one person six questions on unrelated issues from six parts of the assessment. Advance planning means that those questions can be grouped onto one piece of paper and covered in one meeting rather than six.

9   *Record findings as you go*

It is dangerous to trust to memory the findings; make clear notes in enough detail to be able to translate the findings into the report. To not report a finding simply because the notes were not clear may miss an opportunity for risk reduction.

10   *Sufficient depth of investigation*

Ensure the assessment goes into sufficient depth to give confidence that a true picture has been obtained. Do not stop the assessment until you feel you have sufficient information on the adequacy of arrangements in place to control the hazards. A common problem is how much of the documented evidence needs to be read. As the assessor you must satisfy yourself that you have a realistic picture of actual practice and the adequacy of arrangements in place. For example, a Control of Substances Hazardous to Health (COSHH) assessment with individual assessment sheets for chemicals may be available. This can be tested by checking a sample of, say, three chemicals in store to see if assessment sheets are available. However, it is most important that the assessor does not rely on the procedures and documents alone, but observes what is actually happening by being on site. Where it is appropriate, the assessor may also need to investigate further on particular issues within an area, activity or by staff grouping, for example, control of display screen equipment in administration offices, or control of personal protective equipment by grounds personnel.

11   *The report*

Ensure that the report is thorough and supported by factual evidence. There is no model method for preparing the report but it should be clear with priorities for action easily discernible. Generally, a RRN of over a certain value should be prioritized for action with some risks needing to be addressed promptly if not isolated and remedial action taken immediately.

It is also important to emphasize that risk assessment is not a one-off, nor does it constitute a full health and safety audit, which would include analysing safety policy, safety organization, etc. The risk assessment process is simply a management tool to identify and help control hazards.

Venue operations may in essence change very little, but personnel and procedures may. The process should, therefore, be repeated at least every two years as part of the routine management process or sooner, if circumstances change, because problems may be developing or the risk assessment may in some way no longer be valid.

Summary

- Notwithstanding the many other legal requirements, health and safety regulations require a suitable and sufficient assessment of the risks to staff and others who may be affected by a venue operation.
- There are three key stages to a risk assessment:

  (i) identifying the hazards;
  (ii) evaluating the risks; and
  (iii) producing a written report and action plan.

- The risk assessment must be undertaken by a competent person.
- There are eleven basic parameters to observe in commissioning or carrying out an assessment:

  (i) prepare thoroughly;
  (ii) make progress area by area, or activity by activity;
  (iii) address each site or work activity individually;
  (iv) be objective and factual;
  (v) understand the service or product being audited;
  (vi) consider using an independent assessor;
  (vii) concentrate on significant risks;
  (viii) plan and time the audit;
  (ix) record findings as you go
  (x) ensure the assessment goes into sufficient depth; and
  (xi) ensure that the report is thorough and supported by factual evidence.

- The risk assessment should be repeated at least every two years, or sooner, if circumstances change.

Acknowledgement

This chapter was previously published as Wootton, G. and Mills, P. (1996). Don't Take Chances. *Panstadia International Quarterly Report*, **3**(4), 24–26.

15 The evolution of safety management and stewarding at football grounds

Steve Frosdick and John Sidney

This chapter traces the development of safety management and stewarding at football grounds since the Hillsborough disaster in 1989. It shows how football has become a highly regulated activity. It outlines the lower profile role of the police. It goes on to describe the evolution of the football safety management profession and to highlight the role of the Football Safety Officers' Association. It then provides an overview of higher profile stewarding and introduces the football authorities' training package for stewarding at football grounds. Finally, the chapter refers to the advances made in safety facilities and equipment.

Introduction

Throughout the 1970s and 1980s, football match days often resembled military operations. In terms of crowd management, the emphasis was firmly on public order. Huge numbers of police were employed on tactics which achieved control, but at the expense of safety and comfort. This repressive policing style was generally coupled with hard engineering measures such as the high fences still seen in most continental stadia. And the grounds themselves were generally old, poorly maintained and with minimal facilities for the spectator.

The 1989 Hillsborough disaster and the subsequent inquiry by Lord Justice Taylor [1] have been widely recognized as the catalyst for major change in the

British stadia industry. Much of the subsequent publicity concerning the standard of British stadia has focused on the new and refurbished structures and the facilities provided within them. But the actual fabric of the stadium is only half the story. Equally important is the safety culture within the club and the quality of its safety management systems. Even the most modern ground could still be unsafe if the club cannot properly manage the safety of its paying customers.

The changes in stadium structures and facilities have been highly visible, but other less visible although equally important changes in safety management have also been taking place. So what have the principal changes been and what benefits have they brought to spectator safety?

The regulation of football

Football has undoubtedly become one of the most regulated activities there is. Local authorities are responsible for issuing the safety certificate specifying the stadium capacity and the conditions to be met before spectators are admitted, including the appointment of a safety officer and the provision of adequate stewarding. These certifying authorities, encouraged by the Football Licensing Authority (FLA), have become more rigorous in their safety certification and inspection procedures. Many have chosen to follow the modular certificate structure recommended by the FLA [2], although the contents have properly remained a matter for local determination. This has helped to ensure a balance between standardization and taking account of differing local circumstances. The FLA have matured in their role through the issuing of licences to permit the club to admit spectators to the stadium, the monitoring of certifying authorities, the provision of advice and the carrying out of inspection visits. The Football Association (FA), FA Premier League and Football League have their own advisers who frequently visit grounds. Certifying Authority staff often carry out their own inspections, both on match days and at other times, whilst police, fire and ambulance services personnel are regularly in attendance at some matches.

Furthermore, as Chapter 9 on the British stadia safety industry shows, a large number of different government agencies and other bodies have developed their own detailed guidance on managing aspects of public safety at sports grounds. The range of advice and recommendations is complex and clearly illustrates the growing importance of the subject.

Each Certifying Authority also chairs a multi-agency Advisory Group which meets periodically to discuss relevant safety issues. This allows for regular dialogue between the many agencies involved and facilitates improved operational co-operation. There has been a growing realization that the different agencies need to work in partnership in preparing their respective systems and procedures, such as contingency plans. Chapter 5 by Alan Beckley refers to the need for contingency plans to be prepared on a multi-agency basis, and at many grounds, it has indeed been possible for the various agencies to agree joint contingency plans to deal with emergency situations. Many of these groups also include a supporters' representative, ensuring that the fans' voice is also heard. This is important, because the supporters are often concerned to ensure that their enjoyment is not spoiled either by being commercially exploited by the club or by being subject to excessive restrictions by the police and stewards.

Lower profile policing

In the view of the Home Affairs Committee of the House of Commons and many others, higher profile stewarding supported by lower profile policing represented the way forward for the 1990s [3]. And the police have sought to reduce their involvement in policing public events including football matches. This has arisen for reasons of both policy [4] and costs [5], arising from concerns about the extent of their own liability, burgeoning demands for their services and increasing pressure on the public purse. Following the Taylor recommendation [6], each club agreed a statement of intent with the local police, setting out their respective responsibilities for safety management. The general responsibility for safety began to be assumed by the club whilst the police role shifted to concentrate on crime, public order and emergency management.

As the police refocused on public order, so their intelligence systems for dealing with hooliganism became more sophisticated. The police appointed liaison officers for each club, creating a national network of local intelligence officers, co-ordinated by the Football Unit of the National Criminal Intelligence Service. Prior to any match, the liaison officer could call for an intelligence report, including full details and photographs of known trouble-makers, to assist in assessing the likely risk of disorder. This intelligence system was reinforced by the attendance of police 'spotters' representing the away club at appropriate matches.

Football safety officers

The revised police role was reinforced by the authorities repeatedly pointing out that the responsibility for the safety of spectators lay with the Chairman and Directors of the club concerned [7]. Football clubs began to recognize their legal and moral responsibilities for ensuring the safety of their customers and also to seek to reduce the escalating costs of special services of police.

These trends created the need for the appointment of club safety officers who would take operational responsibility for safety management. Initially, some of these appointments were on a part-time basis involving responsibility only for the match day operation and pre- and post-match inspections. But the majority of clubs began to realize that it was not possible to create an artificial distinction between crowd safety on match day and the health and safety of players, club staff and the public both on match day and throughout the week. Thus more and more safety officers became appointed as full-time safety professionals with a wide portfolio of responsibility.

The Football Safety Officers' Association

In the flurry of activity following the Taylor Reports, concerns were raised by both the football authorities and the practitioners themselves that standards of safety performance varied so greatly from ground to ground. Systems and practices had been evolving locally in a piecemeal and ad hoc fashion and there was very little uniformity. Spectators travelling away from home did not know whether they would be treated as an invading army, as valued customers or something in between the two. The Football Safety Officers' Association (FSOA) was inaugurated on 29 October 1992 with the aims of improving safety at football grounds, promulgating best practice, enhancing the role of stewards and continually developing safety officers' expertise.

Full membership of the Association is open to safety officers and their deputies at grounds in the FA Premier and Football Leagues, whilst associate membership is open to any suitable person associated with the responsibility for safety at sports grounds. From an initial gathering of 28, the FSOA has grown into an organization of over 130 members. By October 1996, all professional football clubs except five were represented, together with representatives of the football authorities, several certifying authorities, stewarding companies, major Scottish football clubs, rugby league clubs, consultants and academics.

As its membership has grown, so the Association has become involved in a wider range of activities and become a more influential player in the stadia industry. It holds two national conferences each year at which members can debate safety issues and exchange good practice. These conferences are supplemented by regional meetings which allow for discussion of more local concerns. The FSOA is represented on the Advisory Group Against Racism and Intimidation (AGARI) and receives regular enquiries from companies wishing to promote their goods and services within the stadia industry. Finally, the Association has been extensively involved in working with the football authorities to improve the quality of stewarding at football grounds.

Higher profile stewarding

Great strides have been taken towards the vision of higher profile stewarding supported by lower profile policing. The numbers of police officers deployed at football matches has fallen considerably. At Nottingham Forest, for example, a typical match in 1989 saw over 150 police officers inside the ground, supported by about 75 stewards. Compare this with the 1995 to 1996 season, when most Forest matches were policed by 250 or more stewards, supported by just 22 police officers. Several other clubs, including some in the Premiership, have managed to police selected matches with no police whatsoever in the ground. This role reversal has been driven by three key factors. As well as the concern about wide variation in standards, there was a strong desire within the industry to demonstrate the ability to self-regulate rather than be dictated to. There was also a need to achieve good quality training with value for money.

But what has actually been done to bring about such change? In response to the concerns raised, the Football League published their own stewarding guidelines in July 1991 [8]. This guide, supported by a video, included five outline training modules and provided a useful first set of recommendations for the industry. Subsequent changes, including stadium redevelopments, policing policy, reduced Football Trust grant aid for stewarding, as well as the formation of the FSOA, resulted in a meeting in October 1993, at which a working party was set up to update the Football League publication. As a result of that work, a set of comprehensive guidelines on stewarding and safety management were published by the football authorities early in 1995 [9]. The guidelines recommended six modules for stewards training and set out the aims and objectives of each module, together with the performance criteria the training was intended to achieve. The six modules were:

- General Responsibilities;
- Maintenance of a Safe Environment;
- Response to Spectators;
- Emergency Aid;
- Basic Fire Safety Awareness; and
- Contingency and Evacuation Plan Training.

The six modules provided an excellent framework around which safety officers were able to build their local club training programmes. But there was a will among both practitioners and the authorities to take things a step further. At the FSOA annual general meeting, in March 1995, a second working party was formed with the brief to develop a package of training materials to flesh out the bones of the six modules. This venture was now a partnership involving the Football League, the Football Association, the FA Premier League and the Football Safety Officers' Association, and was undertaken in consultation with the Football Licensing Authority.

The working party received a presentation on the Level 2 National Vocational Qualification (NVQ) in spectator control, which was being piloted at Leeds United, Bradford City, Cambridge United and Scunthorpe United, and which is referred to by Alan Beckley in Chapter 5 on liability issues. After deliberation, the working party felt the NVQ would be too expensive for clubs and also unpopular with many stewards. It was therefore decided to develop a training package using in-house expertise and the idea of a multimedia, computerized package quickly won support. After presentations from several computer companies, the working party decided the package should be prepared using Microsoft PowerPoint® electronic presentation software. This approach was endorsed by the FSOA September conference and a consultant was appointed to undertake the necessary work.

By Christmas, the working party had edited the first draft and a second draft was then circulated to the FSOA membership. The various reviewers' comments were collated and a third draft was presented to the FSOA annual general meeting in March 1996. The draft package was debated, approved and the final product commissioned. The new multimedia package [10] was launched by the Football

League President, Gordon McKeag, at a national seminar at West Bromwich Albion on 5 June 1996. The final package was demonstrated and copies were issued to the representatives of each club. The launch also included a useful session on good practice for trainers in giving presentations.

The package is made up of the six modules set out in the original framework, together with an initial familiarization session and an induction training module for newly appointed stewards. The package comes in a presentation binder and has three main components:

- computer disks containing electronic full-colour presentations;
- black and white slide masters for use in producing acetates; and
- notes pages to help the trainer.

Using the Microsoft PowerPoint® Viewer, the electronic presentations can be used in several different ways. If training a large number of stewards, trainers can hire a liquid crystal display tablet and project the presentations onto a large screen using a high intensity overhead projector. This is a very effective method and gives a very professional impression to the audience. With a smaller group, trainers can sit their stewards round an ordinary computer screen. Alternatively, stewards can be allowed to teach themselves by sitting in front of the computer and operating the presentation alone.

Trainers who have their own Microsoft PowerPoint® software can also edit the package. They can insert clipart, change the colours or rewrite some of the text. But even without a computer, trainers can still show all the slides using an ordinary overhead projector. The package includes a black and white master of every single slide. Trainers can decide which slides they want to reproduce, and simply photocopy them onto acetate.

The modules are made up of topics, each of which is covered by a notes page, containing:

- the relevant slide;
- the instructional objective;
- the suggested instructional content;
    (i) some topics, for example football legislation, are similar for all stadia and in these cases, additional slides and notes are provided for the trainer's use;
    (ii) other topics, for example standards of dress and appearance, are different for each stadium. In these cases, the content will have to be determined locally, although a suitable title slide with clipart is usually provided;

- the assessment criteria, i.e. what the steward is expected to have learned as a result of receiving the training; and
- the suggested assessment method(s).

The introductory modules cover a wide range of topics, including the broad framework of safety management, stadium layout, legislation, ground regulations, stewards' duties and conduct. The next module deals with crowd behaviour, crowd control, stadium safety features and equipment. The following module addresses spectator breaches of safety as well as general customer care issues. The next two modules provide the basic knowledge needed to cope with a medical or fire situation pending the arrival of the emergency services, whilst the final module covers contingency plans, safe evacuation and the accompanying practical exercises. The full list of topics covered in the six principal modules is shown in Table 15.1.

The football authorities recognize that it will take some time for all stewards to be fully trained and it is certainly not intended that all stewards should be trained in every aspect of the package before they are deployed. The timescales recommended are as follows:

- before any deployment whatsoever – an initial familiarization session;
- a minimum of four matches in company with a qualified steward;
- before being allowed to work alone – induction training module;
- within twelve months of Induction Training – completion of all six modules, designation as a qualified steward and award of a certificate;
- within three years – completion of all six modules by existing qualified stewards.

The football authorities have recommended the package as a best practice training aid which represents the minimum requirement for the training of stewards at football grounds. The package is a resource on which trainers should be able to draw in preparing their own courses. They do not have to follow it letter for letter. If they already have their own way of meeting a topic objective, they are free to carry on using it. But most trainers seem to be happy to use the slides and notes pages as the basis for their training delivery.

Facilities and equipment

These many changes in management practice have been supported by widespread investment in modern safety facilities and equipment. Reflecting the growing trend

Table 15.1   Training package modules and topics

Module	Topics
Module One – General Responsibilities	Background History
	Organizations Involved in Safety
	Safety Certificate
	Club Safety Policy
	Statement of Intent
	Safety Management Structure
	Layout of Stadium
	Ground Regulations
	Legislation
	Health and Safety
	Standards of Conduct
	General Duties
	Specific Duties
Module Two – Maintenance of a Safe Environment	Crowd Behaviour
	Crowds - The Three Ds
	Principles of Crowd Control
	Ground Safety Features
	Responding to Crowd Incidents
	Communication Skills
	Safety Equipment
Module Three – Response to Spectators	Safety Issues
	Football offences
	Offences against ground regulations
	Unsociable behaviour
	Customer Care Issues
	Giving directions to seats and facilities
	Dealing with problems
	Treating people equally
Module Four – Emergency Aid	Approaching a Casualty Incident
	Priorities of First Aid
	Responsiveness and Breathing
	Resuscitation
	Some Common Emergencies

(continued)

Table 15.1   Training package modules and topics (*cont.*)

Module	Topics
Module Five – Basic Fire Safety Awareness	Hazard Assessment
	The Fire Triangle
	Fire
	Initial Response
	Fire Fighting Equipment
	Stadium Features
Module Six – Contingency and Evacuation Plan Training	Background
	Contingency Plans
	Coded Messages
	Safe Evacuation
	Evacuation Routes
	Crowd Behaviour in a Crisis
	Access Routes and Rendezvous Points
	Traffic Control
	Practical Exercises

towards multi-agency partnership, many of the newly built control rooms have included sufficient space and equipment for all the agencies involved in the operation. This has allowed for rapid consultation and co-ordination in emergency situations, allowing crises to be resolved at an early stage. The safety operation has been enhanced by the employment of technological life safety systems for access control, communications, emergency warnings, means of escape and surveillance monitoring. Under this latter heading, the installation of modern closed circuit television (CCTV) systems is widely regarded as a key advance in allowing both for crowd safety monitoring and the identification of individuals engaged in criminal behaviour. And many grounds now have properly equipped medical centres to provide for emergency aid.

Looking forward

Whilst total safety can never be guaranteed, ensuring public safety means reducing the risks as far as reasonably is practicable. The major advances made in safety management and stewarding at football grounds demonstrate the industry's commitment to dealing effectively and professionally with the many complex safety hazards involved in stadium management.

But notwithstanding the progress made since Hillsborough, there is much that remains to be done. Stewards' training is becoming more professional, but this is only the first rung of the training ladder. There is ongoing debate about training the trainers, assessment, the training of supervisors, and the professional qualifications of the safety officers themselves.

The drive to lower profile policing seems set to continue. The 1996 Home Office Review of Police Core and Ancillary Tasks proposed that, 'stewards could make a greater contribution to the policing of public events (such as football matches and pop concerts) and be more adequately trained for the purpose [and that] organizers could assume fuller responsibility for the safety and behaviour of spectators and participants' [11]. It seems clear that the ongoing evolution of higher profile and more professional stewarding and safety management remains the way ahead.

Summary

- Prior to 1989, the management of football matches was driven by public order concerns. Control was maintained at the expense of safety and comfort.
- The Hillsborough disaster was the catalyst for radical change.
- Changes in stadium structures and facilities have been highly visible, but other less visible changes in safety management have also taken place.
- Football has become one of the most highly regulated activities there is, with systems for licensing, safety certification, inspection and multi-agency dialogue.
- The police have adopted a lower profile, concentrating on intelligence gathering, crime, public order and emergency management.
- A profession of full-time football safety officers has emerged to take operational responsibility for stadium safety management.
- The Football Safety Officers' Association (FSOA), inaugurated in 1992, has evolved into a increasingly substantial and influential organization.
- Considerable progress has been made towards the vision of higher profile stewarding supported by lower profile policing.
- The training of stewards has evolved considerably. The English football authorities and FSOA worked together to produce a sophisticated multimedia training package for stewarding at football grounds.

- This modular training package was launched in June 1996 and is recommended by the football authorities as a best practice training aid which represents the minimum requirement for football stewards training.
- Changes in management practice have been supported by widespread investment in modern safety facilities and equipment.
- Notwithstanding the advances made since Hillsborough, there is much that remains to be done.

Acknowledgement

This chapter is derived from the authors' previous articles published in *Football Decision* (1996), **2**, July, 48–51 and *Football Management* (1996), **4**(3), Summer, 26.

References

[1] *The Hillsborough Stadium Disaster 15 April 1989 – Inquiry by the Rt Hon Lord Justice Taylor – Final Report* (Taylor Report, 1990). HMSO.
[2] Football Licensing Authority (1992). *Guidance on Safety Certificates.*
[3] House of Commons Home Affairs Committee (1991). *Policing Football Hooliganism*, Vol. 1: *Report together with the Proceedings of the Committee*, p. xxv. HMSO.
[4] Wilmot, D. (1993). *Policing Football Matches*. Greater Manchester Police.
[5] Home Office (1991). *Charges for Policing Football Matches* (Home Office Circular 36/1991).
[6] Op. cit. 1. pp. 37–38.
[7] See Steve Frosdick's discussion of responsibility for safety in Chapter 3 on risk as blame.
[8] The Football League (1991). *Safety at Sports Grounds – a Guide to the Appointment, Training and Duties of Football League Club Stewards.*
[9] The Football League, the Football Association, the FA Premier League (1995). *Stewarding and Safety Management at Football Grounds.*
[10] The Football League, the Football Association, the FA Premier League and the Football Safety Officers' Association (1996). *Training Package for Stewarding at Football Grounds*. Staffordshire University.
[11] Home Office (1996). *Review of Police Core and Ancillary Tasks*, p. 15. HMSO.

16 Playing away in Europe

Steve Frosdick, Mike Holford and John Sidney

This chapter presents a case study of Nottingham Forest Football Club's safety management experiences during the 1995–96 Union of European Football Associations (UEFA) Cup competition. The case study is derived from the authors' personal experiences, notes and reports prepared in their respective capacities as an academic observer, the club safety and security consultant and the club deputy safety officer.

Introduction

During the 1995–96 football season, Nottingham Forest Football Club took part in the Union of European Football Associations (UEFA) Cup competition. Details of the eight fixtures played are included in Table 16.1. This shows that, over the four away matches, some 7200 Forest fans travelled to watch their team playing away in Sweden, France and Germany.

The very high level of sensitivity involved in foreign travel by English football supporters has particularly arisen since the Heysel stadium disaster at the European Cup Final between Juventus and Liverpool in Belgium in 1985. Thirty-eight Italian fans were killed by a wall collapse and a number of Liverpool supporters were later convicted of manslaughter. The Heysel disaster was a national disgrace and English clubs were withdrawn from any European competition for several seasons. Security at matches abroad is thus not only a matter of safety but also of national prestige. Football clubs playing away in Europe carry a heavy burden of responsibility.

There are several official publications setting out the safety and security requirements of the various authorities involved in the regulation of European football competitions [1–4]. Whilst these prescribe what a club must do, there is very little in the way of documented advice or best practice for any club preparing its

Table 16.1   Nottingham Forest in Europe: 1995–96

Date	Fixture	Result	Crowd	Away fans
12/09/95	Malmo v Nottingham Forest	2–1	12 486	700
26/09/95	Nottingham Forest v Malmo	1–0	23 817	372
17/10/95	Auxerre v Nottingham Forest	1–0	18 900	1500
31/10/95	Nottingham Forest v Auxerre	0–0	28 064	30
21/11/95	Nottingham Forest v Olympique Lyonnais	1–0	22 141	1000
05/12/95	Olympique Lyonnais v Nottingham Forest	0–0	31 000	1000
05/03/96	Bayern Munich v Nottingham Forest	2–1	38 000	4000
19/03/96	Nottingham Forest v Bayern Munich	1–5	28 844	2228

Note: the crowd numbers and number of Forest fans at the away matches are the best available estimates. The figures for Forest's home matches are derived from an electronic turnstile monitoring system.

safety and security arrangements for a European fixture, either at home or away. Our purpose, then, in presenting this case study, is not only to inform the student or general reader but also to provide practitioners with a source of reference which we hope may be of help to them as they plan and carry out their own arrangements.

Pre-planning

Towards the end of the 1994–95 season, Nottingham Forest were doing very well in the FA Premier League and seemed to have a good chance of qualifying for a UEFA Cup place. At that stage, therefore, it seemed appropriate to begin discussing what would need to be done and to identify the people from whom useful advice might be obtained.

In the event, the club came third in the League and did indeed qualify. UEFA Cup matches are played over two legs and so Forest and its supporters were guaranteed at least one away match even if they were knocked out in the first round. The club now put into effect those elements of the pre-planning that could be undertaken prior to the draw being made and the first round opponents known. Early contact was made with safety management colleagues at three clubs with recent experience of European competition. One of the clubs, Arsenal, were shortly due to play in the Cup Winners' Cup Final in Paris and the safety officer was kind enough to offer an opportunity for observers to attend the match. All of the clubs offered advice and provided copies of useful documents such as travel planning, notes of meetings and post-match reports.

The local police Football Liaison Officer was consulted and provided a list of the police requirements. The local Police Ground Commander was also contacted and invited to attend all the planning meetings, inspection visits and matches, home and away. A meeting was held with the crowd management personnel at the Football Association to discuss their requirements and, as a matter of courtesy, contact was made with the local Football Licensing Authority Inspector.

As a result of the various regulatory requirements and the advice received from colleagues, a number of policy decisions were taken:

- the club would strictly comply with the UEFA regulations;
- official away travel arrangements would be the club's responsibility;
- one travel agent would be appointed to manage all the official away travel arrangements;
- a full list of all fans travelling on official away packages would be compiled;
- official away travel would be supervised by club stewards;
- all ticketing arrangements would be the club's responsibility;
- the club was (probably) not entitled, on grounds of restraint of trade, to refuse to sell tickets to other travel agents who wished to arrange their own travel packages; nevertheless, the club would wish to retain some influence over the activities of independent travel agents;
- Nottinghamshire Police would be invited to send 'spotters' to all away matches; and foreign police chiefs and 'spotters' would be invited to all home matches.

These decisions reflected the club's intention both to accept their responsibility for safety and security and to manage the associated accountability by having maximum possible control of the arrangements made.

Planning for the away legs

Initial meetings

The draw for each round of the competition was held in Geneva and was attended by the club chairman, secretary and commercial manager. Once the draw was made, the officers of each club were able to hold a preliminary meeting with their opposite numbers to open discussions on such matters as ticket allocation, facilities, VIPs and team arrangements. Following on from the draw, a planning meeting was held to decide on the forms of travel and the arrangements for ticket allocation to be adopted for each leg. Coach travel is popular with supporters because it is usually half the price of a flight package. But the distances involved mean it is not always practicable to provide this option.

Well in advance of each away match, the manager and coach travelled out to the away club to ensure they were satisfied with the hotel accommodation and training facilities being offered to the team. They also visited the stadium to check on the changing rooms and the condition of the pitch.

Travel arrangements

Official travel

Once the first round draw had been made, the commercial manager appointed a recommended travel agent to arrange and manage the travel packages for both the club and for the supporters who wished to travel away. The relationships between the various parties to this arrangement were quite complex and are shown in Figure 16.1. Thus for all four away matches, supporters had the choice of either coach or air travel, with a guaranteed ticket for the match.

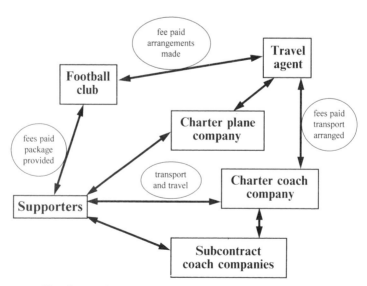

Figure 16.1   Official travel arrangements.

This model, although previously followed by other clubs, proved in our view to be unsatisfactory in practice, largely because the club had insufficient influence over the performance of the transport providers. With the benefit of hindsight, it would, have been better for the club to contract directly with the plane and coach companies and to refuse to allow any further subcontracting. The difficulties experienced resulted from both incompetence and from failures in customer care, which in turn created operational problems for the club personnel acting as couriers. These arose particularly where the coach company used self-employed drivers, who we found to be generally boorish and unco-operative. We also found the travel agents representatives reluctant to intervene when requested to resolve such difficulties.

On one trip, a subcontractor's driver ran out of diesel and, since he had no money with him, one of the club couriers had to pay for the coach to be filled up at a continental service station. On another trip, the supporters had decided their coach would be 'no smoking'. The drivers refused to comply with this, causing great discomfort to many. The same drivers forgot the key to the coach toilet and refused to stop either to try and unlock the toilet or to allow people to relieve themselves.

Approved independent travel

In previous European matches involving other clubs, there have been complaints from both supporters and travel agents that the club refused to sell tickets to anyone other than supporters travelling on the official club trip. In the light of experience from the Malmo and Auxerre matches and from advice received, Nottingham Forest became more convinced that such action was an unlawful restraint of trade and, furthermore, denied supporters the freedom to make their own choice of quality and price.

Several local tour operators and supporters clubs were offering their own coach, rail and flight packages for supporters wishing to travel independently to Forest matches abroad. For the last two rounds, Forest decided to agree to sell tickets to all those parties who could demonstrate that their arrangements for safety and security were acceptable and who agreed to sign a suitable form of undertaking with the club. A list of the club's requirements was drawn up as shown in Table 16.2. A particular requirement was the attendance of travel couriers at formal briefing sessions arranged by the club.

We contend that approved independent travel is good practice. Security arrangements can be undermined by groups of supporters who travel independently, hoping to buy their tickets abroad, or who use devious methods to try and buy

Table 16.2　Example requirements for approved independent travel

- A levy of £1 per head must be paid to the Nottingham Forest Football Club. This charge is to part subsidize the 'dummy runs' that Nottingham Forest have had to perform partly on your behalf.
- The coach company that you use must comply with all regulations that may apply in travelling abroad.
- Every person travelling must be a member of the official supporters branch and also be a season ticket holder at Nottingham Forest Football Club.
- The recognized official of the branch will attend a meeting with the deputy safety officer in order that they may be briefed on the conditions laid down by the FA and UEFA.
- Match tickets must be paid for in advance but will not be issued until every independent coach meets at a designated point.
- Each member travelling must be adequately insured and also sign a document disclaiming Nottingham Forest from all liabilities.
- Any untoward incident that may occur during the course of the trip which can be proven will result in the supporters club branch being held responsible and the branch will be expelled as a member of the supporters club.
- On booking tickets, Nottingham Forest will require a full list of passengers together with their supporters club membership number, season ticket number and passport number.
- Season ticket numbers will be checked by computer in order to establish that travellers are bona fide.
- Passports will also be checked against the manifest by the authorities, again to establish that travellers are bona fide.
- An itinerary of your proposed route and ferry crossing times should also be provided to Nottingham Forest no later than seven days prior to departure.

tickets from the foreign club. At both the first two away matches, it was quite clear that substantial numbers of 'unofficial' Forest supporters had managed to obtain access to various parts of the stadium, where they were not segregated from the home supporters and clearly posed a threat to public order, whether as assailants or as victims. We now believe that facilitating controlled independent travel reduces this risk. At both the Lyons and Munich matches, the Forest supporters appeared confined to the agreed part of the ground.

Site visit to away club

In advance of each match, a site visit was made to the away club. These visits, which were a most essential part of the planning, were made for two purposes. First, they allowed for a full inspection of the stadium and its approaches. Second, they enabled a high-level planning meeting to be held.

Inspecting the stadium and its approaches is vital. Whilst the standards of accommodation and facilities found at English grounds have advanced considerably since 1989, the same cannot be said of many continental grounds. All four away venues had a high pitch perimeter fence. These cause obstructions to sightlines and prevent or restrict emergency egress onto the pitch. The fence at Munich was so high and dense that people seated in the lower rows had virtually no view at all. Inevitably, they all stood up, forcing those behind them to stand up, and thus the whole of the Forest support ended up standing to watch the game. At Lyons, the seating consisted of breeze blocks cemented onto the terraces. The accommodation was just like a standing terrace yet there was no crush barrier provision. At both the French stadia, the toilet provision was woefully inadequate, with just one male and one female WC provided for 1000 spectators at Auxerre. At Malmo, the seats originally offered were without proper segregation facilities, and considerable negotiation was needed before satisfactory accommodation was arranged.

The arrangements for visiting supporter access to the ground are largely determined by the geography of the stadium approaches. For security reasons, it is preferable to have the coaches setting down and picking up as close to the turnstiles as possible. Inspecting the stadium approaches is an important prerequisite to negotiating access and egress arrangements with the local police.

The high-level planning meeting is also essential. The meetings were attended by the Forest club secretary and safety consultant, the Nottinghamshire police commander, a representative from the Football Association, host club officials, the local police and a representative from the British Consulate. Typical discussions covered the team's arrival and departure at the ground, arrangements for the away fans, ticketing issues, intelligence about hooligan activity and the reciprocal deployment of police 'spotters'.

The planning meeting is particularly useful in exposing shortcomings in the arrangements proposed. From experience and discussions with colleagues, it is our view that some foreign police forces' approach to risk assessment and contingency planning is quite inadequate. The police plan may well be as simple as the bare 'if there is a problem, we will deal with it'. The attitudes of some foreign clubs to ticket sales are also unhelpful. On the part of both the foreign club and the local police, there is also a tendency to renege on undertakings made at the planning meeting.

In both Malmo and Auxerre, it was clear that tickets had been sold direct to Forest supporters in contravention of the UEFA security requirements. In Auxerre, the police even insisted on supporters who had arrived without tickets being allowed to pay for cash admission to the ground, making a nonsense of Forest's careful vetting of its travelling supporters. In Malmo, it was agreed that the Forest coaches would park near to the area being used by visiting supporters. These coaches would discharge their passengers close to the turnstiles and would collect them from the same place at the end of the game. The agreement was made by a very senior police officer. On the day, the police commander turned out to be a more junior officer, who decided to make the coaches park several hundred yards away. He promised a police escort for the fans but this was never actioned. This experience highlights the importance of ensuring the actual police commander is in attendance at the planning meeting.

The site visit also allows for a video of the stadium, the viewing accommodation and the stadium approaches to be taken. The video can then be shown to supporters during their flight or coach journey. This is very helpful in familiarizing the supporters on what to expect once they arrive at the venue.

The 'dummy run'

The experience of other clubs has shown that foreign police forces can have an unhealthy view of football supporters. In 1993, for example, Norwich City fans travelling to Munich found themselves unexpectedly met at the German border by a large contingent of riot police. Norwich City fans have no reputation whatsoever for bad behaviour, yet the police insisted on escorting them straight to Munich, with no comfort or refreshment breaks allowed.

Forest were determined to avoid such problems, and therefore decided to 'dummy run' the route the official coaches would take. The 'dummy runs' were undertaken by the deputy safety officer, with representatives from the travel agent and the main coach company contracted to provide the transport. The route was selected and driven. Motorway service stations were visited and negotiations held with their management to ensure that the coaches would be welcome and suitable facilities available. Video footage was obtained so that supporters could be shown in advance where they would be stopping for meals, etc. Timings were arranged so that the coaches would arrive around lunchtime on the day of the match, allowing the supporters some sightseeing time. Locations were established where the coaches could set the fans down and park for the afternoon. Hotel accommodation was identified where day rooms could be booked to allow the courier and stewards to freshen up and make their final preparations.

All of the arrangements decided upon were then agreed with host club's local police who were requested to provide casual supervision at the agreed service stations and afternoon parking locations.

Final preparations for the away leg

Having discussed aspects of the necessary planning and liaison for the away leg, we now move into the final few days leading up the match itself. It is during this phase that final preparations such as ticket distribution and advance briefing need to be completed.

Ticket distribution

Given the club's accountability for the behaviour of its travelling supporters, Nottingham Forest were keen to ensure that away clubs complied with UEFA requirements and did not sell tickets direct to supporters. As we have indicated, the arrangements for the first two away matches did not prove satisfactory, and so the club adopted an even more assertive line for the Lyons and Munich trips.

It is a UEFA requirement that tickets for travelling fans should not be issued to them more than two hours before the match. Since experience shows that foreign police forces will often want to see that coachloads of fans are in possession of match tickets before allowing them to continue their journey unhindered, this means that tickets had to be made available to the various travel organizers in advance of the journey. Thus the ticket distribution system had to reflect the arrangements made for both official and approved independent travel. The system adopted is shown in Figure 16.2.

The tickets received from the away club were thus either held by the club for distribution via club representatives on the official coach and flight parties, or else made available to the approved independent travel organizers at an advance briefing session.

Briefing sessions

About one week before each match, a representative from each approved independent travel organization, together with the club stewards acting as couriers

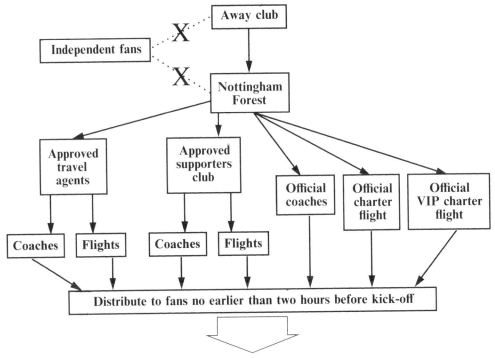

Figure 16.2   Ticket distribution system.

for official travel, attended a meeting to be briefed by the deputy safety officer on the conditions laid down by the English and European football authorities and the specifics of the forthcoming fixture. The approved independent travel representatives and the club stewards were all provided with an information package compiled by the club, including maps, notes and a message from the foreign police.

Documentation

In order to comply with UEFA requirements, match tickets can only be supplied to those supporters who provide their names, addresses, passport details and information about their travel for both the outward and return journeys and their accommodation abroad. Therefore, passenger manifests were compiled by the ticket office at the time of selling tickets and also required from other agencies organizing their own trips. These lists of travellers were passed on to the police for vetting prior to departure, and also forwarded with the travel itineraries for the information of the relevant foreign police force.

Away stewarding arrangements

The shortlist of thirty stewards chosen to act as couriers for the club on coaches and planes were carefully chosen from an initial list of over one hundred volunteers. Account was taken of their stewarding experience, supervisory qualities, availability and, above all, of their teamworking and communication skills and their ability to command the respect of the fans. The choice was more than vindicated by the excellent way in which all those chosen performed their duties and ensured little or no trouble involving the fans in their care.

On the journey

We have no personal experience of the journeys undertaken by the approved independent travel agents and supporters clubs and are therefore unable to comment on them.

Official air travel

Official charter flights were available to all four away matches, with coach transfers provided from the airport to the stadium and back. All four were arranged as day trips, typically arriving in the early afternoon and departing immediately after the match. Although one plane to Munich was delayed by a mechanical fault, all four return journeys were pleasantly free of incident.

Official coach travel

For each of the away matches, the official coach parties met at the Nottingham Forest ground. Any outstanding passenger details such as passport numbers were collected to ensure the passenger manifest was fully completed prior to departure and we got on our way. The deputy safety officer acted as the official club courier for all four trips, supported by the two stewards allocated to each coach. Over the course of the journey, the supporters in each coach were shown the video footage of the service stations, the stadium and its approaches, to help familiarize them with what was to come.

Because of restrictions imposed by the ferry companies, football supporters are only permitted to cross the channel via Dover. This can add considerably to the journey time, as we found when we needed thirty hours to travel to Sweden via Calais for the Malmo match. If the ferries are full, the coaches can be diverted to travel on the shuttle train through the Channel Tunnel. Couriers need to be aware of this possibility so that arrangements can be made to cater for fans who suffer from claustrophobia.

With the exception of the quality of service issues already discussed, arising from the club's lack of adequate control over the performance of the transport providers, the journeys were largely uneventful. Even in modern buses with toilets and refreshment facilities, long distance coach travel is relatively boring and uncomfortable, especially on the way home when all the anticipation of the match is gone. Meals were taken in the service areas identified during the dummy run, and in many cases, the local police sent a car to meet us. It is good practice to have an interpreter travel with the coach party to help the fans in making purchases and to help the courier liaise with the police. Any possible tensions with the police quickly disappear when they can converse with the club courier and receive assurances about the good behaviour of the fans.

Inevitably, a few minor incidents did take place, and this is exactly why it is necessary to steward the coaches. During the Auxerre match, an elderly lady who had had too much to drink fell over in the toilet and broke her leg. She refused to go to hospital in France. The stewards were able to arrange for her to travel back to Nottingham in the front seat of the coach and for an ambulance to be waiting for her at the ground. On several journeys, as the night wore on and many people wanted to try and sleep, friction developed with younger supporters who had been drinking on the ferry and were remaining boisterous. The timely intervention of the stewards prevented any such incidents from escalating into unpleasantness. On one or two occasions, fans had to be reminded that they would not be provided with their match ticket if their behaviour was unacceptable.

As with the other matters, we found that the arrangements agreed with the foreign police did not always work out as planned. On the Munich trip, we were met as agreed by a police escort at a service station north of the city. We were then escorted to a road beside an underground station where it had been agreed that parking would be provided for both our coaches and the coaches transporting our supporters from the airport. When we arrived, no parking space had been kept for any of us and the fans lost over an hour of their sightseeing time whilst the police made alternative arrangements.

Once the fans had set off to view the town, the courier and stewards made their way to the hotel, where day rooms had been booked for a meal, briefing and final distribution of the tickets to the stewards. Thereafter, we all returned to the coaches to meet the supporters. Tickets were only distributed once we were en route, under police escort, to the stadium. There were reports, particularly in Munich, of Forest supporters being arrested during the twenty-four hours before the match. But, on all four trips, not one member of the official travel party was arrested, nor did any fans risk losing their entitlement to a ticket by returning to the coaches having had too much to drink.

At the away matches

UEFA delegates meeting

On the day of any match in a UEFA competition, officials of both clubs meet with the police, the referee and linesmen, the referee observer from the Fédération Internationale de Football Association (FIFA) and the delegate appointed by UEFA to oversee the match. This meeting represents the culmination of all the preparation and planning in the preceding weeks. The UEFA delegate chairs the meeting, which follows a standard UEFA format and covers various refereeing, administrative and security matters. For example, the delegate will want confirmation that the referee is satisfied the two teams' colours will not clash, or will want to discuss the arrangements made to treat players injured on the field of play. The safety and security consultant found that the meetings easily got bogged down with refereeing and administrative matters, and that it fell to him to emphasize the importance of the safety and security arrangements. For example, to avoid dangerous crowd surges, it is vital that players are discouraged from running up to the crowd to celebrate the scoring of a goal. The referee is the key figure here and the UEFA delegate meeting is a useful vehicle for reinforcing this matter.

The meeting also agrees the composition of the small group who will meet to co-ordinate the management of any operational crisis which may arise before, during or after the match itself. For some of Forest's matches, the UEFA delegate had this crisis group meet a couple of hours before kick-off to review whether any difficulties had arisen. Notwithstanding the club's protests, the changed coach parking arrangements at Malmo were imposed by the local police at just such a meeting.

At the stadia

As we have already shown, the quality of the viewing accommodation provided for Forest supporters away from home did not always compare favourably with the excellent views and facilities to which they have become accustomed at the City Ground in Nottingham. And the same was true of the safety and security management systems, which, as Steve Frosdick and John Sidney have shown in Chapter 15, have evolved to a degree of considerable sophistication in the UK.

We have already referred to the lack of contingency planning by some foreign police forces. Proactivity was not a word easily understood by officials at any of the four clubs we visited. They much preferred to wait for problems and react to them. We also found that foreign police may see the English supporters themselves as the principal source of risk, rather than the condition of the stadium or their own lack of experience of policing major events.

At one of the French matches, the Forest supporters mingling outside the ground became very angry on hearing a rumour that several of their number had been sprayed with CS gas in a nearby bar. A group of French riot police were deployed to confront the fans rather than to pacify them, and the situation was only saved by the intervention of the Forest stewards, who placed themselves between the fans and the police and managed to calm things down. At the Munich match, the police deployed to stand in the aisles of the Forest accommodation were all very young trainees, clearly intimidated by the noise and spectacle, and we saw several Forest fans handled very roughly for no immediately apparent reason.

Also at Munich, the very restricted access allowed by the temporary barrier configuration employed at the entrances, coupled with a lack of staff to undertake the searching of spectators wishing to enter, caused considerable crowds to build up on the approaches. Several of the Forest stewards commented on how unpleasant the crowd pressure outside the ground had been.

The home matches

This chapter has particularly focused on Nottingham Forest's experiences away from home, but let us now say something about the particular considerations which made the home legs of Forest's European matches different from playing in a domestic competition.

First, the extra discussions and meetings generated by a European fixture, together with the involvement of additional foreign agencies, inevitably meant that the preparations were more involved. The planning stages we have already discussed all had to take place, although here it was Forest, supported by the Nottinghamshire Constabulary, who hosted the site visits whilst the more detailed responsibility for travel arrangements and final ticket distribution fell to the away club. On match days themselves, the UEFA delegate meetings were held at the City Ground, following the standard agenda.

The involvement of foreign opposition meant there was a need to employ interpreters to support the safety and security operation. During the final preparations, an interpreter was used to prepare foreign language flysheets to welcome the visiting fans and inform them of the ground regulations. On match day, we found it to be good practice to have an interpreter on duty in the control room. Such interpreters were able to assist in making public address announcements as well as in translating the writing on flags and banners to make sure it was not offensive to other fans. It was also useful to have an interpreter equipped with a loudhailer on duty near the away turnstiles to assist in giving directions to the fans and to provide other help where needed.

We found that many away fans wanted to buy souvenirs of their visit to the City Ground. Since the club shop was situated on the opposite side of the ground from the away fans' accommodation, the interests of segregation meant that access to the shop was impossible during or after the match. The club therefore made arrangements for souvenirs to be available from a booth in the away concourse and also from a stand at the East Midlands airport.

The culture of continental fans can be more carnivalesque than has traditionally been the case in this country. We found that supporters wanted to bring drums and air-horns into the ground, and the club's positive experiences in adopting a more liberal line in these matters were helpful in the preparations for the Euro '96 football championships, for which the City Ground was one of the eight competition venues. We also found that greater number of fans wanted to bring banners and flags into the stadium and that it was important to them to have somewhere to display the banners. Recognizing this need, it proved to be a good idea to have stewards briefed to help the fans to place the banners appropriately rather than confront them if they put them in the wrong places.

Nevertheless, the need to exclude flares and large flagpoles meant it was appropriate to supervise the away fans' entry to the stadium more thoroughly than is done with domestic supporters. The sale of alcohol is prohibited at UEFA matches, and this freed the Forest licensing stewards, normally deployed in the bar areas, to provide additional searching capability at the turnstiles. All the away fans were handed a leaflet in their own language telling them what the prohibited articles were, and large bins were provided for the disposal of bottles, cans, large flagpoles, etc. Some supporters were searched before being admitted, but this was selective rather than blanket searching and left to the discretion of the police and stewards concerned.

In the event, the drums, banners and flags all contributed to the atmosphere, and only two flares got into the ground, both let off at the Munich match. Contingency plans had been made to deal with these and a team of ordnance experts were on standby in the stadium for each match.

Conclusion

In concluding this case study, we want to emphasize two points. Football supporters should be treated and respected first and foremost as the customers of the club and not as potential trouble-makers. In the event of any problems, police and club intelligence systems are sufficient to allow for the identification and banning from the club of any convicted hooligans.

Waiting for crises and reacting to them is not good management and exposes travelling football fans to unacceptable risks. Detailed, flexible and well-documented planning is essential to support the proactive identification and management of safety and security risks in European football competitions. English practitioners are now at the forefront of best practice in proactive spectator safety and security. We would wish to commend their expertise to countries such as France, who will host the 1998 World Cup and who wish to move forward from their present systems of reactive management.

Summary

- Foreign travel by English football fans is a sensitive subject and clubs are accountable for the safety and behaviour of their travelling supporters.
- The requirements of the regulatory authorities are well documented, but there is little guidance on how best to comply with these.
- This case study draws on Nottingham Forest's experiences in Europe during 1995–96 to suggest good practice in planning an away match in a European competition.
- In order to maintain control of the quality of service delivered, clubs should contract directly with transport providers.
- In the interests of consumer choice, match tickets should not be restricted to fans travelling with the official club party, but should also be made available to approved independent travel organizers who can satisfy the club's safety and security requirements.
- An advance inspection of the stadium and a planning meeting with the away club officials and police is essential, although regulatory requirements and agreements reached may later be disregarded by the police.
- A 'dummy run' of the coach route is helpful for planning journey times, negotiating stopping places and taking a video to show fans on the journey.
- Ticket distribution must be carefully controlled.
- The UEFA delegate's meeting on the day of the match is an important forum for emphasizing safety concerns.
- Proactivity is an alien concept to some foreign police forces, who are more used to reacting to problems as they arise.
- A home match against European opposition involves more planning than a domestic fixture. Sufficient interpreters should be employed and arrangements made to take account of the more carnivalesque styles of football support found among some foreign supporters.

Acknowledgement

The authors gratefully acknowledge the support of Nottingham Forest Football Club in the preparation of this chapter

References

[1] Football Stadia Advisory Design Council (1992). *Digest of Stadia Criteria.* The Sports Council.

[2] National Criminal Intelligence Service (1992). *Guidelines for Co-operation on the Policing of European Football Matches.*

[3] *European Convention on Spectator Violence and Misbehaviour at Sports Events and in particular at Football Matches* (1985). HMSO.

[4] Union of European Football Associations (1993). *Safety and Security in the Stadium for All Matches in the UEFA Competitions.*

17 Policing Euro '96

Bryan Drew

The European Football Championships held in England in June 1996 have been widely regarded as a great success. This success can be attributed not only to the good humour of the many supporters who attended the championships, but also to the extensive and careful planning undertaken by the many agencies involved. This chapter reflects on the security related aspects of that planning and its outcomes.

Introduction

Between 8 June and 30 June 1996, England hosted the European Football Championships (Euro '96), the largest sporting event to be held in this country since the 1966 World Cup Finals. The tournament has been widely regarded as a great success and as the springboard for a possible bid to stage the World Cup Finals in 2006.

Some of the facts and figures associated with the championships are set out in Table 17.1. The competing countries are shown in Table 17.2, whilst the details of the eight venues are set out in Table 17.3. The schedule of matches played is shown in Table 17.4.

Background

Because foreign travel is now relatively cheap it was anticipated that the championships would attract in excess of 250 000 visitors to the UK, many of whom would stay for varying lengths of time, depending upon how far their country progressed. During the planning it was anticipated that the majority of police forces in the country would be affected to a greater or lesser extent by the many visitors who

Table 17.1   Euro '96 facts and figures

- Euro '96 was the third largest sporting event in the world after the World Cup and the Olympic Games.
- It was hosted by The Football Association under the authority of the Union of European Football Associations (UEFA) – the European governing body of the sport.
- It was exactly thirty years since a major football tournament was last staged in England.
- For the first time, sixteen nations competed in the finals.
- There were 1.3 million tickets available for the tournament.
- The cumulative worldwide audience was projected at seven billion people.
- It was originally estimated that the tournament would attract in excess of 250 000 supporters from the competing countries.
- The championships commenced at Wembley on 8 June 1996 with an opening ceremony and the England v Switzerland match.
- The final between Germany and the Czech Republic was played at Wembley on 30 June 1996. Germany won.
- There were a total of thirty-one matches played at eight different venues.
- There were a total of 1148 arrests notified for offences broadly related to the championships, whether in or near the venues or elsewhere.
- The majority of the arrests were for minor drink-related offences or for ticket touting.

Table 17.2   The sixteen competing countries

Bulgaria	Netherlands
Croatia	Portugal
Czech Republic	Romania
Denmark	Russia
England	Scotland
France	Spain
Germany	Switzerland
Italy	Turkey

would use the opportunity of visiting England for Euro '96 to take in the many tourist sights when not watching football matches. The planning strategy therefore catered for a considerable number of supporters travelling around the country on a regular basis.

Previous experience of major international tournaments in Europe identified that criminal elements could be expected to travel to the United Kingdom to take advantage of a wide spectrum of criminal opportunities. Our preparations therefore had to take account of this likelihood.

Table 17.3   Euro '96 venues and capacities

Group	Venue	Capacity
Group A	Wembley Stadium	76 000
	Villa Park, Birmingham – Aston Villa FC	39 000
Group B	Elland Road, Leeds – Leeds United FC	39 000
	St James' Park, Newcastle – Newcastle United FC	35 000
Group C	Old Trafford, Manchester – Manchester United FC	43 000 +
	Anfield, Liverpool – Liverpool FC	41 000
Group D	Hillsborough, Sheffield – Sheffield Wednesday FC	40 000
	City Ground, Nottingham – Nottingham Forest FC	30 500

Our planning process sought to build upon experiences from the 1988 European Championships in Germany, the 1990 World Cup in Italy, the 1992 European Championships in Sweden and the 1994 World Cup, which was held in the USA. These previous championships highlighted the way in which international co-operation and the sharing of information and intelligence were vital elements in ensuring that the primary objectives of the police service were achieved. These were to ensure:

- that the championships took place in a safe and peaceful environment;
- that the opportunity for any organized criminal activity was minimized;
- that the hooligan element were targeted in a proactive manner; and
- that genuine supporters, particularly those from other countries, were able to travel throughout the country in safety.

Reinforcing the importance of international co-operation, both prior to, and during the period of the Championships, members of the French 1998 World Cup Organizing Committee were keen observers of all aspects of our preparations. In addition, representatives from both the Netherlands and Belgium, who jointly host the next European Championships in the year 2000, also attended as observers.

The National Criminal Intelligence Service

The day-to-day work of the National Criminal Intelligence Service (NCIS) Football Unit involves extensive international co-operation and the sharing of intelligence,

Table 17.4   Schedule of matches

Round	Date	Match	Venue/time
First round matches	Saturday 8 June	England v Switzerland	Wembley, 3 pm
	Sunday 9 June	Spain v Bulgaria	Elland Road, 2.30 pm
		Germany v Czech Republic	Old Trafford, 5 pm
		Denmark v Portugal	Hillsborough, 7.30 pm
	Monday 10 June	Netherlands v Scotland	Villa Park, 4.30 pm
		Romania v France	St James Park, 7.30 pm
	Tuesday 11 June	Italy v Russia	Anfield, 4.30 pm
		Turkey v Croatia	City Ground, 7.30 pm
	Thursday 13 June	Bulgaria v Romania	St James Park, 4.30 pm
		Switzerland v Netherlands	Villa Park, 7.30 pm
	Friday 14 June	Portugal v Turkey	City Ground, 4.30 pm
		Czech Republic v Italy	Anfield, 7.30 pm
	Saturday 15 June	Scotland v England	Wembley, 3 pm
		France v Spain	Elland Road, 6 pm
	Sunday 16 June	Russia v Germany	Old Trafford, 3 pm
		Croatia v Denmark	Hillsborough, 6 pm
	Tuesday 18 June	France v Bulgaria	St James Park, 4.30 pm
		Romania v Spain	Elland Road, 4.30 pm
		Scotland v Switzerland	Villa Park, 7.30 pm
		Netherlands v England	Wembley, 7.30 pm
	Wednesday 19 June	Turkey v Denmark	Hillsborough, 4.30 pm
		Croatia v Portugal	City Ground, 4.30 pm
		Russia v Czech Republic	Anfield, 7.30 pm
		Italy v Germany	Old Trafford, 7.30 pm
Quarter Finals	Saturday 22 June	Spain v England	Wembley, 3 pm
		France v Holland	Anfield, 6.30 pm
	Sunday 23 June	Germany v Croatia	Old Trafford, 3 pm
		Czech Republic v Portugal	Villa Park, 6.30 pm
Semi-Finals	Wednesday 26 June	France v Czech Republic	Old Trafford, 4 pm
		England v Germany	Wembley, 7.30 pm
Final Sunday	30 June	Germany v Czech Republic	Wembley, 7 pm

and so the informal planning for Euro '96 could be said to have begun as soon as it was known that England would be hosting the tournament. In planning for the championships, staff from the Football Unit sought to build upon the established and excellent working relationships that already existed with colleagues in many law enforcement agencies throughout Europe. In a few cases, for example Croatia, no such relationships existed and their nurturing and development was essential.

It is not appropriate to give details of the extensive intelligence work carried out in the years and months leading up to Euro '96. However, the fact that the known European hooligan groups did not travel to the UK during the competition and the almost complete absence of any disorder from the eight tournament venues, must be regarded as a successful outcome. The disorder which did take place in London's Trafalgar Square and in other English towns and cities after England's defeat by Germany in the semifinal was anticipated and was a recurrence of the problems experienced after the same fixture in the 1990 World Cup in Italy.

The national plan

The formal national planning began in earnest in early 1994 when the Football Association, as the organizers, established a 'Safety and Security Working Group', comprising representatives of Government departments, the police service, and other participating agencies such as The Football Trust. This group was responsible for the strategic co-ordination of the entire tournament and all the associated issues which would impact upon it, such as transport, liquor licensing, international liaison, media, supporter accommodation, and the role of government departments. The full group met on eight occasions in the two years preceding the championships, however its various subgroups and members were in contact with each other on an almost daily basis.

The work of this group played an invaluable part in the successful staging of the championships, and in providing leadership and direction to the various agencies involved.

Police service planning

In parallel with the national safety and security working group, the Association of Chief Police Officers (ACPO) Public Order Sub-Committee formed a steering group to co-ordinate strategic planning for the police service. Malcolm George, an Assistant Chief Constable from Greater Manchester Police and Secretary of the

ACPO Public Order Sub-Committee, was appointed National Co-ordinator for the Police Service and Chair of the Steering Group. Membership of the group comprised an Assistant Chief Constable from each of the eight forces responsible for a tournament venue.

At regional and local level, all eight police forces formed their own planning groups and liaised closely with the local authorities, hoteliers, travel companies and other organizations involved with Euro '96. Again, this extensive liaison was a prime factor in the success of the tournament.

National co-ordinating centre

A National Co-ordinating Centre (NCC) was established at New Scotland Yard in London, the headquarters of the Metropolitan Police Service. It was operational twenty-four hours a day between 1 June and 30 June. Each competing country was requested to provide their own national police liaison officer to work in the NCC for the duration of their country's interest in the championships. On the basis of previous experience in other tournaments, the request emphasized that officers nominated should have a background in football crowd control and intelligence matters.

Additionally, the Belgian *Gendarmerie* sent a liaison officer at their own request, first because they were the only major transit country whose national team had not qualified for the championships, and second, because they were due to host Euro 2000 and wanted to learn from our experience. The Russian government thought it unlikely that any significant number of supporters would attend from their country. They promised their full co-operation but elected not to provide a liaison officer.

The foreign liaison officers worked alongside staff from the NCIS Football Unit and a number of other football intelligence officers (FIOs), seconded to the NCC for this period from twelve police forces who were not directly involved in policing one of the match venues. These FIOs are responsible for monitoring and developing intelligence on criminals whose activities impact on safety at or near football grounds.

Each national liaison officer was provided with their own dedicated telephone line for contact with law enforcement agencies, government departments and other agencies; such as their own football associations, travel operators, etc. The primary role of the NCIS staff and the FIOs in the NCC was to ensure that all incoming supporter travel information and criminal intelligence, from whatever source, was evaluated, analysed and disseminated as quickly as possible to the appropriate police force(s) or other relevant agencies.

Police command centres

Policing in the United Kingdom is not a national function, but is carried out by forty-three individual police forces in England and Wales. The same was true of the policing of Euro '96.

Each of the eight police forces with responsibility for one of the Euro '96 venue grounds established its own police command centre, which was also operational twenty-four hours each day until the matches at that venue had been completed. It was these eight police command centres, and not the NCC, that were responsible for all the operational deployments made within their respective force areas in connection with policing the tournament. The role of the NCC was very much to provide the intelligence to support the operational decision making undertaken by the individual forces. A number of other non-venue forces, for example those which had responsibility for a team training ground or hotel, also established their own command centres to co-ordinate the necessary deployments within their own force areas. Although the organizational structure of policing in England and Wales meant that these operational command arrangements were complex, nevertheless they worked very effectively in practice.

Operational police assistance

As well as requesting police liaison officers from the competing countries, operational support in the form of a police intelligence officer was requested from Scotland, Holland and Germany. These officers worked in the police command centre of the force with responsibility for the venues where their own national teams were playing. Additional assistance was also requested from certain countries in the form of 'spotters', as they are referred to in the UK. These are officers who are familiar with, and able to identify known trouble-makers and who were therefore able to provide practical operational support to the UK policing operation.

Intelligence co-ordinators

Both the national co-ordinating centre and each of the police command centres had an intelligence co-ordinator on duty at all times. This was an experienced senior detective whose role was to evaluate the intelligence received and to advise on the deployments which should be made in response to it.

Senior investigating officer

Similarly, each of the eight venue forces appointed a senior investigating officer (SIO). Again this was a senior detective, and in some cases the same officer performed the dual role of intelligence co-ordinator and SIO. The role of the SIO was to deploy intelligence gathering teams, including teams of 'spotters' made up from English FIOs and their foreign colleagues, and to undertake the investigation of any major incidents, for example serious disorder, the murder of a supporter or a road or train crash involving football fans connected with the competition.

With the exception of the nationwide cases of disorder which followed England's elimination from the championships, there were thankfully no other major incidents related to Euro '96.

Security for competing countries

The Football Association were responsible for the security and accommodation of players and match officials and this included the team hotels and training grounds. Police involvement was limited to where there was a specific threat to a team or an official. An English police liaison officer was attached to each competing national team for the duration of their involvement in the championships. This officer provided the link between the national team, the officials from each country and the local police, as the team moved from venue to venue or visited local tourist attractions on non-match days.

No significant incidents involving any of the teams took place throughout the competition.

Refusal of entry to the UK and deportation

Police throughout the country liaised closely with colleagues in the immigration service, both prior to and throughout the championships. Under European law there are grounds for refusing entry to the UK to both European Economic Area (EEA) and Non-EEA members. The government publicly announced that these powers might be used on selective occasions, and indeed they were, although this was in respect of just one individual on one occasion only.

Crimestoppers campaign and the NCIS Hooligan Hotline

The NCIS Football Unit operate a national freephone Hooligan Hotline (0800 515 495) which is widely advertised nationally and encourages the public to provide information on hooligan activity. In addition to this, the Crimestoppers Trust launched an initiative specifically targeted at Euro '96, but aimed at a wider audience than the NCIS Hooligan Hotline. This initiative had the support of all agencies involved in the planning process, including the Football Association, the Football Trust and the police service. Assistance from the public, through a number of calls received through both these sources, provided valuable information, in some cases usefully confirming matters already known to the police.

UK football offences

On purchasing their tickets, supporters from the qualifying countries were provided with a leaflet advising them of public order and other legislation relevant both to their stay in the UK and to football matches. Unlike the majority of other European countries, we in the UK no longer have fences surrounding the pitches in our stadiums. To prevent pitch invasions, we have legislation introduced in 1991 making it a criminal offence to enter the field of play without lawful authority. This absence of fences was identified as being a major cultural difference for the supporters of other competing countries. Also, unlike a number of other European countries, it is a criminal offence to possess or use fireworks and flares at a football stadium.

In support of the information leaflet distributed with ticket sales, searches were conducted at all of the venue stadiums. The agreed policing policy was that anyone found in possession of fireworks or flares would be arrested and charged and the items would be confiscated.

The publicity circulated and policies adopted were clearly effective. There were only three arrests during the championships for persons running onto the pitch and no reported incidents of fireworks or flares being set off during any of the matches.

Organized crime

It was recognized that any event of this scale was liable to attract an element of organized criminality, such as organized drug dealers, distraction thieves who operate at air and sea ports and hotels, and prostitutes, or those who control them. Contingency plans were prepared to both prevent and detect this type of criminal activity. The services of both Interpol and the Metropolitan Police Service Hotel Squad were particularly helpful here in being able to identify known travelling criminals who engaged in these types of criminal activity.

Information technology

The primary objective of the IT strategy for Euro '96 was to provide a secure communications link which would allow the fast and efficient exchange of both data and images between the National Co-ordinating Centre and the eight United Kingdom venue police forces. A secondary objective was to extend these communication links to as many other UK and European police forces and other law enforcement agencies as possible.

Two systems were originally identified which met this criteria. The first of these systems was the European Police Information Centre (EPI-Centre), developed by the Police Scientific Development Branch of the Home Office Science and Technology Group. EPI-Centre is accessible by police forces world wide and provides:

- general policing information;
- access to special interest groups (such as Euro '96);
- access twenty-four hours a day;
- extensive search and retrieval facilities; and
- e-mail and an ability to attach files to messages.

The major benefit of EPI-Centre was that it was available, free of charge, to every police force in the UK, Europe and beyond. This meant that police and other law enforcement agencies involved in Euro '96, whether the NCC, local police command centres or police forces abroad, were able to exchange information electronically and on one system. Although Euro '96 was the first occasion on which the system had been employed in such a large scale operational way, its successful use during the championships has now established its credibility and it will continue to be used on both a domestic and international basis.

The second system identified was Photophone, an image storage and transmission system that simply plugs into a single standard telephone line to transmit both voice and pictures. Images can be captured using any video device, such as a camcorder or CCTV camera. Photophone can use all types of telephone lines as well as satellite or portable cellular communications. The benefits of Photophone were that:

- it was a fast effective method of transmitting high quality colour, or black and white images;
- the cost of transmission were no more than the cost of the telephone call itself; and
- it was already used extensively throughout the world by Interpol and other law enforcement agencies.

Application was made to the Football Trust (which provides grant aid to the football industry) who generously funded 75 per cent of the costs of the Photophone equipment. The system proved a most valuable and effective tool and, since the equipment remains *in situ*, its benefits will continue to be enjoyed by the venue forces for years to come.

EPI-Centre was intended as a national and international system, but because it was untested operationally on this scale, a third system, a specialist criminal intelligence database used by the Metropolitan Police Service, was also used to provide additional computing capability. Although more sophisticated than EPI-Centre, its networking was restricted to the eight venue forces, British Transport Police and the National Co-ordinating Centre.

The efficient and effective use of all this technology played a major part in reducing the opportunity for organized crime and disorder during Euro '96.

Reflections on Euro '96

Although it had been anticipated that a large number of the 250 000 visitors expected for Euro '96 would stay in this country for the duration of their own teams involvement in the tournament, this did not in fact prove to be the case. Whatever the reasons, considerable numbers of fans from France, Germany, Holland, Denmark, Switzerland and Spain – who between them provided the majority of the spectators at the matches – actually travelled into the UK on the day of the match and returned home the same day. It appears that the low costs of air travel competed very effectively with the costs of staying several nights in hotel or other accommodation.

In general terms, for countries such as Bulgaria, Croatia, Russia and the Czech Republic, the costs of travel and match tickets proved to be beyond the means of many ordinary supporters. Relatively few fans attended from these countries, many of whose supporters in the grounds proved to be expatriates living in the UK, although more Czech fans sought to travel once their country reached the Final.

Finally, notwithstanding some of the negative reporting in the popular press in the weeks prior to the tournament, it must be said that, as the championships drew nearer, all the intelligence suggested that the known foreign hooligan groups had been dissuaded from travelling to the UK because of their awareness that the policing arrangements would thwart their criminal intentions. This intelligence was fully confirmed once the NCC was open and the foreign liaison officers were in post. It was not anticipated that there would be any disorder other than following England's elimination from the competition, and this intelligence proved to be correct.

Summary

● The 1996 European Football Championships was the third largest sporting event in the world. The sixteen competing countries were involved in a total of thirty-one matches played at eight separate venues.

- Careful planning coupled with the good humour of the supporters meant that the Euro '96 tournament has been widely regarded as a great success.
- Preparations for Euro '96 were based on the assumptions that:

  (i) there would be considerable numbers of foreign supporters travelling around the country;

  (ii) criminal elements, for example drug dealers, thieves, prostitutes and hooligans could be expected to travel to the UK; and

  (iii) international co-operation was essential for planning a safe and peaceful tournament.

- Co-ordinated police service planning was undertaken in consultation with many other agencies at both national and local levels.
- Operational police deployments were made by eight police command centres, supported by a national co-ordinating centre, sophisticated information technology and a network of police liaison and intelligence officers.
- With the exception of the nationwide disorder, which had been anticipated, following England's elimination from the tournament, there were no other major incidents related to Euro '96.
- The absence of pitch perimeter fences and the prohibition on fireworks in the UK presented a cultural difference for some foreign supporters. The publicity arrangements and policing policies adopted were effective in preventing any problems.
- There were only 1148 arrests associated with the tournament, the majority for minor drink-related offences or ticket touting.
- The extensive liaison and intelligence work undertaken by the NCIS Football Unit proved to be successful in deterring organized criminals and hooligan groups from attending the championships.

PART 5 VISION

Overview

Part Five outlines the editors' vision of where sport and safety management should perhaps be heading in the approach to the millennium. Options are presented for the strategic development of the industry and methodologies offered for undertaking strategic risk assessments and for managing change through the vehicles of programme and project management.

Chapter summaries

In Chapter 18, Steve Frosdick sets out a strategic vision for the development of sports safety management. The chapter opens with an overview of the idea of strategy and introduces an established tool for analysing options for strategic development. It goes on to suggest possible future roles for the Football Licensing Authority and Football Safety Officers' Association and, in particular, to outline how sports safety management might continue to evolve in the approach to the millennium. Finally, it suggests the contribution which programme and project management could make to the process of managing change and development.

In Chapter 19, Steve Frosdick sets out a framework for strategic risk assessment in public assembly facilities. The chapter takes account of both management accountability for safety and of the need to balance the competing demands of commerce, safety, enjoyment and the outside world. It illustrates the cultural complexity of the hazards perceived and provides a worked example of a simple risk assessment.

In Chapter 20, Lynne Walley looks at the way in which effective project management can assist sports clubs to identify, plan and evaluate initiatives. She sets out a clear methodology for implementation as well as looking at the project-based culture.

18 The strategic development of sports safety management

Steve Frosdick

This chapter sets out a strategic vision for the development of sports safety management. The chapter opens with an overview of the idea of strategy and introduces an established tool for analysing options for strategic development. It goes on to suggest possible future roles for the Football Licensing Authority and Football Safety Officers' Association and, in particular, to outline how sports safety management might continue to evolve in the approach to the millennium. Finally, it suggests the contribution which programme and project management could make to the process of managing change and development.

The need for strategic vision

Strategy is about vision. It is something that shapes the long-term scope of an organization's activities. It seeks to match an organization's resources to the world in which it operates and to meet the expectations of all those who have an interest in what it is doing [1]. The process of managing strategy is the process of bringing about that vision. It is made up of the three components of strategic analysis, strategic choice and strategy implementation [2], which are often represented by the three questions:

- Where are we now?
- Where do we want to be?
- How do we get there?

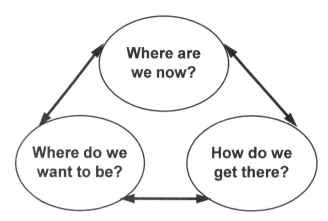

Figure 18.1   The components of strategic management.

Figure 18.1 shows these three components of strategic management. Although, in theory, these three components could follow a linear form — analysis followed by choice followed by implementation — in practice, the three stages are all involved with each other. As Johnson and Scholes point out [3], analysis may be an ongoing activity, whilst one way of working out whether to choose a particular strategy may be to start to implement it and see what happens.

The first four parts of this book have sought to provide a broad position statement on how the safety at sports grounds industry, particularly within football, has evolved since the 1989 watershed of Hillsborough, and on where it finds itself in 1997. We know something of where we are now.

There is a general acknowledgement within the industry, reflected in several of the chapters in this book (including my own contribution with John Sidney — Chapter 15) that there is much that still remains to be done. We have embarked on a journey. We have begun to climb a ladder. We have begun to implement something. This is all fine, but I believe that now is the right time for the sports safety management industry to debate and more clearly articulate the strategic direction it wishes to follow.

So what I want to try and explore is this. Where is the journey headed? What's at the top of the ladder? In short, where do we actually want to be? And when we've decided on our destination, how are we actually going to get there? This chapter allows me to set out my own thoughts on the strategic development of sports safety management. My comments are derived from my ongoing involvement as an observer, academic and consultant in the world of sports safety management since

1992. I think I understand enough about the industry's resources, its environment and its stakeholders to be able to express an informed view. But I am expressing only my personal opinions on where I think sports safety management ought to be in the year 2000, and how I think it ought to try and get there. My purpose in doing so is simply to make suggestions and to stimulate the very necessary debate.

Strategic choice

Figure 18.2 [4] is a strategic management tool (known as the 'Ansoff matrix') which summarizes the strategic directions which the industry could take. Through consideration of the dimensions of 'product/service' and 'market', both existing and new, it provides some guidewords to help generate possible options.

'Do nothing' and 'withdraw' are self-explanatory. 'Consolidate' does not mean standing still but 'implies changes in the specific way the company operates although the range of products and markets may remain unchanged' [5]. I am taking the idea of 'market development' to refer to the wider world of public assembly facilities (PAFs) beyond football. The notion of 'product/service development' refers not only to products and services, such as the stewards' training

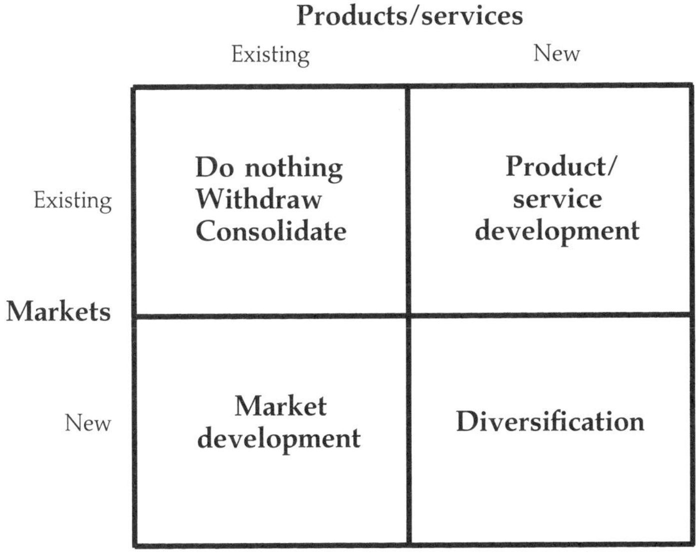

	Products/services	
	Existing	New
Existing (Markets)	**Do nothing Withdraw Consolidate**	**Product/ service development**
New	**Market development**	**Diversification**

Figure 18.2   A model for generating options for strategic development.

package or national vocational qualification (NVQ) in spectator control, but also to an extension of an organization's role or terms of reference. 'Diversification' describes options which go beyond the present products and markets. An example could be a stadium manager who decides to form a new business to use the club stewards to work as security guards in a shopping centre.

I want to use this tool to examine the three issues which I believe to be of the greatest importance, namely:

- the future role of the Football Licensing Authority (FLA);
- the evolution of the Football Safety Officers' Association (FSOA); and
- the general football-led evolution of safety management in PAFs.

The Football Licensing Authority

The role of the FLA has been comprehensively set out in Chapter 6 by its chief executive, John de Quidt. He shows how the FLA has shifted its emphasis from the physical redevelopment of grounds to the positive promotion of proactive safety management. He sees it being able to reduce its supervisory role in relation to some clubs and local authorities, whilst maintaining a high profile advisory role. This reflects the idea of 'consolidation'. The FLA could continue to operate with its existing terms of reference within the football market, but with a gradual change away from active supervision to providing a source of expertise.

In view of John de Quidt's comments, the options of 'doing nothing' and 'product development' through extending the FLA's range of regulatory activities do not appear to merit further discussion. But what about 'withdrawal'? It is conceivable that a future government might be persuaded that the FLA will have outlived its usefulness by the year 2000. The vast majority of grounds may have been rebuilt or refurbished with all seated stands. All football clubs may have fully accepted their accountability for safety and put in place comprehensive and professional safety management systems. Local authorities may be fully capable of providing all the necessary supervision and advice.

Whilst 'withdrawal' might be viable, I believe it would be a mistake. The FLA has considerable experience and expertise, not only in questions of management, but also, since the demise of the Football Stadia Advisory Design Council, in matters of structural safety and design. Through quiet persuasion, it has been the catalyst for much of the change that has taken place since its inception. It has taken the lead in important matters such as the revision of the *Green Guide* to safety at sports grounds [6]. Thus in my view it would not be sufficient to consolidate the FLA's role. I believe this should be extended – 'market development' – beyond the world of football. This represents a strong parallel with the Health and Safety Executive (HSE). What is needed is a PAFs safety authority which has a regulatory function in overseeing local authorities but which also acts as the standard setting and advisory body.

Taking the example of the Welsh national stadium at Cardiff Arms Park, it may be argued that there is no logic in the present situation. The FLA licence the venue, undertake supervision and provide advice when the ground is being used to stage football matches, generally involving the Welsh national team. Yet when the same ground is being used for rugby union, again usually involving the Welsh national team, and often with a substantially larger crowd, the FLA have no role at all. Moreover, different rules apply regarding the use of standing accommodation and the consumption of alcohol. These differences apply at all grounds shared with other sports such as rugby league and American football.

In my view, therefore, the FLA role should be extended to include responsibility for all public assembly facilities which require safety certification, either of the whole ground (for sports grounds designated under the Safety of Sports Grounds Act, 1975) or of one or more stands (for stands designated under the Fire Safety and Safety of Places of Sport Act, 1987). This would ensure that venues used for spectator sports such as rugby league, rugby union, cricket, horse racing and motor racing, together with sports with large crowds accommodated in temporary facilities such as golf, were brought under the same regulatory framework as football. Thus my vision is one of a 'Sports Safety Executive', paralleling the work of the Health and Safety Executive in other sectors of the leisure industry.

There may be some scope for the FLA to undertake some 'product development' and even 'diversification', not in a regulatory direction, but in its advisory, guidance and training role. For example, in October 1996 the FLA were invited to make a presentation on UK-style stewarding to an international audience at the Council of Europe in Strasbourg, France. The same month, following the death of over eighty people during a World Cup qualifying football match in Guatemala, South America, the FLA were invited to send two Inspectors to assist in the post-disaster inquiry. Whilst the role of the FLA is determined by Government, through the Department of National Heritage, it might make sense to consider bringing together the safety work of the FLA and the grant-giving role of the Football Trust and the National Lottery. These are controversial matters and should therefore be seen as secondary to the main 'market development' option.

The Football Safety Officers' Association

I want to turn briefly to the role of the FSOA, described in my earlier chapter with John Sidney (Chapter 15). The FSOA is already considering some consolidation of its role, by debating the options for dealing with the growing workload faced by its officers. If appropriate funding can be found, I believe that it would be appropriate to establish a small head office, with one part-time employee to provide administrative support.

But the key question facing the FSOA is this – should it develop the products and services it offers within the world of football, seek to expand its membership to include safety managers from other PAFs or indeed diversify to offer a more comprehensive range of services in the wider world of PAFs management?

A number of well-established national and international professional bodies already exist for PAFs managers. These include the Institute of Leisure and Amenity Management (ILAM), the International Association of Auditorium Managers (IAAM), the Association for Sport and Leisure Facilities Development and Management (AFDM), the Institute of Sport and Recreation Management (ISRM) and the Sport Playwork and Recreation Industry Training Organization (SPRITO). In addition, the Rugby League facilitated the formation of an association for safety managers within its own sport in late 1996.

Within the world of football, the professional bodies which represent the interests of other managers, namely the Commercial Managers Association, the Managerial Staffs Association, the Football Administrators Association and the League Managers Association, have created their own umbrella structure, the Institute of Football Management and Administration (IFMA). Football safety officers are probably the only management personnel not represented within IFMA.

Given that the world beyond football is already well catered for, and given the existence of a professional umbrella organization within football, it seems to me that the FSOA would do well to seek to affiliate to IFMA, thus taking the strategic decision to remain within the world of football with an enhanced professional status. This is not to deny the appropriateness of maintaining close liaison with colleagues in other sports or even permitting them to become associate members of the FSOA.

My personal view, then, is that the FSOA should seek to consolidate its role within the world of football in the short term, and in the medium term to debate the type of professional services it should be offering its members. Long term, I believe it should seek to become a recognized professional body, thus allowing those whom it admits to membership to reflect their professional status with the designatory letters 'MFSOA'.

Safety management

I think it is clear from this book that the strategic development of sports safety management has been driven by practitioners and regulators within the football industry. So I want to take the documentary products produced within football – the *Green Guide* [7], *Red Book* [8] and *Blue Pack* [9] – as the starting point for exploring the options for the future. Thus referring back to Figure 18.2, the three documents are the existing products/services and football is the existing market place.

Do nothing/withdraw?

This option implies that the industry has done enough to discharge its accountability for the safety of its customers. It has invested time and effort in the production of the documents. The job is done. We have the finest stadia in the world and our management systems stand comparison with any other country you could name. Accidents hardly ever happen and are never our fault.

Let me refer the reader back to my earlier chapter with Dominic Elliott and Denis Smith (Chapter 2), to their analysis of management attitudes (Chapter 7), and to the words of Lord Justice Taylor. Not only are accidents and continued near misses a regular occurrence, but too many clubs are too crisis prone and still need reminding that 'all those responsible for certifying, using and supervising sports grounds should take a hard look at their arrangements and keep doing so. Complacency is the enemy of safety' [10].

The essential need to avoid such crisis-prone complacency means that the only way is forward. But the process of radical reactive change imposed as a result of occasional disaster has got to be replaced by a process of ongoing, proactive, incremental change, informed by best practice and the results of relevant research.

Consolidate

All three products are quite new and some consolidation is surely therefore appropriate in the short to medium term. This implies such matters as the updating of the products to reflect any changes in procedures or legislation. For example, the basic fire awareness module in the training package will need updating to reflect new EC standards on the colour of fire extinguishers. Post-implementation review of the three products may well also be appropriate to establish whether they have delivered the benefits envisaged in their production.

Market development

Although the preparation of the revised *Green Guide* was carried out for the Government by the FLA, its intended application will be the same as the previous edition, namely 'to cover grounds where sporting events of all kinds are held and where the gathering of large crowds is likely to present a safety problem' [11]. This implies that the revised product will need to be marketed to the wider world of PAFs management.

Similarly, the football authorities have found other sports bodies and regulatory agencies, both at home and abroad, wishing to purchase copies of the guide to safety management and have stockpiled a number of copies of the training package to meet a similar anticipated demand.

This suggests that there is some scope for involvement in new markets, however I believe that this should be secondary to the primary strategic direction of ongoing incremental improvements in management systems and practice – the product/ service development option.

Product/service development

I want to discuss the theme of ongoing, proactive incremental improvement under four headings:

● assessment of stewards;
● baseline standards;
● professional training and qualifications; and
● accreditation.

Assessment of stewards

I am convinced that the work started with the training package will not be completed until the question of assessment has been addressed. I believe that it would be a good idea to commission an assessment package, prepared by a small working party with consultancy support, made up of one smaller and two main modules:

- advice on recruiting and interviewing potential stewards to ensure that the process includes a basic assessment of relevant demeanour and attitudes;
- assessment of knowledge through the provision of a set of properly tested and validated multiple choice examination papers, ensuring that the steward who passes the exam at one club is of the same level of competence as the one who passes at another; and
- assessment of skills through the preparation of a set of baseline performance standards for use for self-assessment by individual clubs, with some moderation from external verifiers.

Baseline standards

Risk assessment and baseline standards may be seen as complimentary approaches to the question of proactive safety management. Several chapters of this book are devoted to risk assessment, and I have set out my own thoughts on this theme in a later chapter. The baseline standards approach can be helpful in two contexts.

First, it recognizes that, where current safety arrangements are not considered satisfactory – for example in countries such as Zambia or Guatemala, both of which suffered football-related disasters in 1996 – there is a need to do something as a stopgap pending the carrying out of a comprehensive risk analysis. Thus systems are benchmarked against a yardstick of minimum standards and immediate action taken to improve those areas which do not measure up. Second, the approach would allow for the development of both a self-inspection module within an assessment package and also a comprehensive management tool against which to undertake safety audit and inspection.

So what might be the areas for which baseline standards could be developed? I want to suggest that the key issues can be considered under the following headings.

Documentary infrastructure – certificates, licences, meeting minutes, records and other documents which make up the safety library archives at the venue.

Management of the venue structure and fabric – the activities carried out by the stadium or PAF's manager.

Management of technology – vehicles, plant, and general equipment as well as the communications and IT systems at the venue.

Human resource management – the systems for staff recruitment, selection, training, welfare and discipline.

Financial management.

Pre-event planning – planning and preparatory activities which take place prior to the
venue being opened to the public.

Event operations – the management of public access to the venue, the event itself, and
public egress after the event.

Post-event issues – once the venue has closed down after the event.

Management services – a catch-all to include such matters as ethics, customer service
and performance review.

By way of stimulating debate on the usefulness of the approach, let me suggest two
areas for which standards might be developed under each heading. These are listed
in Table 18.1. And there are dozens more important issues for which standards
might also be developed in support of a standard framework for PAFs' safety audit
and inspection.

Professional training and qualifications

PAF's safety management is a highly complex and involved business. The associated
professional training inevitably requires a degree of complexity in its structure and
most certainly in its content. This was reflected in the comprehensive human
resource development strategy developed in 1995 by the Stadium and Arena
Management Project [12].

Although a number of football safety officers have undertaken a basic awareness
course run by the Greater Manchester Police, the need, in my view, is for something
beyond the basics, which deals with both the formal qualification and the continuing
professional development of safety officers. A formal qualification will need to offer
something equivalent to the Level 4 National Vocational Qualification (NVQ),
towards which several FSOA members were working in 1996. I believe there are a
number of possible approaches. Either the FSOA could choose to encourage its
members to go with the Level 4 NVQ, or an award-making institution could be
asked to design and accredit a customized qualification, probably at certificate rather
than at diploma level. For example, a university might be willing to offer a distance
learning certificate in management, customized to include a special module on
stadium safety.

Turning to the question of ongoing professional development, there are a variety
of seminars, conferences, etc. which offer such opportunities. Between 1995 and
1996, for example, FSOA members have had the opportunity of attending the
Home Office Emergency Planning College at Easingwold, the Institute of Local

Table 18.1   Example baseline standards for PAFs safety management

Area	Suggestions
Documentary infrastructure	Is there a safety policy document, including the written policy required under the Health and Safety Act, a safety organization plan and a safety responsibilities plan?
	Is safety considered as an agenda item at Board or management meetings?
Management of the venue and fabric	Is there a system for checking the venue for damage after an event?
	Is there a system for inspection and certification of engineering structures?
Management of technology	Do the size and sufficiency of control room workstations meet recognized ergonomic standards?
	Has the CCTV system been performance tested against its operational requirement?
Human resource management	Is there a written code of conduct for stewards or attendants?
	Are the training syllabus and training materials properly documented?
Financial management	What is the level of remuneration for stewards or attendants?
	Does the safety manager have control of a budget?
Pre-event issues	Is there a system for ensuring liaison with other agencies?
	Is there a mechanism for determining the number of stewards or attendants to be on duty for an event?
Event operations	Is there a system for screening the public to prevent dangerous items being brought into the venue?
	What is the policy for dealing with spectator incursions onto the area where the event is being held?
Post-event issues	Is there a system for ensuring staff are debriefed from the event?
	Is there a mechanism for analysing the lessons from critical incidents taking place at the venue?
Management services	Is there a system for dealing with customer complaints?
	Is there a mechanism for assessing both the individual and the collective performance of stewards or attendants?

Government Studies (INLOGOV) at the University of Birmingham, Staffordshire University, the *FC Magazine* seminar at Anfield in Liverpool, the Soccerex '96 conference and Loughborough University, as well as the FSOA's own conferences.

Some of these events will have been more useful than others and it is well-established practice for industries to accredit such events using some form of points system, often based on the number of days' training received. I see no reason why FSOA members should not be encouraged as a matter of best practice to participate in (say) three days professional development activity each year.

Accreditation

From my point of view, accreditation is the name of the station at the end of this train's journey. It is the word written on the top rung of the ladder. I believe that, by the year 2000, safety certificates should only be granted to PAFs in which the safety management system has been properly accredited by an appropriate body. Following the regulatory principles laid down in other fields such as the railway or off-shore industries, I believe that PAFs' managers should be required to make a 'safety case' in order to obtain such accreditation.

Such a 'safety case' could be substantiated by evidence of such matters as:

- compliance with recognized standards of training and assessment;
- the appointment of professionally qualified managers;
- the undertaking of audit in accordance with agreed baseline standards;
- comprehensive documented risk assessment; and
- appropriate plans for risk reduction and management.

Diversification

It must be acknowledged that the UK football industry has acquired substantial safety experience and expertise since 1989. The ongoing process of continual improvement, which I am arguing is essential, can only serve to heighten that expertise. The option of diversification, however, implies a deliberate strategy of developing new products and services specifically for new market places and I do not believe this would be appropriate. I have argued for the industry to have a secondary strategy of making its existing expertise available both at home and abroad, but this requires the particular expertise to be first developed within football, as I have described.

Strategy implementation

Having thus sought to articulate where the train is heading or what is to be found at the top of the ladder, I want to turn now to the question of how the journey should be carried out. The issue here is one of managing change. This is a complex and substantial topic in its own right. Burnes [13], for example, highlights the considerable problems that organizations can and do experience in bringing about change.

There can be real difficulties in co-ordinating all the activity needed to bring about the benefits sought, and an increasing number of organizations in both the public and private sectors have looked to programme and project management as their preferred vehicle for managing change. I want to suggest that programme and project management offers a useful way of supporting the delivery of the strategic vision set out in this chapter.

Programme and project management

Programme management is 'the co-ordinated management of a portfolio of projects to achieve a set of business objectives' [14]. It operates in the environment shown in Figure 18.3 [15]. Strategies are shaped by stakeholder expectations and the outside world − the external business environment. Strategy informs the selection and planning of programmes, which are designed to move the organization towards the blueprint identified for its future. Projects deliver the benefits of change into the business operations.

Thus the project to develop the stewards training package should be delivering benefits into the front-line stewarding operation at football grounds. But because that project was carried out in isolation, without being part of a co-ordinated plan of work seeking to deliver a clearly articulated strategy, the opportunity for maximizing the project's benefits, in synergy with any other projects, has not been fully realized.

There are a variety of models for project management, for example the PRINCE (PRojects IN Controlled Environments) methodology [16], and Lynne Walley offers a framework for project management in Chapter 20. So I will confine my comments here to suggesting the establishment of a programme for advancing safety in public assembly facilities.

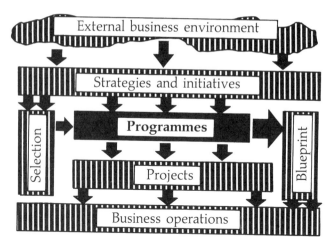

Figure 18.3   The programme management environment.

A programme for safety in public assembly facilities

This book provides a first attempt to analyse the environment within which the business of PAFs' safety management operates. Together with the outcome of other relevant research, some of which has yet to be commissioned, the book should be able to help inform the devising of a strategy and blueprint for the industry in the year 2000 and beyond. The strategy and blueprint in turn should inform the selection of programmes for such matters as training, assessment, accreditation, audit and inspection. Each of those programmes should commission projects to move towards the blueprint and deliver benefits into operational safety management.

What is needed, then, is the establishment of a programme executive for safety in public assembly facilities. The key activities of such an executive would be to:

● commission the relevant research;
● devise the appropriate strategy;
● define the necessary programmes;
● initiate suitable projects; and
● monitor the delivery of the benefits of change.

The programme executive could also act as the accreditation body for approved safety management systems.

Such a programme executive could comprise:

- A programme director with overall authority and responsibility for leading the programme. This could be a senior figure from any sector in public life who had sufficient credibility to champion the programme.
- A full-time professional programme manager, with day-to-day management responsibility.
- One or two business change managers, with suitable business skills, responsible for realizing the benefits of change.
- One to four technical or professional advisers, bringing the expert perspective of stakeholders such as the governing bodies of sports, regulatory agencies and spectator organizations. Each of these might chair a small working group from within their own constituency to act as a forum for wider consultation and quality assurance of the work of the programme.
- A full-time programme support office for day-to-day administration.

The thinking around these matters is still very much in its infancy within the industry. In the absence of a clearly defined strategy, I do not believe it is appropriate to do more than offer the concept of a programme executive, with a possible role and structure. The location of such an executive - for example should it be co-located with the office of any 'Sports Safety Executive' - would no doubt be a matter for some discussion. I hope that this chapter and this book will stimulate others to carry the debate forward.

Conclusion

My views on the strategic development of sports safety management are summarized in Figure 18.4.

The FSOA's primary strategy should be one of consolidating an enhanced professional status within the world of football. The FLA should both consolidate its activities and also move out into the wider world of PAFs' safety management as the recognized sports safety executive. There is also some scope for the FLA to extend and even diversify its advisory role. In the interests of professional independence, both the FSOA and FLA should take the lead in establishing their own programmes for strategic development.

Products/services

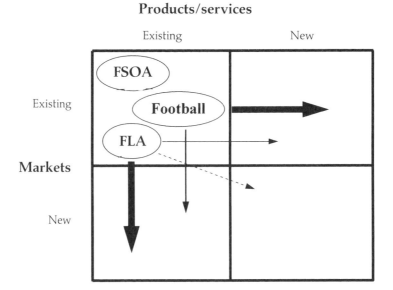

Figure 18.4 Strategy summary for sports and safety management.

The world of football should build on the three guidance documents already produced with a primary strategy of continuous incremental product development, with some secondary activity in making expertise available to other PAFs markets both at home and abroad. This strategy should be co-ordinated through a programme management structure in which all the stakeholders are properly represented.

Summary

- Strategic management is made up of three questions: 'where are we now?' (strategic analysis); 'where do we want to be?' (strategic choice); and 'how do we get there?' (strategy implementation).
- This book provides a broad outline of where we are now.
- The public assembly facilities (PAFs) safety industry is evolving but there is a need for a clearly defined strategy to steer that evolution.
- A tool from strategic management can be used to consider the various options for choice of strategic development.

- The Football Safety Officers' Association should choose to consolidate an enhanced professional status within the world of football.
- The Football Licensing Authority should be empowered by the Government both to consolidate its activities and also move out into the wider world of safety management as the recognized sports safety executive.
- The world of football should choose a primary strategy of continuous incremental improvement in safety, with particular reference to assessment, professional training and qualifications, baseline standards and accreditation.
- This strategy should be implemented and co-ordinated through a programme management structure in which all the stakeholders are properly represented.
- Secondary activity should make the expertise developed in football available to other PAFs markets at home and abroad.

References

[1] Faulkner, D. and Johnson G. (1992). *The Challenge of Strategic Management*, pp. 17–20. Kogan Page.

[2] Johnson, G. and Scholes, K. (1988). *Exploring Corporate Strategy* (2nd edn.), p. 10. Prentice Hall.

[3] Ibid.

[4] Ibid. p. 153. Adapted from Ansoff, H. (1968). *Corporate Strategy*, p. 99. Penguin.

[5] Ibid. p. 155.

[6] Department of National Heritage (1997). *Guide to Safety at Sports Grounds*. HMSO.

[7] Ibid.

[8] The Football League, the Football Association, the FA Premier League (1995). *Stewarding and Safety Management at Football Grounds.*

[9] The Football League, the Football Association, the FA Premier League and the Football Safety Officers' Association (1996). *Training Package for Stewarding at Football Grounds*. Staffordshire University.

[10] Home Office (1990). *The Hillsborough Stadium Disaster – 15 April 1989 – Inquiry by the Rt. Hon. Lord Justice Taylor – Final Report*, para. 25. HMSO.

[11] Home Office and Scottish Office (1990). *Guide to Safety at Sports Grounds*, p. 5. HMSO.

[12] Wootton, G. and Stevens, T. (1995). *Into the Next Millennium: A Human Resource Development Strategy for the Stadia and Arena Industry in the United Kingdom*. Stadium and Arena Management Unit, Swansea Institute of Higher Education.

[13] Burnes, B. (1992). *Managing Change*. Pitman.

[14] Government Centre for Information Systems (CCTA) (1993). *An Introduction to Programme Management*, p. 3. HMSO.

[15] Ibid. p. 6.

[16] Government Centre for Information Systems (CCTA) (1990). *PRINCE Reference Manuals*. NCC Blackwell Ltd.

19 Managing risk in public assembly facilities

Steve Frosdick

This chapter sets out a framework for strategic risk assessment in public assembly facilities. It takes account of both management accountability for safety and of the need to balance the competing demands of commerce, safety, enjoyment and the outside world. It illustrates the cultural complexity of the hazards perceived and provides a worked example of a simple risk assessment.

Introduction

In the discussion of accountability in Part Two of this book, we have seen how management have a moral and legal duty of care towards participants, performers, spectators and staff alike. They have a statutory duty to deal with risks to the health and safety of people who might be affected by the operation of their facility. Following a number of high profile legal cases, there is growing awareness of the civil and even criminal liability of public assembly facilities (PAFs) management in the event of a disaster precipitated by negligent preparations. Dealing with safety hazards and the risks to which they give rise must therefore be seen as an important part of PAFs management.

Thus the importance of risk assessment has been brought into ever sharper focus and the earlier chapters by Mel Highmore, Clive Warne and by Glyn Wootton and Peter Mills (Chapters 12, 13 and 14, respectively) have offered considerable advice on this subject. What I want to do in this chapter is to offer my own thoughts on the management of risk process, drawing particular attention to the need to take account of differences in perceptions of risk.

The management of risk

The overall management of risk process [1] shown in Figure 19.1 comprises the three main components of analysis, management and monitoring, each of which has a number of subsidiary processes. This offers us a framework for identifying hazards, estimating their likely frequency and consequences and evaluating their acceptability. Where appropriate, we can go on to plan what needs to be done. We allocate resources to progress the plans and thus take the necessary management measures to control the risk, whether by reducing it, avoiding it altogether or perhaps transferring it to another party. Finally, we monitor how we are doing.

In my earlier chapter on risk as blame (Chapter 3), we have seen that there are different views about the idea of risk. Having acknowledged the debate, let's start with a simple definition of risk as 'the chance of exposure to the adverse consequences of future events' [2]. There are therefore three elements to be assessed in a risk:

● the future event which may occur;
● the probability of the event occurring; and
● the adverse consequences if it does occur.

Identifying the future event is the hazard identification process.

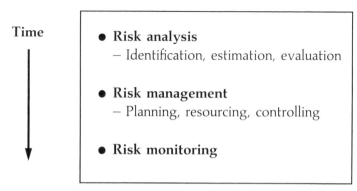

Figure 19.1   The management of risk framework.

Hazard identification

Understandably, the emphasis has been on public safety hazards, and whilst these must be paramount, it can be shown that looking at them in isolation can create operational difficulties for PAFs management.

As we have seen in the analysis in Part Three of this book, the problem is that managers are faced with the cultural complexity of four competing demands. Commercial pressures require them to optimize the commercial viability of the venue and its events. Spectator demands for excitement and enjoyment require credible events staged in comfortable surroundings. Regulatory and other requirements for safety and security must also be met, whilst any negative effects which the venue and event may have on the outside world must be kept to a minimum. Each of these areas contains sources of hazards and risks. Successful PAFs management means striking an appropriate balance between these differing demands and perceptions.

My argument is that the PAF's manager needs to adopt a more strategic and holistic approach to hazard and risk assessment. As I concluded in my chapter with Gerald Mars (Chapter 8), what this means in practice is an acceptance that nobody is wrong either to perceive a particular issue as a hazard, or to evaluate a risk in a particular way. It is therefore important to ensure that a broad range of perspectives are adequately represented in any risk assessment exercise. Three points are key here. First, any exercise should be undertaken by a group of people, rather than just one or two. Second, representatives of each of the four groups: commercial, regulatory, spectator and local resident, should be identified and invited to participate. Third, such representatives should be drawn from those with direct hands-on experience of the issues, rather than their senior managers.

To illustrate the potential richness and diversity of this approach, I want to look again at the PAF as a system, broken down into zones, such as we saw in my earlier chapter on stadium design (Chapter 11). For the purposes of this illustration, I shall concentrate on the most commonly perceived hazards in the zone where the event is held (the pitch, track, or court, etc.) and the perimeter between it and the viewing zone.

The commercial perspective

Threats to the interests of advertisers and sponsors form the principal sources of event area hazards perceived from a commercial perspective.

It is important to ensure that perimeter advertising is clearly visible to the television camera and conflicts can arise between commercialism and safety when supporters drape their banners over the hoardings.

Since accredited sponsors will have paid substantial fees to be associated with the event, there is also a perceived need to prevent 'ambush marketing' by other brands. At the Portugal v Turkey match in Nottingham during the Euro '96 Football Championships, several banners advertising Portuguese products were brought into the stadium and displayed whenever play and thus the cameras went in their direction. Stewards had to be more active dealing with these banners than they did with the well-behaved crowd!

Television companies also pay handsomely for their access and are inevitably anxious to minimize the risks of high installation costs and poor broadcast quality in their choice of camera positions and cable runs around the event area perimeter. Conflicts arise when these choices create trip hazards or obstruct spectator sightlines.

The spectator perspective

Since their main purpose is to watch the event, any deficiencies in sightlines, in the physical event area, in lighting and in the event itself provide sources of hazard to the enjoyment of the spectators. Restricted views arise from old PAF designs, with roof props and even floodlight pylons around the perimeter of the event area. Unusually high perimeter hoardings, cage-type fences, inappropriately sited television cameras or excessive deployments of police and/or stewards around the perimeter represent further sources of hazards to sightlines.

Sports events may either become a farce or else be unplayable if surfaces, particularly grass, become too wet. The high jump section of the women's pentathlon competition at the 1996 Atlanta Olympics, where standing water was not properly cleared from the runway, adversely affecting the athletes' performances, provides an example.

Enjoyment may also be threatened by a lack of credibility in the event itself. In boxing, a number of 'big fights' have ended in the first round because of the mismatching of opponents. The early dismissal of a star player, even if justified, denies spectators the chance of enjoying that player's skills and may lead to their team adopting boring defensive tactics for the remainder of the match.

The external disruption perspective

Whilst it is clearly the zone beyond the venue which provides most hazards perceived by the outside world, nevertheless the event area itself provides two main sources.

First is the noise created by the participants or performers. This is a particular issue with music events staged in stadia, where the sound travels beyond the stadium through the open air.

Second is the threat of articles from the event area being projected beyond the facility. Cricket balls 'hit for six' or parachutists trying to land on the event area as part of a display can cause damage to property or injury to passers-by outside the ground. Pyrotechnics set off on the event area provide a further source of hazard. During an early satellite television broadcast from a Premiership football ground, some of the pre-match fireworks landed, still burning, on the forecourt of a petrol station down the street!

The safety and security perspective

The principal sources of hazards from this perspective involve perimeter obstructions and the potential for adverse interaction between spectators and participants in the event. Television cables, perimeter hoardings, fences and gates all provide tripping or obstruction hazards which may delay spectator egress onto the event area in emergency evacuations. The 1989 Hillsborough stadium disaster in which 95 football fans were crushed to death against a perimeter fence provides an extreme example.

Incursions onto the event area are the other principal concern. The perceived hazards range from attacks on officials or players, for example the on-court stabbing of tennis star Monica Seles in Germany, to damage to the event area, such as at Wembley Stadium after a notorious England v Scotland football match in the 1980s. Conversely, participants leaving the event area cause similar concerns. Players who run into the crowd to celebrate goals or points scored frequently cause the crowd to surge towards them. And who could forget the pictures of Manchester United's Eric Cantona leaping into a stand to karate kick a spectator? Team benches provide a source of similar hazards, either because spectators misbehave towards them or vice versa.

Finally, as Mel Highmore has shown in his Chapter 12, we have the health and safety hazards which the event, the event area or the perimeter pose to the participants themselves. For safety reasons, the English football team nearly refused to play on a poor surface in China in 1996. And several boxers have died in the ring. Looking at the remaining zones — the viewing accommodation, concourses and curtilages — would illustrate the different perspectives in further detail. But from the event area alone, it can be seen that strategic risk assessment requires a broader focus than safety and security alone.

An example

What I want to do now is to run through the remaining processes within the management of risk framework, and, as we go along, to demonstrate their practical application through a simple worked example.

For our worked example, I want to stay with the playing area zone in a football stadium, and look particularly at the away team bench, which is one area within that zone. To keep things simple, we will assume that the hazard identification process has resulted in just four hazards, as follows:

- A missile will be thrown at the away team personnel on the bench.
- The substitute players will obstruct the front of an advertising hoarding while they are warming up.
- A spectator will shout verbal abuse at the away team personnel on the bench.
- The away team personnel will shout abuse at the referee or linesmen.

So we have our list of hazards. Now we need to get an estimation of their probability and consequences.

Risk estimation process

Each hazard should be considered by the team who carried out the identification process and a collective judgement made about the probability of the risk occurring. The probability should be judged on a five-point scale ranging from none to low to low/medium to medium/high to high. A collective judgement should then be made about the potential adverse consequences if the hazard did occur. I would suggest that there are four types of adverse consequences to consider, corresponding to the four competing demands faced by PAF managers, namely:

- for public safety and order;
- for the profitability of the business (including its exposure to liability);
- for the enjoyment of the spectators or participants; and
- for the community and environment in the outside world.

All four types of consequence may be tackled in one exercise, or there may be a focus on just one type. However the exercise is approached, each type of consequences should also be judged on a separate five point scale. Going back to

Table 19.1　Example of a hazards register

Ref.	Hazard	Probability	Consequences			
			Safety	Profit	Enjoyment	Community
A	A missile will be thrown at the bench	3	4	2	2	0
B	The subs will warm up in front of an advertising hoarding	2	1	3	1	0
C	A spectator will shout abuse at the bench	4	2	0	2	0
D	The bench will shout abuse at the referee	3	0	0	1	0

our example, let's imagine that the estimation process has come out with a hazards register something like Table 19.1.

This shows how the different hazards can have different implications for the four different types of consequence. Such a hazards register should provide a substantial reference document to support the running of the venue. But the operator cannot reasonably be expected to tackle all the hazards, nor will it be cost-effective to try to do so. So we need to prioritize the hazards. This prioritization process is called risk evaluation.

Risk evaluation process

Having estimated probability and consequences, in however many dimensions, each risk in the hazards register should be plotted onto a five by five matrix. The distribution of the hazards on the matrix should then be evaluated by an appropriate forum, which may well be the board of directors of the company running the venue.

The general principle governing risk evaluation is that risk should be reduced to a level which is 'as low as is reasonably practicable' (ALARP) [3]. In general terms, those risk issues which have been judged to be of lower probability or consequences will be designated as 'low risk' and will be accepted as residual risks. At the other end of the scale, those risks which have been estimated as higher probability and consequences will be designated as 'high risk' and therefore intolerable. These risks will have to become subject to remedial action, almost irrespective of cost, through

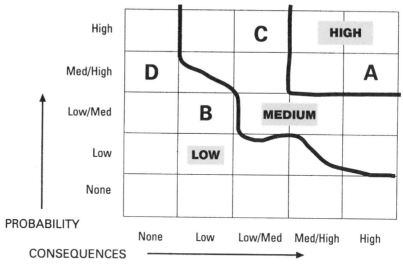

Figure 19.2   Example risk evaluation matrix.

the preparation of appropriate risk management plans. Where the boundaries fall between these two categories will be a question of management judgement, and, once decided, will determine which issues are designated 'medium risk'. These risks may require careful monitoring and incorporating into the risk management plans if appropriate, for example where something can be done at a cost less than the benefit of the risk reduction.

The boundaries should then be added to the matrix. In the interests of simplicity, and since the demand for risk assessment is often safety related, only the consequences for safety and order for the worked example have been plotted in Figure 19.2.

It can be seen that one of the hazards – the throwing of the missile – has been designated as high risk, whilst one – verbal abuse by a spectator – is medium and the other two are low risk.

The outcome of the risk identification, estimation and evaluation processes should then be reported as the formal risk assessment. This risk assessment documents which hazards have been identified as priorities and how and why those decisions have been made. So the risk assessment is an exercise in accountability.

Risk management process

In respect of each high risk or relevant medium risk, an appropriate group of people should meet to consider what action can be taken to control the risk and reduce the probability and/or consequences to a tolerable level. Again, the group should in my view be comprised of representatives of each of the four different cultural constituencies, although in this case it would be appropriate for more senior management to be involved in the exercise.

The countermeasures defined, the resources assigned and the responsibilities allocated should be recorded. The outcome of the process will be the risk management plan. Taking the high risk issue in our example we can ask ourselves what could be done to reduce the probability of a missile being thrown at the away bench. We might decide to sell the tickets in the surrounding area only to season-ticket holders or Family Club members. We would be able to vet applicants and would know who was in what seats in that area every game. Thinking about reducing the consequences for safety and order if a missile was thrown, we might decide to build a polycarbonate shelter around the bench and thus protect the occupants from harm. Turning to the medium risk, the verbal abuse, we might decide that the same ticketing policy would reduce the probability a little. We might also decide to locate a steward adjacent to the bench. This would have a modest opportunity cost but would ensure that a member of staff was available to nip any problems in the bud and so reduce the consequences of the abuse escalating into potentially harmful disorder. Thus the implementation of the countermeasures identified should result both in increased protection for our guests and customers and reduced exposure to liability for ourselves.

Risk monitoring process

But the management of risk process is not a 'single shot' to be forgotten after it is completed. Regular monitoring is important to ensure that the risk implications of any changes are considered and appropriately acted upon. A formal review of the hazards, their estimated probabilities and consequences, tolerability and any risk management measures proposed, should therefore be carried out at appropriate intervals, for example after major building work. The hazards register, risk assessment and risk management plan should be amended as appropriate and reissued accordingly.

Summary

- The management of risk process comprises risk analysis, risk management and risk monitoring.
- Risk is the chance of exposure to the adverse consequences of future events.
- Cultural complexity means that public assembly facilities managers face competing demands for commercial viability, spectator enjoyment, safety/order and minimum external disruption.
- Each of these four areas contains sources of risk and the different perspectives need to be captured in the risk assessment process.
- Hazards should be identified and risks estimated by a team in which all four perspectives are represented.
- Management plans should be put in place to reduce risks to a level which is as low as is reasonably practicable.
- Risks should be monitored on a regular basis.

Acknowledgement

This chapter is derived from arguments set out in the author's previous work, namely:

Frosdick, S. (1997). Danger, disruption, finance and fun. *Stadium and Arena Management*, **1** (1), 26–30.
Frosdick, S. and Odell, A. (1997). Practical management of programme and project risk: A case study of the national strategy for police information systems. *Information Management and Computer Security*, **4**(5), 24–34.
Frosdick, S. (in press), Sports and safety: Leisure and liability. In *Leisure Management* (I. Cooper and M. Collins, eds.). CAB International, Oxford.

References

[1] Scarff, F., Carty, A. and Charette R. (1993). *Introduction to the Management of Risk*, p. 23. HMSO.
[2] Ibid. p. 88.
[3] Health and Safety Executive (1996). *Use of Risk Assessment Within Government Departments*, p. 16. HSE Books.

20 How are we doing? where are we going?

Lynne Walley

This chapter looks at the way in which effective project management can assist sports clubs to identify, plan and evaluate initiatives. It sets out a clear methodology for implementation as well as looking at the project-based culture.

Project management

Safety management is an integral part of business management, and any projects initiated should form part of the overall strategic management plan. Project management can be incorporated in the strategy that a sports club has. It is a new culture which enables new projects to flourish in an effective management hierarchy [1].

However, we can query the knowledge that many boards of directors may have regarding the operations or projects at a lower level. As we saw in my discussion of corporate manslaughter liability in Chapter 4, levels of management can 'filter out' vital elements of management information, leaving questions such as 'do the management really need to know this?' or conversely 'do the workers really need to know this?'

Organizational management

Sporting organizations are now large and complex beasts and Figure 20.1 gives an example of a typical management structure. The layers of management and the

Figure 20.1 A typical sports club management structure.

communications flow mean that not only should the organization have predetermined objectives but that they should be effectively communicated to all levels of staff. One club's marketing team had arranged with the local newspaper that free copies would be placed on each seat on the morning of a match; no consultation had taken place with the safety staff and a potentially dangerous incident was avoided when the safety manager pointed out that a few thousand free newspapers distributed in a old and partly wooden stand presented a high risk to the public. Seemingly, the marketing team had not considered either the fire hazard or the waste aspect of papers blowing around the ground or being wet and soggy underfoot.

A team undertaking a specific project should have quantifiable objectives with clearly identified performance indicators and monitoring systems which address the ongoing cost of the project and the effective measurement of the human resources. This is achieved by effective management and administration at all levels. Coordination and integration of projects is carried out by senior management.

Organizational development has meant that many companies now run their operations and projects on a parallel plane. This management style is particularly relevant to sporting organizations where they have to consider the following:

- customer demand for better service;
- customer awareness of new technology;
- communities becoming more concerned about the environment and social safety; and
- pricing set against other available entertainments.

These points underlie strategic management and drive organizations towards more effective use of resources. Clearly, organizations that respond to these elements will be working in a customer-orientated structure which seeks to address the needs of the staff and the customer. They will exhibit a great responsibility towards management and a greater level of communication will operate within the company. Using these management tools then enables the company to meet new markets and monitor those initiatives already implemented.

Many elements of projects involve not only the organization but often an external element, namely the public as spectators, supporters, etc. Projects must have an objective which may be anything from attracting more fans to effectively coordinating visiting teams and supporters at a special event. Operational activity is that which is ongoing and the daily business of the company, whilst project activity relates specifically to goals or set objectives.

Objectives have to be set that are realistic and achievable. They also have to be matched against resources, both financial and human. An objective must also be set against time and costs factors.

Project costs have to be measured against benefits to the club or company. How is 'value for money' measured? Is it set against purely financial benefits in terms of increased tickets or sales of merchandise? A project may be carried out in collaboration with a local authority or other interested party, for example a sponsor. Here the distribution and spending levels can come under further scrutiny.

Methodology

In order to determine a clear view of a project and its objectives it is necessary to look at what is to be achieved and how those goals will be reached. Berry and Carter [2] set out a ten-point plan for the effective methodological approach to identifying, implementing and monitoring a project. Figure 20.2 sets out this approach.

First, it needs to be clearly established at the beginning that assessment of the project is entwined with the management of the project. This ensures continuity, ease of monitoring and the identification of the life cycle of the project. Second, there needs to be a clear identification of management personnel and staff and communication structures for the project. It needs to be established who has initiated the project and which staff will see it through, during whatever stages.

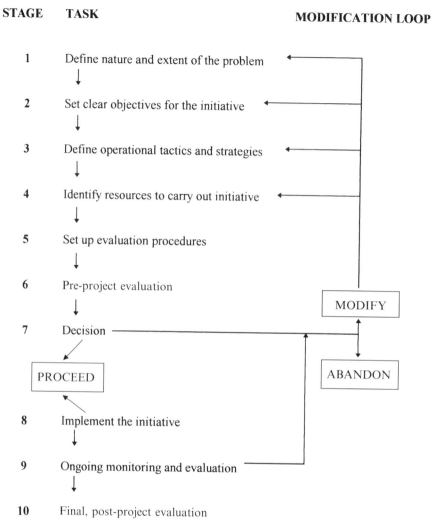

Figure 20.2   Project methodology.

Berry and Carter set out their ten-point plan as follows.

1   Problem definition – where are we now?

Here the aim is to focus on the current situation, for example, car parking around a ground may be bad, merchandise sales may be poor, thefts from spectators' vehicles may be unreasonably high.

2   *Clear objectives – where do we want to be?*

Any objectives set here must be clear, understandable and measurable and they must be set against realistic targets. Ideally a time frame will be set and the main objectives communicated to all relevant parties. These objectives should be limited and may, in some instances, run parallel to other initiatives currently being operated. The project manager should then ensure that there is no duplication of resources.

3   *Define strategies – how shall we get there?*

The problem definition and objective setting exercises should have led to an identification of potential tactics. The strategy may be one that has been identified by other departments within the company who may have different objectives. Again there is a need to avoid duplication and open clear communication channels within the organization.

4   *Identify resources – who does it and who pays?*

Having identified the initiative, objective and strategy there is a need to determine staffing levels and funding. It may well be discovered at this stage that due to restrictions on both staff and funds there may need to be some redefinition of the objective to realistically fit the resources.

5   *Assessment – how shall we measure how we are doing?*

At the outset it is essential to ensure that the project can be effectively managed and evaluated throughout. It is necessary to determine what performance indicators are to be used and what information will be available to assist the monitoring process; in the sporting sense they may well be attendance figures, sales in the club shop or corporate functions held in club facilities. Other factors which need to be considered are the depth of the assessment practices as well as the decision on the dissemination of the results and how they will be presented and to whom. This is an essential stage in the process of project assessment as many important factors need to be determined at this point.

6   Pre-project assessment – will it be worth it ?

A rational view needs to be taken of the viability of the project. This exercise will incorporate consideration of factors such as all resource assessment as well as environmental and contextual issues.

7   Decision making – shall we do it?

Having looked at the previous six stages, the project manager can then make an informed decision as to the effectiveness of the project and the viability of it reaching its set objectives. It is not too late at this stage to abort the project based on the facts obtained from the pre-project stage.

8   Implementation – let's do it!

Putting the identified resources and project plan together means that the only way is forward.

9   On going monitoring – how are we doing?

The identification of the life cycle of the project means that an ongoing evaluation can be done at any time. Regular monitoring is set against resource allocation, time scales and milestone targets. Project life cycle is dealt with in greater detail below.

10   Final assessment – how have we done?

A final assessment can determine whether targets have been hit and can also allow for measurement against any baseline data that was taken at the start of the project.

Project life cycle

Figure 20.3 sets out the project life cycle and identifies the various stages through which a project passes. It looks at differing features of the project life cycle than those illustrated in Figure 20.2.

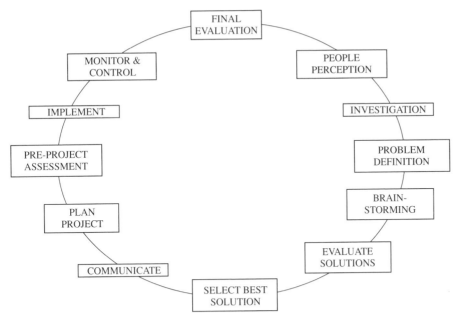

Figure 20.3 Project life cycle.

Two essential factors need to be considered at the outset: first, what aim or objective will address the benefit to the organization and the community in which it sits; second, what features have to be identified in order to determine the feasibility of the project from the point of the organization. In other words, how will senior managers or the board of directors view this project as one which will be successful and which has merits over other proposals. Further factors to consider include the selling aspects, in the form of the profit margin, and also the intangible benefits to the club in terms of raised public perception or heightened image.

Setting milestones can often be done in an arbitrary way, but a statement that a monthly update will suffice often does not address the effective progress of the project. It should be noted that projects have a 'shelf life' and that they have an introduction, a growth, a maturity, saturation and decline. Also set against these factors are limited resources, both financially and human resources and the ever-increasing need to see 'instant' results.

The pitfalls during the project life style, decline in motivation and reduction of resources, can be planned for at the outset. Any loss of motivation falls to the project manager to regenerate and any foreseeable reduction in resources can be planned for. Constant monitoring of the project mean that shortfall in any area can be addressed immediately it occurs. Regular planning sessions also mean that if the project is not on target it can quickly be corrected.

Multi-agency projects

Increasingly nowadays many projects involve a number of interested parties; sporting clubs no longer operate in isolation, they often embark on projects with local authorities, local residents and sponsors to name but a few. The nature of this mixture can mean that parties are entering into projects with entirely different agendas and with widely different perceptions of the problem or objectives. However, many agencies now have similar working practices, including the police service, which necessitates budget approval, resource permission and planning meetings; this can be time consuming and the project manager has to ensure that any time limitations set take all these factors into account.

It is particularly important that the project leader or champion is aware of all the facets of different working practices and that the objectives are both clearly set out and attainable. It is they who will be responsible for the lines of communication and an agreed cultural 'terminology', ensuring that any jargon used in a particular department or agency is clearly understood by all parties.

Where multi-agency programme management is taking place complications arise in a number of areas, not least that at any one time a particular agency will be involved in a number of projects. Project leaders from the different agencies need to establish their own lines of management and communication to ensure their authority. They should be able to come to project meetings and express the opinions of their own agency without prejudice, irrespective of rank or seniority.

Equally any external consultant who is brought in to work either with a single organization or with a multi-agency partnership must be made aware, by the project manager, of the differing managerial aspects of the projects as well as the different culture and funding bases concerned.

Summary

- Project and safety management should be integral parts of any organization. Both should have clear aims and objectives and be communicated to all those responsible for the management of the club.

- Projects should be monitored and evaluated with clearly identified performance indicators set at the beginning of the project.
- Sports clubs initiating projects have to take account of the needs of a number of interested parties. Because their sports grounds are fixed venues they also have to consider environmental issues.
- Having clearly defined the problem which the project is to address, it is then possible to move on to set clear objectives, determine strategies and resources and establish assessment procedures.
- From this platform it is then possible to decide either to progress with the project or, having reviewed the viability, to decide not to proceed.
- Implementation, monitoring and final assessment would then follow in the project life cycle. It is essential to have the project manager focused on matching resources to the project life cycle and on monitoring all stages of the project.
- Within the commercial world of sport it is now highly likely that many projects will have a number of partners from different agencies, all of whom may have differing resources, personnel, aims and objectives. This places greater emphasis on the project manager being able to negotiate within the partnership, to maintain clear lines of communication and to keep the project objectives focused.

Acknowledgement

The author acknowledges her grateful thanks to colleagues at Staffordshire University, Geoff Berry and Jim Izat, for their assistance with this chapter.

References

[1] Berry, G., Izat, J., Mawby, R. and Walley, L. (1995). *Practical Police Management*, pp. 165–185. Police Review Publishing Company.
[2] Berry, G. and Carter, M. (1991). *Assessing Crime Prevention Initiatives: the First Steps*. Home Office Crime Prevention Unit Paper 31.

Useful addresses

International Football Associations

Fédération Internationale de Football Associations (FIFA)
PO Box 85
8030 Zurich
Switzerland
Tel: 0041 1384 9595
Fax: 0041 1384 9696

Union of European Football Associations (UEFA)
Chemin de la Redoute 54
Case Postale 303
CH-1260
Nyon
Switzerland
Tel: 0041 2299 44444
Fax: 0041 2299 44488

National Football Associations

The Football Association (FA)
16 Lancaster Gate
London W2 3LW
Tel: 0171 262 4542
Fax: 0171 402 0486

Irish Football Association (IFA)
20 Windsor Avenue
Belfast BT9 6EE
Tel: 01232 669458
Fax: 01232 667620

Scottish Football Association (SFA)
6 Park Gardens
Glasgow G3 7YF
Tel: 0141 332 6372
Fax: 0141 332 7559

Welsh Football Association (WFA)
3 Westgate Street
Cardiff CF1 1DD
Tel: 01222 372325
Fax: 01222 343961

Senior football leagues

FA Premier League Ltd
16 Lancaster Gate
London W2 3LW
Tel: 0171 262 4542
Fax: 0171 402 0486

The Football League Ltd (FL)
319 Clifton Drive South
Lytham St Annes FY8 1JG
Tel: 01253 729421
Fax: 01253 724786

The Football League of Wales
3 Westgate Street
Cardiff CF1 1DD
Tel: 01222 372325
Fax: 01222 343961

Irish Football League (IFL)
96 University Street
Belfast BT7 1HE
Tel: 01232 242888
Fax: 01232 330773

Scottish Football League (SFL)
188 West Regent Street
Glasgow G2 4RY
Tel: 0141 248 3844
Fax: 0141 221 7450

Other public and football related bodies

Football Licensing Authority
27 Harcourt House
19 Cavendish Square
London W1M 9AD
Tel: 0171 491 7191
Fax: 0171 491 1882

Football Safety Officers' Association (FSOA)
c/o John Sidney
Nottingham Forest FC
City Ground
Nottingham NG2 5FJ
Tel: 0115 952 6000
Fax: 0115 952 6003

Football Supporters Association (FSA)
PO Box 11
Liverpool L26 1XP
Tel/Fax: 0151 737 2385

The Football Trust
Walkden House
10 Melton Street
London NW1 2EB
Tel: 0171 388 4504
Fax: 0171 388 6688

Health and Safety Commission (HSC)
Rose Court
2 Southwark Bridge
London SE1 9HS
Tel: 0171 717 6000
Fax: 0171 717 6717
Website: http:\\www.open.gov.uk\hsehome.htm

Institute of Football Management and Administration
1A Chapel Court
Holly Walk
Leamington Spa CV32 4UF
Tel: 01926 882313
Fax: 01926 886829

National Federation of Football Supporters' Clubs
87 Brookfield Avenue
Loughborough
LE11 3LN
Tel/Fax: 01509 267643

Professional Footballers' Association (PFA)
2 Oxford Court
Bishopsgate
Manchester M2 3WQ
Tel: 0161 236 0575
Fax: 0161 228 7229

Scottish Sports Council
Caledonia House
South Gyle
Edinburgh EH12 9DQ
Tel: 0131 317 7200
Fax: 0131 317 7202

Scottish Professional Footballers' Association
Fountain House
1–3 Woodside Crescent
Charing Cross
Glasgow G3 7UJ
Tel: 0141 332 8641
Fax: 0141 332 4491

Sir Norman Chester Centre for Football Research
Department of Sociology
University of Leicester
University Road
Leicester LE1 7RH
Tel: 0116 2522741

The Sports Council
16 Upper Woburn Place
London WC1H 0QP
Tel: 0171 273 1500

Sports Council for Northern Ireland
House of Sport
Upper Malone Road
Belfast BT9 5LA
Tel: 01232 331222
Fax: 0232 331757

Sports Council for Wales
Welsh Institute for Sport
Sophia Gardens
Cardiff CF1 9SW
Tel: 01222 397571
Fax: 01222 222431

Governing bodies of sports

All England Women's Hockey Association
Harold Fern House
The Stadium
Silbury Boulevard
Milton Keynes MK9 1NR
Tel: 01908 689290
Fax: 01908 689286

Amateur Swimming Association
Derby Square
Loughborough LE11 5AL
Tel: 01509 230431
Fax: 01509 610720

Auto Cycle Union
ACU House
Wood Street
Rugby CV21 2YX
Tel: 01788 540519
Fax: 01788 573585

British American Football Association
Southrey House
Church Road
Freiston PE22 0LA
Tel/Fax: 01205 761508

British Athletic Federation
Athletics House
225A Bristol Road
Edgbaston
Birmingham B5 7UB
Tel: 0121 440 5000
Fax: 0121 440 0555

British Cycling Federation
National Cycling Centre
Stuart Street
Manchester M11 4DQ
Tel: 0161 230 2301
Fax: 0161 231 0591

British Equestrian Federation
British Equestrian Centre
Stoneleigh Park
Kenilworth CV8 2LR
Tel: 01203 696697
Fax: 01203 692351

British Olympic Association
1 Wandsworth Plain
Wandsworth
London SW18 1EH
Tel: 0181 871 2677
Fax: 0181 871 9104

Central Council of Physical Recreation
Francis House
Francis Street
London SW1P 1DE
Tel: 0171 828 3163
Fax: 0171 630 8820

English Basketball Association
48 Bradford Road
Stanningley
Leeds LS28 6DF
Tel: 0113 2361166
Fax: 0113 2361022

The Hockey Association (Men's)
The Stadium
Silbury Boulevard
Milton Keynes MK9 1NR
Tel: 01908 689290
Fax: 01908 689286

The Jockey Club
42 Portman Square
London W1H 0EN
Tel: 0171 486 4921
Fax: 0171 935 8703
E-mail: jockeyclub@nettec.co.uk Website: http:\\www.nettec.co.uk\jockeyclub\

Lawn Tennis Association
Queens Club
West Kensington
London W14 9EG
Tel: 0171 381 7000
Fax: 0171 381 5965

National Greyhound Racing Club
24–28 Oval Road
London NW1 7DA
Tel: 0171 267 9256
Fax: 0171 482 1023

RAC Motorsports Association Ltd
Motor Sports House
Riverside Park
Colnbrook
Slough LS3 0HG
Tel: 01753 681736
Fax: 01753 682938

Royal and Ancient Golf Club
St Andrews
Fife KY16 9JD
Tel: 01334 472112
Fax: 01334 477580

Rugby Football League
Red Hall
Red Hall Lane
Leeds LS17 8NB
Tel: 0113 232 9111
Fax: 0113 232 3666

Rugby Football Union
1 Rugby Road
Twickenham
Middlesex TW1 1DZ
Tel: 0181 892 8161
Fax: 0181 892 9816

Scottish Rugby Union
Murrayfield
Edinburgh EH12 5PJ
Tel: 0131 346 5000
Fax: 0131 346 5001

Squash Rackets Association
PO Box 1106
London W3 0ZD
Tel: 0181 746 1616
Fax: 0181 746 0580

Test and County Cricket Board
Lords Cricket Ground
London NW8 8QZ
Tel: 0171 286 4405
Fax: 0171 286 5583

Welsh Rugby Union
Cardiff Arms Park
PO Box 22
Cardiff CF1 1JL
Tel: 01222 390111
Fax: 01222 378472

Professional associations and institutes

Ambulance Service Association
Department of Health
Erleen House
80–94 Newington Causeway
London SE1 6EF
Tel: 0171 972 2939

Association of Building Engineers
Jubilee House
Billing Brook Road
Weston Favell
Northampton NN3 8NW
Tel: 01604 404121
Fax: 01604 784220

Association of Chief Police Officers (ACPO)
New Scotland Yard
London SW1H 0BG
Tel: 0171 230 2456

Association of Chief Police Officers Scotland (ACPOS)
Police HQ
Fettes Avenue
Edinburgh EH4 1RB
Tel: 0131 31 3051
Fax: 0131 311 3052

Association of Consulting Engineers
Alliance House
12 Caxton Street
London SW1H 0QL
Tel: 0171 222 6557
Fax: 0171 222 0750

Chartered Institute of Building Services Engineers
222 Balham High Road
London SW12 9BS
Tel. 0181 675 5211
Fax. 0181 675 5449
E mail: secretary@cibse.org

Chartered Institute of Environmental Health Officers
Chadwick Court
15 Hatfields
London SE1 8DJ
Tel: 0171 928 6006
Fax: 0171 827 5866

Chief and Assistant Fire Officers Association
10–11 Pebble Close
Tamworth B77 4RD
Tel: 01827 61516
Fax: 01827 61530

Chief Leisure Officers Association
c/o I. K. Hook
Head of Leisure Services
Mansfield District Council
Chesterfield Road South
Mansfield NG19 7BH
Tel: 01623 663074
Fax: 01623 420197

Institute of Building Control
21 High Street
Ewell
Epsom KT17 1SB
Tel: 0181 393 6860
Fax: 0181 393 1083

Institute of Civil Engineers
1–7 Great George Street
London SW1P 3AA
Tel: 0171 222 7722
Fax: 0171 222 7500

Institute of Fire Engineers
148 New Walk
Leicester LE1 7QB
Tel: 0116 255 3654

Institute of Groundmanship
19–23 Church Street
The Agora
Wolverton
Milton Keynes MK12 5LG
Tel: 01908 312511
Fax: 01908 311140

Institute of Leisure and Amenity Management
ILAM House
Lower Basildon
Reading RG8 9NE
Tel: 01491 874 222
Fax: 01491 874 059

Institute of Lighting Engineers
9 Lawford Road
Rugby CV21 2DZ
Tel: 01788 576492
Fax: 01788 554 0145
E-mail: ile@dial.pipex.com

Institute of Sports and Recreation Management
36–38 Sherrard Street
Melton Mowbray LE 13 1XJ
Tel: 01664 65531
Fax: 01664 501155

Institution of Electrical Engineers
Savoy Place
London WC2R 0BL
Tel: 0171 240 1871
Fax: 0171 240 7735

Insitution of Mechanical Engineers
1 Birdcage Walk
London SW1H 9JJ
Tel: 0171 222 7899
Fax: 0171 222 4557

Institution of Structural Engineers
11 Upper Belgrave Street
London SW1X 8BH
Tel: 0171 235 4535
Fax: 0171 235 4294

International Association of Auditorium Managers
4425 West Airport Freeway
Suite 590
Irving
Texas
USA
Tel: 001 214 255 8020
Fax: 001 214 255 9582

Police Federation of England and Wales
15–17 Langley Road
Surbiton KT6 6LP
Tel: 0181 399 2224
Fax: 0181 390 2249

Royal Incorporation of Architects in Scotland
15 Rutland Square
Edinburgh EH1 2BE
Tel: 0131 229 7545
Fax: 0131 228 2188

Royal Institute of British Architects
66 Portland Place
London W1N 4AD
Tel: 0171 580 5533
Fax: 0171 225 1541

Royal Institution of Chartered Surveyors
12 Great George Street
London SW1P 3AD
Tel: 0171 222 7000
Fax: 0171 222 9430

Royal Town Planning Institute
26 Portland Place
London W1N 4BE
Tel: 0171 636 9107
Fax; 0171 323 1582

Index